ABOVE
SUSPICION

ABOVE
SUSPICION

ABOVE
SUSPICION

JOE SHARKEY

OPEN ROAD
INTEGRATED MEDIA
NEW YORK

Copyright 1993, 2017 by Joe Sharkey

Cover design by Andy Ross

978-1-5040-4176-8

This edition published in 2017 by Open Road Integrated Media, Inc.
180 Maiden Lane
New York, NY 10038
www.openroadmedia.com

1

The baby threw up just as the eighteen-wheel coal truck with the word *Jesus* on its front plate barreled out of a blind switchback and bore down on them like a forty-ton avalanche of soot.

It was a drizzly, cold afternoon in February 1987. Skidding on the slick mountain road, Mark Putnam managed to pull the 1980 Oldsmobile far enough off to the side, where he slowed to a crawl, the passenger door nearly scraping the granite wall that went a hundred feet up. The coal truck rumbled by with its horn shrieking.

"Oh my God," Kathy Putnam said in a slow, low voice from the back seat, where two-year-old Danielle lay across her lap, miserable with car sickness and fatigue.

When they caught their breath, Kathy cleaned up with a diaper. Her gaze met her husband's dark eyes in the rearview mirror. "Listen, Kat, we don't have to do this," he said with a grimace, and added, only partly in jest, "Do you want to turn around and go back to Connecticut?"

Kathy was nothing if not a good sport. Three years before, when she and Mark had dashed off to get married in New York City, she had known very well what she was getting into. Mark was a young man with one overriding goal: He intended to be an FBI man. And together, they had accomplished that. Theirs was a marriage remarkable for its synergy—her hard-nosed realism applied to his unchecked zeal, his fortitude to her diffidence, creating a force that augmented their individual strengths. If Mark's first assignment out of the FBI Academy was a forlorn outpost in the isolated mountainous coalfields of eastern Kentucky—in Pikeville, a town neither of them had heard of until two weeks earlier—well, they would make a go of it and wait for a better assignment in years to come.

Kathy smiled, tickled the baby's chin, and said, "It's going to be okay. You'll see." Mark guided the old car, its engine straining, up the steep mountain road.

"We keep going up," he said disconsolately from the front seat, where he was wedged uncomfortably between the door and a stack of pillows on top of a picnic cooler and some cardboard boxes that claimed the passenger.

"Gotta go down eventually," she replied cheerfully.

In a while, they were relieved to see a road sign, **CON-GESTED AREA**, but it only marked the truck pull-off for a coal-mine operation below the blasted rocks and stepped contours of a strip-mined mountain. Heaps of coal chunks clattered noisily on conveyor tracks that crisscrossed down from outcrops high up the ridge. Broken trees and shattered boulders lay scattered on the site in huge heaps. Staring in wonder, they drove past and started another steep climb.

Kathy frowned at a Triple-A road map, but it was clear there was no real choice except to go straight ahead on the winding two-lane. There weren't any intersections, and few pull-offs. But after a while, they saw evidence of a settlement: unpainted little frame houses set onto shelves of land hacked into the hills; tumbledown bungalows and rust-streaked trailers pushed up close against the highway, as if waiting to pull out into traffic. On a sagging front porch, a woman in a faded print housedress and muddy field boots studied them from a rocker.

A mile farther, the highway bored down abruptly and swept open into four lanes at the base of a deep gorge blasted through the rock, with walls one hundred feet high, the surfaces of which were veined with glistening narrow seams of coal that might have been drawn in by a thick black marker. They sped past another road sign, **PIKEVILLE—POP. 4,500**, and past an exit that wound around into a small community shadowed by surrounding mountains and skirted by a narrow meandering brown river. A jumble of neat buildings dominated by a brick courthouse with a weather vane on top, Pikeville looked like a village in a model railroad display, except for another billboard at the entrance to town, this one bigger, that said:

HILLBILLY DAYS!!!
Fun filled weekend carnival celebrating the heritage of
PIKEVILLE, KY
Rides! Handicrafts! Good eatin's.
April 24-25-26
Ya'll Come!

On either side of the billboard's message were cartoon images of stereotypical shotgun-wielding hillbillies with ratty straw hats, patched overalls, big gnarly bare feet, and goofy smiles showing missing front teeth.

"Is this us?" Kathy said, taking this sight in with some amusement.

Mark looked anything but amused. He drove on slowly. A mile beyond the exit, the road narrowed and began to climb once more. Mark made a U-turn and drove back to the little town in the coalfields of Kentucky where their lives would change forever. In 1997, Kathy Putnam was twenty-seven years old, six months younger than her husband. She and Mark had both grown up in Connecticut, where they had met five years earlier. With their daughter, they made a handsome and cozy family—Mark, dark and sensitive, a muscular young man who had been a star athlete in college and stayed in shape by running and lifting weights; Kathy, with her delicate features and untamed light brown hair, hopelessly unathletic; and amiable Danielle, already chatty, with her mother's quick smile and her father's flashing eyes. If the FBI had commissioned a recruitment commercial to get young families to consider a career in the bureau, the Putnams would have been in it.

But that commercial probably would have shown the family arriving somewhere other than isolated Pikeville, the seat of Pike County, Kentucky, a corrugated chunk of land shaped, in fact, like a lump of coal. It sprawls over 785 square miles, most of them situated between two rivers, the Levisa Fork and the Tug Fork, which tumble out of the high watershed of the western Appalachian range down into the Cumberland Plateau. They flow north for about a hundred miles and join at the old railroad town of Louisa to form a river known as the Big Sandy, which then plunges northward under rocky escarpments forming the border between Kentucky and West Virginia, and finally empties into the Ohio River.

It is a land extravagantly endowed with mineral and other natural resources—and thus cursed with plunder. After the Civil War, timber barons cleared the mountains of their magnificent hardwood forests, and when they were gone, coal barons came in to dig for the wealth underneath. Under a thin veneer of modest prosperity in small towns such as Pikeville, the toll of over a century of feverish exploitation was evident, both physically and socially, as Appalachian historian Harry M. Caudill put it, in "exhaustion of soil, exhaustion of men, exhaustion of hopes."

"Dogpatch" was what some new arrivals called the place. The term, though a misnomer with origins in Al Capp's classic *Li'l Abner* comic strip set in a fictional Arkansas hamlet, conveyed the disdain outsiders often bring to their first encounters with "hillbillies" and the condescension that has always seeped down the map to rural southern Appalachia from the urban media centers. During the heyday of the sensationalist press in the late 1880s, big-city newspapers from the East were drawn to southern Appalachia by the colorful narratives afforded by the Hatfield–McCoy feud. The stories gave birth to the stereotype of hillbillies as perpetually befuddled lummoxes engaged in contentious disputes, surrounded by sexually amenable Daisy Maes, bumptious elders, and assorted comic shotgun-toting wild men, all coexisting in dim-witted timeless bliss in a junkyard Eden where tranquility is regularly shattered by thumping mountain quarrels.

As with most enduring stereotypes, there is always authentication available to those who look for it. Pikeville and the neighboring Tug Valley along the border with West Virginia were in fact the locale for the Hatfield and McCoy war that raged here after the Civil War and continued into the first years of the twentieth century. In the hilly rural areas outside of town, welfare has been a way of life for generations, the teenage pregnancy rate is among the highest in the country, abuse of both illegal and legal drugs is rampant, and feuds lasting generations simmer like stew pots.

The geography itself explains much of the history. It was here in southern Appalachia that the liberal imagination stumbled into the back alley of the industrial revolution, on a vast, fan-shaped plateau of deep, sinuous valleys and hulking mountains where wealth has been found, and carted off, since the days when the first agents of capitalism descended with pockets full of coins to claim the land.

The settlers of this place were pioneers who came through the Cumberland Gap seeking not the rich farmland of the Ohio Valley, but the nearly impenetrable hills to the east, hacking their way along animal trails into the Tug Valley, a rugged terrain that offered no guarantees except solitude. This is the hillbilly stock, described by Caudill as "a population born of embittered rejects and outcasts from the shores of Europe, as cynical, hardened, and bitter a lot as can be imagined outside prison walls."

It is a place whose young people have long plotted to leave, as soon as they can. According to Caudill, by the end of the 1950s, three-quarters of the annual crop of high school graduates were migrating out of the plateau. What they left behind was a society as stratified as its landscape, one still nearly feudal in its relationships between rich and poor—the rich clustered in small towns like Pikeville, among the banks and courthouses, the marginalized poor clinging stubbornly to life in smoky hollows and along the ridges, with walls of granite at their backs and thick veins of the richest bituminous coal in North America underfoot. Long accustomed to the appraisal of outsiders, inured to flash floods, mudslides, mine explosions, and rockfalls, alert as guerrillas this remarkably homogeneous population includes some of the most cantankerous and individualistic humans alive on the continent.

These were the people Mark Putnam, rookie special agent of the Federal Bureau of Investigation, twenty-seven years old and all of one week out of the academy, was sent to serve. Being a federal law enforcement agent in such a place meant encountering a long legacy of futility left by the land-deed agents, railroad cops, coal-company detectives, government revenuers, federal officials, and social reformers who had trampled the hills for a century, outsiders attempting to exploit—or in some cases, to save—indigenous interests. Mark brought with him an analytical wariness unusual for a young cop off on what others might have looked forward to as a great adventure.

Just before graduation from the sixteen-week training course at the academy, when he got his orders to Pikeville, he had approached an agent who had lived in Louisville, in the bluegrass flatlands of Kentucky two hundred miles across the hills. The agent had whistled softly as he looked over the rookie's papers. "Pikeville? I can't believe they're sending you there, a pretty Yankee boy in his first office! It's the mountains, Mark. You don't know what you're in for. Just watch your young ass down there, buddy."

In fact, Mark was worried not by the potential dangers of the post, but by the apparent lack of supervision. Pikeville was a two-agent office, nearly a three-hour drive from the regional office in Lexington, and farther yet from the FBI's main Kentucky office in Louisville. Shortly after the Putnams arrived, the senior agent from the Louisville office, a man seldom seen from year to year in Pikeville, drove down to offer the new arrivals a welcome. He told Mark frankly that he would have been better off in a more central office like Lexington, where there were dozens of more experienced agents to teach him the ropes. But the supervisor pointed out the bright side to Mark's situation. A small isolated office such as Pikeville offered certain career opportunities for a rookie looking to make a name for himself. It was the political and administrative center of a region that always ranked at the top for the sorts of crime and mayhem that can keep a cop's life interesting. And besides, he would not be following a tough act.

"I'll be right up-front with you, Mark. You're right out of the academy. This is an office that needs new blood. It has a lot of potential that hasn't been worked at for years. We thought that you would benefit from this. You could do a lot of screwing around down there, but you're obviously gung ho, and there's a lot to keep you busy if you want to work it. Anything that comes out of there is a bonus for us because we don't expect much from Pikeville. Look at it as a potential career-maker."

"I'm going to bust my ass for you," Mark assured him.

"Just do your caseload. You don't have to bust your ass."

It puzzled Mark not to have heard at least a robust pep talk. The senior agent left him instead with this: "I won't kid you—nobody else wants to come here, which is why you got it. Luck of the draw, I guess."

There was another, unspoken, reason for the assignment. The FBI, with its deeply entrenched love of detailed record keeping, liked to insist that its files be as neat as its agents' attire. But over years of indifference, the Pikeville Bureau had become an administrative disaster. The office needed more than new blood and a degree of supervision—it needed a clerk to straighten out the mess. Whatever his nascent abilities as a crime-fighter—and Mark Putnam had been considered one of the most promising rookies in his graduating class—he had another skill that put him at the top of the list for a vacancy to be filled in Pikeville. For four years after college, while he and Kathy worked toward getting him accepted as a special agent, Mark had toiled as a clerk in the busy FBI office in New Haven, Connecticut, where he had soaked up everything he could learn from the fifty agents assigned there, while shrugging off a depressing bureaucratic refrain: "Clerks don't make good agents." Now, having overcome that prejudice to finally gain admission to the ranks, he realized that he also had to demonstrate the obverse—that in his case, at least, an agent must also make a good clerk.

It was characteristic of the Putnams' marriage that Kathy had been the one to shore him up and motivate him for the assignment—after initially intervening and trying to have it changed. Before they packed up the car in Connecticut, Mark had told her about his apprehensions, saying, "I'm afraid I'm going to screw this up and ruin my career before it gets going. I'm a rookie and a Yankee, with no law-enforcement experience." So his wife had called the special agent in charge in Louisville to point that out, but she was told that the assignment was firm. "Tell him the Pikeville office can be a career-maker if he handles himself well," she was told.

Resigned to labor night and day to do just that, Mark reported to work on a Monday morning in late February 1987. The Pikeville FBI office was a tiny room on the ground-floor front of the federal building, with a window that looked out on Pikeville's sleepy Main Street. It was still staffed by Mark's two predecessors, Dan Brennan and Sam Smith, who were awaiting transfer to more appealing locales, with Sam headed out within a month. The new man had to squeeze past their desks to get to his makeshift work area, which consisted of a chair, a telephone, and a cleared space on the table that held the paper-shredder, mail bin, and answering machine. There was no secretary; after Mark settled in to the work routine, Kathy would begin to fill that role for him, fielding calls and passing on messages from home. When she came in to visit during Mark's first week on the job, she was surprised by the humble surroundings, which she thought looked like the cubbyhole in an automobile showroom where the customers sign the loan papers.

The office transportation fleet consisted of a beat-up Dodge Diplomat with nearly a hundred thousand hard miles on it and a four-wheel-drive Bronco, both of them already claimed by the two veteran agents. Kathy needed the Olds to get them settled in their new home. With a territory of several thousand square miles to cover in Pike County and adjoining counties in eastern Kentucky and West Virginia, Mark resented having to arrange for a bureau car like a teenager asking his father for the keys.

"Where are you going? I need to know where you're going," he would be told by one of the other agents.

"I need to go out and interview this guy. You're not using the car, dammit."

"Why don't you wait till tomorrow? We'll go out and do it together."

"Come on, man. Days are passing! I want to get rolling."

Again and again, he heard the same frustrating message. "Relax. You've got a big career ahead of you. You're not supposed to go overboard down here—this is a sleeper office that nobody cares about," as Sam Smith told him.

Yet he wasn't prepared to accept that. He finally talked Dan Brennan into a compromise arrangement to fit the twelve-hour days he'd already begun to work, every day but Sunday. Late in the afternoon, he would drive his colleague home. Then he'd use the Dodge well into the evenings to get into the hill towns to do investigative work on the cases that piled up. Because Mark reported to work at seven in the morning, two hours earlier than his colleagues, he would leave the car in Brennan's driveway that night and jog home, then jog the mile back to work the next day.

On Saturdays, he often brought little Danielle into the office, installing her at a desk to draw with crayons while he went through the mail and official dispatches, lining up the coming workweek. Sundays were family time.

"Mark went to church and usually took Danielle with him," Kathy recalled. "We actually acclimated pretty quickly to the new environment. He had the job he'd dreamed about, that we both had worked so hard for. Danielle was the center of our lives. It didn't matter if we were in Pikeville, Louisville, or Florida at that point because we had each other. When he came through the front door, she'd be right on top of him; he'd scoop her up. We read to her together every night, without fail. When he wasn't working, there was no time for anyone else but the three of us."

But Mark's long workdays left Kathy largely on her own to establish their home in a place where many things about her, not least her flat Connecticut accent, marked her as an outsider. She worked gamely at it. Thanks largely to her skills at managing money, they had had enough saved up to make the down payment on an $89,000 two-story colonial on Honeysuckle Lane, the sole street in a small development called Cedar Creek that had been built within a narrow valley between two mountains at the northern edge of town, accessible across a sway bridge over the Levisa Fork. The house, which had been on the market for over a year, was of "modular" construction; that is, large sections had been trucked in and assembled on site. Kathy's father, a building contractor in Connecticut, had inspected it with an experienced eye and pronounced the house solid and well-built when her parents came to visit for a week not long after they arrived—but a neighbor soon set her straight. "The reason the house was a bargain is, if a house isn't 'stick-built,' people think it's like a glorified trailer," Kathy was told. Their new neighbors—dentists, small-business people, accountants, and faculty members at the tiny Christian college in town—had, in fact, filed an unsuccessful lawsuit to block construction of the house years before. Later, seeing rusted trailers sagging precariously against mountain roads in the desolate hollows of the hills, Kathy understood the cultural prejudice.

Kathy, however, loved that house. "We could never have afforded a place like that in Connecticut," she said. "It had seven rooms, with hand-embroidered curtains, a nice kitchen, two full baths, nice appliances, lots of room, nice landscaping. It seemed perfect for a small family like ours."

Mark's only objection, which Kathy soon came to understand, was the mountain that loomed over the backyard. Kathy remembered him the day they moved in, standing at the sliding glass door and staring at the great muddy hulk that left the house in a cold, damp shadow for most of the afternoon. She felt a chill as she watched him.

Mark had little time to brood because he started in on his first case a few days after he reported to work. Several months earlier, a roadside bank had been robbed in a tiny mountain town on Johns Creek called Meta. The robber got away with $18,000 in cash. Since the days of Dillinger, bank robbery had been classified as a federal crime.

"We got a call from this lady who believes the guy she lives with did the robbery," his new partner Brennan told him. It looked like a break had arrived in the case. The two agents took the car and bumped along mountain roads to the trailer where the woman lived. She invited them inside. Brennan took out his notebook.

"Why do you think it was him?"

"Well, he come home that day with a potful of money."

"How much money?"

"It must of been over ten thousand dollars."

"Why are you telling on him?"

"The dirty son of a bitch won't share none of it. He's been going out, drinking it away. I need a new dress and he won't get me one. I'm mad at him, is why."

"Where is he now?"

"I ain't seen him in three days. He done took off, and he took all the money I had saved up, too."

Mark listened, thinking back to his training: the strategy of interviewing, the criminal mind, the psychology of informants. He plunged in:

"Ma'am, I'm kind of confused about something. What exactly is your relationship with this guy?"

For the first time the woman regarded him.

"I think I'm married to him, is what," she said a bit defensively.

"What do you mean, you think you are?"

"Well, we was talking about getting married, and he wrote out a piece of paper that he was going to be bringing down to the courthouse in Pikeville with twenty-five dollars that he borrowed from me. And he went down there and come back later that day and said we was married. I still have the note here with the writing on it."

She went to a drawer, withdrew a wrinkled sheet of paper, and showed it to Mark. "I don't read," she said casually, as if she were declining milk and sugar with her coffee.

The scrawled note said: "*By this hereby, advices that these two are legally married*," and below that both names were handwritten.

Mark surmised that they had their robber, but Brennan warned him not to jump to conclusions.

In a few days, they discovered that the man had a different story. He said he had gone into town to file for divorce against his actual wife, and he needed the $25 as a filing fee. He volunteered to take a lie detector test and passed it without any problem. The woman in the trailer had named him as a bank robber only in retaliation for his reneging on a marriage promise. To a young agent who still studied his notebooks from the academy at night, it was a small but important lesson in gratuitous deceit, banal revenge, hidden agendas, and the perils of easy assumptions.

Without supervision, desperate to assimilate and learn, Mark soon found a way to get into the hills during the day without reliable availability of a car. He surprised some local law enforcement officers, who tended to resent the FBI for its haughtiness and its preoccupation with its image, by asking to tag along on their patrols. At the academy, the value of good relationships with the local cops had been stressed. Mark's purpose was to see and be seen—he wanted to cover eastern Kentucky like a Bible salesman. It amused him that the cops who befriended him from the beginning were actually named Hatfield and McCoy. Paul Hatfield, Fred McCoy, and Bert Hatfield, all of the Pike County sheriff's office, let him ride with them and introduced him to the old coal towns and hill settlements. Bert, a tall, laconic young sheriff's deputy who also sold used cars from a small lot in Freeburn, an old coal company town on the bank of the Tug across from West Virginia—"three mountains away from Pikeville," as he called it—became a particularly good ally.

Bert was endlessly amused by the young FBI man's driving skills, or lack of them. "That the way they teach you to drive up in Connecticut?" he joked one afternoon as Mark cautiously maneuvered the sheriff's car around a blind curve on a narrow asphalt road cut into a sharp ridge high above the treetops. On the way back to town, Bert took the wheel and showed him how it was done, racing around the switchbacks with tires squealing. "This is the way us hillbillies drive," he said. Still, Bert was pleased to see that Mark Putnam learned fast.

Before long, Bert and Mark had forged a friendship working together on bank robberies and other cases in the rural mountain belt around Pikeville. Bert was amazed that the new FBI man was often without transportation.

"We'd use my car. I'd even drive into Pikeville and pick him up, which was pretty sad, if you ask me," Bert recalled many years later. "I liked working with the guy. He wasn't standoffish like other FBI can be in dealing with local police. He was a natural law-enforcement officer, but green. I'd say he had knowledge and instincts, but no skill at first. That boy came out here when he'd never had a single day's experience, but he sure did work hard. Very fast, he learned how and how not. He was ready and he was gung-ho."

Bert added, "One thing about some law enforcement guys is they're lazier than shit, and they're always looking at the clock. But not me and him. We'd go till all hours. We never said, hell it's quitting time."

Yet as he got to know local cops, Mark found that the lines of his dealings with them could get just as tangled as they had been in the trailer of the woman who reported the bank robber. Once, deep in the coalfields to serve a federal fugitive warrant he was approached by a local police officer.

"I hear you're looking for this boy."

"Yeah, I am."

"Well, can you kind of leave him alone?"

"What do you mean, leave him alone?"

"Well, he's my second cousin. He's a real good boy."

"Hey, man, I got a warrant for him. I can't do that!"

"Hell, sure you can."

When he didn't, word got around.

Money talks, as cops know, but its voice carried particular resonance in eastern Kentucky, where information has long been a commodity. All law enforcement agencies, including the county sheriff's office that Bert worked for, paid for information, but the FBI had especially deep pockets. Money was readily available for most criminal investigations. All an agent had to do was recruit a potential informant and, once that recruit provided information that proved to be valuable, make a request to the central office to designate that person as a working informant. Then the agent would fill out a voucher with the amount and a few sentences describing the new information likely to be yielded. Within a week a check for $500 or $1,000 would come from Louisville, and the agent would be expected to hand that money over to the informant.

Later, Mark would recall his amazement at discovering how the system worked. "I'd go to an informant, 'I've got something for you.' And then the guy would be just awe-struck that I was actually giving him the whole five hundred or thousand dollars and not holding out like two hundred dollars of it for myself. It was incredible how fast the word got around that I was good for the money. People would actually call the office offering information for sale.

After a while, I didn't have to go out anymore and drum up business—it just came to me."

By summer, Mark felt a long way from the academy. While his rookie classmates were still processing paperwork or working routine details under the supervision of senior agents in Chicago, Miami, or Denver, Mark had already set up a network of informants and, he thought, established himself as a streetwise crime-fighter who was living the life that he had always dreamed about.

One sultry morning while he was at his desk, gazing out at Main Street, he heard the crackle of gunfire, and a federal probation officer burst in from the hall shouting, "Boys, there's bodies on the ground!"

Gun drawn, heart pounding, Mark tumbled outside with Brennan, who ordered, "Watch the buildings, Putnam—snipers! I'm going up to the bank." The bank was a block away.

Mark scampered across the street where two women lay on the sidewalk. Outside the bank, Brennan was crouched over the body of a man.

The older woman was dead, but the younger one was still alive, bleeding heavily with gunshot wounds to the neck and shoulder. "Don't let me die . . . help me," she gasped as Mark crawled to her side. He reached her and said, "It'll be okay. *Look at my face.* Hold on to my hand."

She grabbed his hand tightly. She was still alive when the paramedics came.

When they took her away, the agents pieced together the story with help from state police officers who arrived on the scene. The gunman was the young woman's husband. He had shot her and her mother as they were on their way to the county courthouse to file for a restraining order against him. Then he had turned the gun on himself.

"Family feud," one of the state cops said with a shrug. "We see a lot of it."

2

To a bank robber, eastern Kentucky offers unusual challenges and unusual opportunities. In some ways, it is not an ideal place to rob a bank. For one thing, the region has an FBI office charged with investigating bank robberies. For another, robbing a bank is usually a daylight pursuit requiring the capacity to get away in a car—not an easy task in a place where narrow roads run up one side of a mountain and wind down the other, and the nearest interstate was two hours of bad road away.

But on the other hand, in the 1980s, before big national banks swallowed up nearly all of the local ones, most banks in the eastern Kentucky coal regions were independently owned, sometimes as mom-and-pop operations. In many impoverished towns where business and real-estate activities were minimal, the main purposes of the tiny local banks were to act as a check-cashing agency for welfare, coal miners' union pension, and Social Security disability insurance payments, and to accept cash deposits. By the 1980s, drug dealers were also depending on local banks to stash their cash. In any case, independent banks in isolated mountain settlements tend to be guarded with about as much fortification as a hot dog stand.

Such banks, naturally, drew freelance opportunists in the form of robbers wanting money in a hurry but who haven't always clearly thought through their plans—such as the robber who hid on a bank roof to pounce on the driver for the Piggly-Wiggly store making his night deposit—and missed, knocking himself out cold in the parking lot. Or the hapless gang who held up a bank on Peter Creek, found themselves stranded when the getaway driver got lost en route, politely borrowed a teller's car keys, and then ran out of gas a half mile down the road.

This atmosphere, however, underwent a change during the late spring and summer of 1987 in the hill towns of the Tug Valley when there was an unusual spurt of bank robberies. Small banks in the mountain towns on both the Kentucky and West Virginia sides of the Tug were being knocked off, not only efficiently, but in a similar manner, by a robber using a sawed-off shotgun, with accomplices wearing ski-masks with crudely cut holes for their eyes. The modus operandi was familiar enough to local cops like Bert Hatfield, who guessed that their suspect was a well-known hometown rogue, Carl Edward "Cat Eyes" Lockhart. Cat Eyes was recently released from prison and on probation for robbing banks; he'd apparently gone back to his line of work, probation be damned.

As bank robbers go, Cat Eyes was an unusual case. He had much of the audacity of John Dillinger, only a little of the skill, and absolutely none of the discretion. A proud man, when he got out of prison, Cat Eyes Lockhart had announced his return to work in the Tug Valley to virtually everyone he knew. What's more, Cat Eyes was spending his loot freely, on things like a used Pontiac Firebird Trans Am with the classic gold "Screaming Chicken" stenciled on the hood, much like the one Burt Reynolds drove in the 1977 movie *Smokey and the Bandit*. If Cat Eyes had $5,000 in cash to spend on a flashy used car when he was only a few weeks out of prison, Hatfield had a pretty good idea where that money came from.

Cat Eyes had savoir faire, definitely. He was a soft-spoken, dark-haired young man with luminous green eyes that provided him with his nickname and helped establish his amiable reputation. From childhood on, his stated goal in life had been to be a bank robber. Having achieved that, he had just been released from a Virginia penitentiary after serving seven years of an eighteen-year sentence for a brazen robbery in 1980. In that case, he had gotten away with $300,000 from a bank in Grundy, Virginia, a small town at a crossroads near the corner of the Appalachians where the borders of Virginia, Kentucky, and West Virginia touch.

Cat Eyes was a legend in the Tug Valley, mostly for having spent that $300,000—*all of it*—in a wild three-month spree driving through several Southern states in a white Cadillac El Dorado with a friend. The desperadoes' odyssey had culminated in a truly epic week of debauchery and gambling in Nashville, where the boys dropped their last $50,000 before turning up, frazzled and broke, back home. There they were promptly arrested.

Cat's favorite haunt was the small wood-frame house just across the Tug Fork River in Vulcan, West Virginia, where Kenneth and Susie Smith lived. The house sat next to a little bridge that crossed the Tug to Freeburn on the Kentucky side. Beside that bridge was Bert Hatfield's car lot. Cat Eyes even had the courtesy to wave when he drove past in his Pontiac Firebird.

In June, Bert called up his new friend Mark Putnam and told him he thought he knew who was behind the latest spurt of bank robberies.

"Who's that?" Mark said.

"A fella named Lockhart. Cat Eyes Lockhart." Bert described the man.

"How do you know it's him?"

"Well, all of a sudden, he's rich. One thing about the guy, he spends it." Bert explained that all the reports mentioned the robber's bulky coveralls and ski mask, Cat Eyes's favored disguise.

"Any ideas on how we catch him?"

Bert had a good one. He offered to introduce Mark to Kenneth Smith, Cat Eyes's boyhood friend, unabashed admirer and, it now appeared, host.

Cat Eyes's chief virtues were gregariousness, loquaciousness, and generosity—qualities admirable in law-abiding citizens, but problematic in bank robbers. Cat was so likable that many people would hide him when he required sanctuary, but he was also so gracious that he made it a point to publicly acknowledge the hospitality. Cat liked to think of himself as Robin Hood, without considering the fact that the ancient English outlaw stayed out of custody by hiding in a forest. Cat preferred a more public role. When Cat had money, his friends prospered. He would not only share booze, cocaine, and cash, but also make other gestures certain to gain both admiration and attention, such as buying sneakers and clothing for their wives and children.

After Cat was paroled, Kenneth Smith—himself on probation for drug possession—had graciously invited Cat and his girlfriend, Sherri Justice, to move out of the tent where they had been living in Cat's mother's backyard in Kentucky and come to stay awhile. Kenneth had been married to a Freeburn girl from Barrenshee Hollow, Susie Daniels, for five years, and though they'd divorced a few years earlier, they still lived together, off and on. Susie claimed that it was for the sake of the two children, although people close to her knew that the drugs Kenneth usually managed to get were part of the allure. Kenneth liked cocaine and booze. Susan preferred pills, which were readily available in the region, where many doctors ran "pain management" clinics catering to patients on welfare, disability, Medicaid, and Medicare. The four-room bungalow just across the river where Susan, Kenneth, and the two children lived had long been a social center for the disaffiliated, a place to drop by, borrow clothes, drink beer, smoke cigarettes, or snort cocaine at the kitchen table, and, for those so inclined, crash for the night on the couch.

Oblivious to Susie's haphazard efforts to maintain a household like the suburban ones she saw on television sitcoms, Kenneth invited Cat and Sherri to "stay on the place, do odd jobs for your keep," for as long as it took them to find their own place and settle down—a goal that Cat set out to finance the way he knew best.

Cat liked to embellish his legend by discussing bank-robbing strategy to the shifting population around the Smiths' kitchen table: when banks opened and closed, whether they were constructed of brick or clapboard, where the alarms were located, how many employees they had, when they got the cash deliveries for "check day," when welfare checks arrived at the start of the month. A thorough appreciation of such minutiae, Cat maintained with elaborate gravity, was what separated the amateur from the professional. All summer long, Kenneth and Susie Smith listened with fascination. Susie, who thought of herself as a practical woman, was especially taken with Cat's investment advice: "Trailers. You buy a bunch of them and sit back and collect the rent."

As both a car salesman and a part-time cop, Bert Hatfield made it a point to keep informed on who had spending money in the small universe of the upper Tug Valley. He suggested to Mark that Kenneth Smith, chronically broke but with expensive tastes, might be open to the kind of persuasion the FBI's deep pockets could provide. In August, there was another small bank robbery. Mark and Dan Brennan spent several days visiting dozens of bank branch offices to warn them of the robbery spree and discuss security. Meanwhile, Bert had Kenneth come to Pikeville to see Mark.

The meeting wasn't promising. Kenneth had a list of demands. He would cooperate—without specifying as to exactly what that would entail—only in exchange for being removed from probation and given protective custody. He also wanted a weekly salary, with bonuses for specific information, such as the activities of Cat Eyes. Afterward, Mark contacted Kenneth's parole officer, who said, "Forget it. The guy is totally unreliable." Besides, for a smalltime drug dealer, Kenneth had a notoriously bad memory. His ex-wife was the one who kept track of the details.

Bert, who had known twenty-five-year-old Susie Smith all her life, suggested to Mark that they approach her instead. He warned Mark that Susie "ran her mouth" frequently and did not have a good reputation for telling the truth. Still, with the suspected bank robber living in her house, she had the right connections, and she had secretly provided Bert with useful information in the past. Bert thought she would be worth pursuing for information on the bank robberies and the chief suspect.

By this time, Susie had begun to weary of her houseguests anyway. She liked having people around, but Cat ate like a wolf and ran up the phone bill calling his former prison buddies long-distance. Having his girlfriend in the house created extra tension because Susie was pretty and Cat flirted with her incessantly. Besides, Cat was broke again and needed not only a place to stay with his girlfriend, but gas money for his car. Even though Susie at the time was working a common Tug Valley welfare scam and collecting monthly checks from both West Virginia and Kentucky, money didn't go far with six people in the house—more, if you counted Tennis Daniels, a troublesome younger brother of Susie's, and the others who drifted in and out on a regular basis. She also worried about the effect on her two young children, Miranda Lynn, five years old, and Brady, who had just turned two. By the summer, she and Kenneth were fighting openly over what Susie had come to regard as an intolerable domestic arrangement.

First, Bert decided to introduce Mark to Tennis, whom Bert had also used as an occasional informant, paying him with pittances of fifty or a hundred dollars that the sheriff's department reluctantly agreed to part with from time to time. On the night before they were to get together, however, Bert called Mark at home.

"We got big problems. Tennis shot somebody."

The next morning, they drove directly to Susan's house. It had been a family dispute. Tennis had fled after the shooting, but while they were there, he walked in. Mark persuaded him to give himself up, saying, "They'll be a hell of a lot easier on you. We'll try our damnedest." They called the West Virginia state police barracks just a few miles up the river past Matewan. As they waited for the troopers to arrive, Susie Smith, her eyes blazing with resentment, took the occasion to unload on this self-assured young FBI agent who had barged into her house. Who was he to be looking for a new informant for the FBI? A relative of hers had once helped the FBI in a case, she told Mark sharply, and never got the money that was promised. Fair, she said, hands on her hips, was fair.

As they drove back to Kentucky, Mark reflected on Susie. "Bert, that girl is trouble."

"You're right about that," his companion replied.

Mark said, "Keep working on her, will you?"

Bert nodded, but he was a little annoyed. He'd known Susie since they were both kids. He'd been working her as an informant for years.

A few days later, Mark managed to get the bureau car and made some calls. He found Cat Eyes himself fishing in a dirty pond near a strip-mine site halfway up a mountain. He said hello, and the two young men chatted for a while. Cat, ever cordial, denied robbing banks, but added that he appreciated the courtesy of an introduction.

Not long afterward, when another bank was robbed in a mountain town just across the river Bert called Mark and said Susie had reconsidered, "Okay, she wants to meet."

They drove to a small restaurant in Williamson, a gritty river town in the rocky coalfields on the West Virginia side. Susie arrived accompanied by Kenneth and Tennis, now out on bail on the manslaughter charge. They sat at a table, Kenneth dominating the conversation while Mark made eye contact with Susie, who at least gave him a smile. After a while he asked her quietly, "Listen, could I talk to you alone for a minute?"

Kenneth stopped talking long enough to glower when his ex-wife, defiantly tossing back her brown hair, followed the FBI man out to the parking lot. Through the window, he watched them get into Bert's car and have a conversation.

Mark tried to size her up. She was street-smart, that was obvious. There was an edge and an attitude to her, something he liked in women. She wasn't about to be pushed around. He didn't think she was particularly attractive, although she was generally considered in town to be fairly pretty, with small features, a trim figure that she liked to flaunt, and a smile that was definitely engaging when she turned it on. Like most young women in the Valley, she put on makeup every morning whether she was going somewhere special or not.

"So what do you want to talk about?" she asked, amused.

"Listen, I want to know if you're interested in helping me."

"Now, why would I want to do something like that?"

He explained that money was available. She shook her head disdainfully. He kept at her, thinking, *I am going to break this girl.*

She changed the subject.

"I see you're married. Tell me what your wife looks like."

"What does that have to do with anything? We're talking about—"

"Pretty?"

"Yes, she's pretty."

"She have a good body?"

"She keeps herself in very good shape, Susie," he said, glancing at her tanned legs, exposed in high-cut shorts. Momentarily flustered, she placed her palms unconsciously across her thighs. At five feet five and 125 pounds, she was a bit self-conscious about the ten pounds she had put on during the spring.

"Don't call me Susie. I hate it. It's Susan."

"Okay, Susan." He smiled at her. "Will you help?"

She said she'd think about it, and they went back to the restaurant, where Kenneth and Tennis sat glumly waiting.

Over the next week, Mark and Susan met twice more, privately, and as an understanding evolved, he explained the payment process: "First, you have to give me something to take back." Taking out a notebook that she eyed nervously, Mark got her talking about Cat Eyes.

"Him? Oh, he might be involved in them bank robberies; I surely don't know." She crossed her arms. "He is a robber, after all."

She doled out information in careful increments, and he let her talk. Mark, like many naturally quiet men, was an exceptionally good listener, and it was apparent to him that this was a woman as accustomed to giving attention as getting it. From time to time, he would ask a pertinent question, and she would add a pertinent piece of information. It was a complicated negotiation of egos. Before long, they had arrived at an accommodation. Yes, she finally said, she definitely thought that Cat Eyes was planning on robbing another bank.

"How do you know?"

"He's living with me and Kenneth. Him and his girlfriend."

She knew that Mark was well aware of that, but he played the game. "How come?"

"He's broke. Kenneth likes him."

"Do you?"

"I suppose. I just don't want to adopt him. I already got two kids."

"Doesn't he pay you?"

"No."

"I thought he was so generous."

She shrugged. "He is when he has it."

"Sounds to me like he's taking advantage of you. Exploiting you, like he doesn't give a shit about you."

That got her attention. She agreed to meet Mark the next time in Pikeville. And before long, they were meeting two and three times a week, in a pattern that would continue for the rest of her short life.

Mark knew the basic procedures for working with informants. In sixteen weeks of training at the FBI Academy, new agents received a few lectures on what motivates informants: greed, money, revenge, or occasionally even a sense of duty. The delicate business of actually developing and maintaining relationships with informants, the backbone of the FBI's investigative process, was passed over with a few rhetorical nostrums, the most important of which was, "Don't get personally involved with your informants." Yet even the dullest rookie recognized this as pure bullshit, since the only way to develop a worthwhile informant was through personal trust and loyalty—underscore the word personal.

Money paved the way. To "open" a new informant once that person received initial approval, an agent was allotted five thousand dollars to be distributed at the agent's discretion, and more down the road, with virtually no limit on the amount, depending on the usefulness of the information in gaining convictions. From the beginning, Susan understood that she could earn thousands of dollars for cooperating, if she could deliver. But while Mark was prudently nervous about spending the government's money, he had determined that Susan was willing to talk, that she could provide specific information in a criminal case, and furthermore, she could probably open doors to him in future investigations. So he wrote out a requisition and sent it to his nominal supervisor, Terry Hulse, who ran the Covington branch office near Cincinnati, more than two hundred miles away. When Hulse phoned to talk about it, Mark wondered uneasily if he had done something naïve.

At first, Hulse did not sound encouraging when he asked on the phone, "Mark are you sure about this money for this informant?"

"What do you mean?"

"You're only going to give this girl five hundred dollars?"

"Talk to me some more."

"Well, I mean, she's giving you information on this guy—you know this guy's doing this robbery, don't you?"

"Yeah, I'm about ninety-five percent sure he's doing it."

"So keep her on board. Give her more money."

Mark thought about that for a moment, then said, "This girl's holding back—we're playing a kind of cat-and-mouse game right now. I just want to get her in the habit."

"Okay, I'll buy it. I like it. But let me tell you something: The money is there. Use it. Especially in your area. Don't feel like you're prostituting yourself by giving these people money. They want it. You've got it to give."

"Thanks."

At their next meeting, when he gave Susan the five hundred dollars, she seemed a little rattled, which was the first time he had seen her so.

"Hey, there's more, but the information has got to back it up," Mark said. "My boss is a real prick when it comes to this money."

Mark didn't realize that to Susan, taking the money was a major step. He wouldn't understand until it was too late that once she took money from the FBI there would be no turning back.

Susan Smith was born in 1961 in Matewan, West Virginia, an heir to two famous legends of the Tug Valley. Her mother, Tracy, was directly descended from the McCoys of the Hatfield–McCoy feud. And her birthplace, which had the nearest hospital to Freeburn, about eight miles away on the Kentucky side of the Tug Fork, was the scene of one of the great dramas of the bitter coal-mine union organizing wars, the 1920 "Matewan Massacre," in which nine men died in a shoot-out after a force of private detectives working for Tug Valley coal companies evicted miners and their families from company houses. The hero of that insurrection was the police chief, Sid Hatfield, who stood with the miners. Sheriff Hatfield, of course, was descended from the Hatfield side of the feud.

The Matewan Massacre was historical fact. The Hatfield–McCoy feud is one of those curious specimens of American folklore that, like much of the popular mythology of the Wild West, owes a certain amount of its historical longevity to the invention of the high-speed rotary printing press and the coinciding imperatives of market capitalist expansionism. Which is to say that while the Hatfields and McCoys did indeed shoot and kill each other over a period of many years from their respective turf on either side of the Tug Fork, the commotion would have gone largely unnoticed if it hadn't been exploited by outsiders looking for profit.

The two legends are nevertheless closely related. "In American history and folklore the Hatfields and the McCoys symbolize the backwardness and family violence most Americans associate with Appalachian mountain culture," the historian Altina L. Wailer wrote. The Hatfield–McCoy saga, the most famous of many long-running mountain feuds, is actually "a story involving competition over rich timber resources and the desire of Eastern corporations and the state government to foster economic development in the region. The feud was more a foreshadowing of the era of the bloody coal-mine wars than it was the final gasp of traditional mountain culture."

The Hatfields lived, by and large, on the West Virginia side of the Tug Fork and the McCoys kept to the Kentucky side, although the boundary has never been regarded seriously by the people who live there, isolated together by mountains at their backs. (The boundary was in fact drawn somewhat arbitrarily during an all-night drinking session in 1799 by members of a joint commission.)

There were long-standing animosities between the Hatfields and McCoys, as is inevitable in places where generation after generation of rival families literally face each other, keeping track of grudges over decades. Like many neighbors, the clans sometimes fought over property. In a time just before outside industrialists would begin plundering the Appalachians for hardwood, both families made money from cutting and selling timber on their lands, and deeds were not always firmly fixed in mountain areas. But the trouble really came to a head with the theft of a pig.

In 1878, a Hatfield boy was accused of stealing a hog from the patriarch of the less-prosperous McCoy clan, a cantankerous man known as Old Ranel McCoy. The dispute went to trial in Kentucky, but the Hatfield boy was acquitted thanks to a not-guilty vote by one of six McCoys on the jury, introducing an element of betrayal into the rancor. A few years later, acrimony escalated when Old Ranel's daughter, Roseanna, ran off with Johnse Hatfield, a son of Devil Anse Hatfield, the ferocious but generally law-abiding patriarch of the Hatfield clan. Over Johnse's protests, Devil Anse adamantly refused to allow his son to marry her; the girl was sent back home across the Tug, literally barefoot and pregnant.

Roseanna's brothers set out to avenge the family honor by kidnapping the Hatfield boy, whom they intended to transport to Pikeville and charge with the only criminal violation they could prove, moonshining. But the lovesick Roseanna thwarted them by stealing off at night on horseback to warn Johnse. Meanwhile, on election day, when whiskey flowed freely and voters stumbled across the river to cast ballots on both sides, tempers flared. During a brawl between the young men of both families, Devil Anse's brother, Ellison, was beaten and stabbed by Hatfield boys, one of whom finished him off with a shotgun. A Pike County judge, on the scene to purchase votes, ordered the arrest of the perpetrator and several other McCoy boys. But on the long horseback ride to Pikeville with the boys in custody, a posse of Hatfields, led by Devil Anse himself, overtook the party, kidnapped three of the McCoys, and shot them on the riverbank, near what is now Matewan.

There were sporadic instances of violent retaliation between the two families, but the feud didn't reach its full intensity until five years later. That was when Perry Cline, a Pikeville lawyer who had once fought a legal battle with Devil Anse over five thousand acres of disputed land, decided to reopen his claim, since the property's value was rising sharply as the timber industry expanded and the railroads blasted through the hills into the Tug Valley. Cline prevailed on Kentucky authorities to press the five-year-old murder indictments against the Hatfields, who soon had lucrative bounties on their heads offered by lumber and railroad interests. Devil Anse and his men fled into the hills, pursued by hordes of private detectives and other bounty hunters. Their exploits were celebrated in newly established mass-circulation newspapers like Joseph Pulitzer's *New York World*, where the legend of "white savages" clinging to a primitive region "as remote as Central Africa" caught the fancy of millions of urban readers. By the time the feud died out at the turn of the century, a dozen or so Hatfields and McCoys had been killed, and one of the most enduring caricatures in American culture—the bellicose hillbilly—had been created. Significantly, according to Waller, "many Appalachians themselves had been convinced of the inadequacy of their own culture, and industrialization proceeded with little opposition." Within decades, the largest hardwood forest on the continent—seven million mountainous acres of virgin tulip poplars towering 150 feet over walnuts and white oak, hickories and maple, buckeyes, basswoods, ash, cedar, and pine—had been reduced to less than a thousand acres.

Two hundred million years ago, the Cumberland Plateau of eastern Kentucky was a plain that had risen from the floor of an inland sea. The earth cracked, leaving a jagged fault, pushing up mountains of limestone and slate, seldom more than three thousand feet high, that ripple like a rug bunched against the northern watershed of the Appalachians. As the ancient sea receded, it left a vast trough of peat that would ultimately curse the land and its people when the overlying mountains compressed it into what regional historian Harry M. Caudill called "a mineral the steel age would esteem more highly than rubies"—coal.

Timber had been hauled out chiefly by push boats and steamboats along the swift currents of the Tug and Levisa forks to the Big Sandy River, and thence to the thousand-mile sweep of the Ohio River. The railroad arrived in 1881 in Louisa, where the two forks meet, ushering in a new era of exploitation. This time the prize was the region's vast resources of high-quality, low-ash bituminous coal that lay in fat four- and six-foot seams. Gangs of immigrant construction workers, whose prowess would become embodied by mythical steel-driving men such as John Henry, slashed rights-of-way through ridges and laid bridges between cliffs as the railroad pushed inexorably up the valley, crisscrossing the hills with an intricate web of spurs and short lines. With the railroad came the speculators, agents of Wall Street and the mineral companies. These "foreign lawyers," as they were called, were expert at providing slick legal documentation, often certified at the courthouse in Pikeville, to lay claim to tenuously deeded property.

The greatest entrepreneur of them all was one John Caldwell Calhoun Mayo, a Pikeville prospector. After studying the newly completed federal geological surveys and obtaining financial backing from banks, he tramped the hills securing claims from gullible—and naturally hospitable—hillbillies with an innovative contract that acquired mineral rights independently of surface land rights. Such deeds, thousands of which remained in existence well into the 1980s, gave to the developers broad rights to all minerals in the land—including the perpetual right to make roads, knock down trees, buildings, and even cemeteries, pollute water supplies, or do anything else "necessary or convenient" to exploit the minerals, without liability. A standard rule of thumb among the speculators was that fifteen thousand tons of coal could be gouged out of an acre of such land. On many of his forays shortly after the turn of the century, Mayo was accompanied by his wife, Alice, who had dresses specially made with pockets for $20 gold pieces, which she ceremoniously dropped into the hands of hillbillies, who sold their rights for as little as fifty cents an acre. To attract Eastern capital, Mayo even arranged "safaris" into the hills of the Tug Valley for parties of bankers and developers, who were outfitted in khaki and pith helmets, with meals on the trail whipped up by the world-famous New York chef Oscar of the Waldorf.

From Mayo's expeditions, which within ten years would lay claim to mineral rights on more than 90 percent of the land in Kentucky counties such as Pike, Floyd, Harlan, and Letcher, sprang scores of coal-company camp towns—some well-maintained, many others squalid, all featuring rows of houses arranged in monotonous similarity—with names like Jennings, Neon-Fleming, Happy, Sassafras, McRoberts, and Freeburn. In these vast regions of what became known as the Thacker Coalfield, the coal camps sprang up independently of normal migratory patterns, in the isolation of the hills and backwaters. Their economies were based on company issued "scrip," currency usable only in the company store, with sharp social distinctions between the miners and their families in their squat company houses, and the "big bosses," the executives and foremen, who lived in comfortable and sometimes luxurious residences, typically built on higher ground with a commanding view of the dust-covered shacks, coal tipples, and slag heaps below.

Freeburn, by the time Susan Smith was born, had long since been abandoned by a succession of coal companies that had maintained it until machine-driven strip-mining revolutionized the industry in the 1950s. But there were still a few old-timers in town who could remember the days when patriotism and company loyalty were inseparable, when coal miners, their wives, and children would leave their company houses in town and gather at the company auditorium, known to all as simply "The Building," where in unison they would recite the Freeburn Creed:

I believe in Freeburn, its splendid traditions, its present greatness as a mining prospect, its magnificent prospects for the future.

I believe in the Portsmouth By-Product Coke Company, its high ideals in matters of relations between the employer and the employed, its earnest and just consideration for the happiness and welfare of its workmen, the policy of its officials to deal foursquare with everyone.

I believe in the people of Freeburn as among the best created.

*I therefore believe it is my duty to my own town to love
it, to support it, to respect it, to boost it, and to defend it.*

The Building and the company store had burned down before Susan was born. Even the union, which had transformed miners' lives in the Depression, was barely a factor now. By the 1980s, the United States was producing more coal than ever—85 percent of it going to produce cheap electricity in the United States, Japan, and Europe. But coal prices dropped by more than a third in the first half of the eighties, and unemployment in the region sometimes exceeded 40 percent. Federal relief funds that had poured in with the Great Society programs of the 1960s—most of that spending actually went to build roads—had virtually dried up in the Reagan era. The pace quickened to mine what was left. Coal trucks thundered down mountain roads, overloaded by as much as fifty thousand pounds, with drivers speeding to make two trips a day, getting $1.30 a ton to haul coal to the Ohio River port at Catlettsburg. Ironically, in the urban areas of America where the cheap electricity provided by low-priced coal was being devoured, it cost as much as $100 a ton at this time to haul garbage.

Throughout Susan's lifetime in the Appalachian Mountains, creeks and streams flowed red with toxic runoff from strip mines. Mudslides, on hills now denuded of topsoil and trees, routinely roared down in heavy rains to cut off populated hollows for days. Impoverished mountain hamlets, which themselves had no trash-removal services, were inundated with applications from outside companies who wanted to use the land for dumps, incinerators, and nuclear waste disposal.

Even the land itself had become unstable. Mountains gutted for coal sometimes settle like sand castles; fissures tear open like earthquake faults; there are stories about hunters who have lost good dogs into a sudden break in the earth. The noise of settling mountains, frightening even to those who are used to it, is a hell-ish, primordial cracking of rock.

Such places breed a certain wariness and even resentment of outsiders. In 1992, for example, two unrelated columns appeared on the same feature page of the *Floyd County Times*. One defended the area against a central-Kentucky newspaper account "about how we barefooted, nasal-whining, whiskey-drinking, cock-fighting, illiterate, illegitimate scumbags have become full-fledged dope addicts." Another excoriated a two-year-old TV network news report on Appalachia that focused on a local town: "Pretty much everybody else in the country thinks we're nothing more than toothless hicks playing the banjo on the front porch of our shacks while we stare out at our front yards filled with rusted-out car bod-ies, old washing machines and outhouses with half-moons crudely carved into the doors." One local wag, however, took exception to at least one aspect of that and commented in a letter, "That cannot be true because we all know that anybody that could play the banjo got the heck out of here."

But facts tend to feed the stereotypes. Not long afterward, a Mingo County, West Virginia, newspaper reported on a shoot-out between two local families that left one dead and nine oth-ers wounded. The argument was over a woman who had dated a member of the rival family.

A woman of Susan's age who grew up on the Barrenshee Hollow remembered sharing a room with four sisters in two beds, and fetching water on winter mornings from a well whose chain was caked with ice. Clothes were laundered outside in the butter-churn and hung on long lines up the hill like battleship flags in the wind. She recalled school days hiding from the truant officer because she had no shoes; breakfasts of biscuits and gravy for the week after check day; bread and milk the rest of the month. She remembered her father trudging home across the mountain from the mine in Majestic at night, his face black with soot. Like many of the old miners, he died of black lung disease, an oxygen tank by his bed.

A child who grew up in such circumstances learned early about physical, natural, and economic and social hazards. By the summer of 1987, Susan had already lived a hard fifteen years since she had announced at the end of seventh grade that she had "better things to do" and dropped out of school. If she'd gone on to eighth grade, she would have had to ride a school bus each day along Peter Creek and around the mountain to Phelps, a settlement somewhat more lively than decrepit old Freeburn. She had already been in a couple of physical altercations with girls in elementary school; Susan fought readily and ferociously enough to be ostracized among her better-mannered classmates. In a household where a smack across the face was a routine response to even minor transgression, in a social world where a young girl with a fast mouth sometimes had to defend herself with her fists, Susan had reached adolescence with physical threats already firmly established in her life.

She was poor—her family was on welfare nearly all of her life, and she was ashamed of it. Susan had grown up the fifth of nine children of a chronically unemployed coal miner, Sid Daniels, and his long-suffering wife, Tracy Eldridge Daniels. The children shared clothes and even shoes, in a drafty house high up Barrenshee Hollow in Freeburn, a gloomy mountain gulch that some locals called, more pungently, "Lonesome Holler."

It was a place where trouble never was far away. Susan started school in 1966, at a time when cheap oil was flooding the country and the Appalachian coal industry, already battered by unemployment caused by the growth of efficient strip-mining, sank into one of its cyclical severe depressions. At that time, only one in four students in Pike County finished high school; the majority had already dropped out by ninth grade. In back country areas like the one where she grew up, the high school graduation rate was as low as 7 percent. Dropping out of school came naturally to Susan, a smart girl who had already ascertained that the only way to escape the hard times was to pounce on any opportunity she came across—or simply flee. In 1960, the population of Pike County was 81,154; ten years later, it would be 61,059.

Natural peril intensified a child's sense of fatalism in a mountain hollow, in a place where mine disasters were a routine part of life, and spring rains often unleashed great mud-banks of strip-mine debris and boulders from eroded mountaintops. Catastrophic floods devastated the Tug Valley twice during her youth, in 1963, and again in 1977, when she was fifteen. That year the river, swollen by fifteen inches of rain that fell on still-frozen ground, crested at fifty feet and swept away hundreds of homes in the Valley.

In Freeburn, few of the four hundred or so residents even had telephones during Susan's childhood years—but many acquired television sets, at a time when the initial business of regional cable TV companies was to provide service to rural places. When she was a little girl, Susan decided that she wanted to be a secretary like the ones she saw on television shows. Well-heeled men respected secretaries. Secretaries dressed beautifully and lived fashionably in cities. Secretaries were *helpers,* and Susan, when she was at her best, was a helper. When some of her siblings got into a jam, Susan was the one they turned to for help.

Like most out-of-work miners, her father drank hard. Like most women in the hollow, her mother remained in the background. Susan had few friends. "She was like a stray kitten with a temper," one woman who grew up with her would later recall sadly. "A girl with fancy ideas and an attitude and a temper to boot don't make a lot of friends."

Instead, Susan nourished what were referred to as "notions." The highlight of Susan's grade-school years was her belonging to the Patriotettes, the school's all-girl drill team. No one in town knew the history well enough to enlighten her, but that drill team had actually been organized early in the century by the Portsmouth-Solvay Coke Company, the firm that had built the squat rows of miners' houses along the Tug Fork and named the town Freeburn, after the valued properties of the indigenous bituminous coal. The little girl from Barrenshee Hollow loved her red-and-white Patriotettes uniform and wore it proudly in ragtag holiday parades. In her seventh-grade yearbook, Susan's picture stands out among those of her classmates with pigtails and scrubbed faces. She is the only one wearing a beret.

In 1977, the year of the big flood, fifteen-year-old Susan saw her first opportunity to get out. She met twenty-two-year-old Kenneth Smith, a good-looking local boy who could be charming when he wanted something—the kind of young rogue a girl's father warns her about, if the father is paying attention. When Kenneth spotted her in town and whistled, Susan hopped on the back of his motorcycle and rode off with him to a trailer he rented on the far side of the mountain, in another old coal company town called Majestic.

Kenneth, who fancied himself a successful gambler, actually earned his money by selling drugs. Like most dealers, he visited big cities from time to time. Susan resolved to go with him, and he was smart enough to realize that she was an asset, since she had a good memory, an affinity for numbers, and the kind of engaging personality that was useful in sealing deals. She helped him with small-time transactions of cocaine, marijuana, acid, and bootleg prescription depressants and stimulants, known locally as "nerve pills." In time, she began referring to herself as Kenneth's "executive assistant," a phrase she had picked up from television. Another favorite term she began using was "charming," a word that none of Kenneth's friends had heard anyone actually utter in real life before.

For the first time in her life, Susan was able to go up to Matewan, the nearest town with stores, and buy the clothes she liked—not only for herself, but also for friends and relatives, because Susan was always generous. But the prosperity didn't continue. When Susan was seventeen, Kenneth was arrested for drug possession, jumped bail, and fled, sending her on to Louisiana to stay with one of his brothers and his wife. While there, broke and miserable, she worked for a time in a fast-food restaurant. When that didn't pay enough, she turned to occasional prostitution on an as-needed basis.

In time, Kenneth came back to her. They later moved to Indiana, where they married and had a daughter, Miranda. Thrilled at being parents, they tried to settle into respectability. Kenneth, promising to straighten himself out, took a job as a carpenter's assistant. They were living in a trailer, but Susan worked hard to decorate it with frilly curtains, throw rugs, and pillows. She liked good restaurants; he hated them, suspecting, correctly, that waiters looked down on his crude manners. As the novelty of parenthood passed into drudgery, they again turned to drugs for recreation and then, after Kenneth lost his job, they began fighting. Kenneth would beat her and vow in the morning to reform. It was a pattern from which Susan never managed to break.

From Indiana, they moved for a while to a cheap apartment in Cicero, Illinois, a run-down suburb just outside of Chicago, where the gangster Al Capone once had his business headquarters. In the Chicago area their small-town drug-dealing expertise acquired some big-city sophistication as they established contacts that would later keep them supplied down in the Tug Valley. Among their friends in Cicero were some men who held up a bank. Susan had been fascinated listening to them planning the robbery at her kitchen table. It was like something she had seen on television.

By the time she was twenty-four, Susan and Kenneth had run out their string up north and were back in the Tug, in a life once more squeezed between looming mountains. Facing trial on the old drug charge, Kenneth pleaded guilty and got probation. At home, the fighting got so bad that Susan ran away from her husband and daughter to live with a sister in West Virginia. From there, she wandered for months, staying with friends and relatives who would sometimes find her curled up on their couch in the morning like a child.

During this time, she began showing up regularly at a raucous country and western bar that attracted a spirited crowd on Route 23, the main highway through Pikeville, across from a road called Harmons Branch. The owner, who was also the featured singer, was a burly man named Marlow Tackett, who had hopes of making it as a star in Nashville. Borrowing clothes from her sister, Susan sat at a table night after night and pined for Marlow as he wailed his sad country songs. Once he gave her an autographed publicity picture of him in his cowboy costume, and she cherished it. She told people that she was planning to become his manager and help take him to the big time. Years later, when asked about her, Marlow would barely remember the girl from Freeburn.

Miserable and destitute, Susan finally returned to Kenneth. A second child, Brady, was born in 1985. She and Kenneth formally divorced soon afterward, which enabled her to get better welfare benefits, but they were still living unhappily together in the rented house beside the river in 1987—which was when Mark Putnam came into Susan's life, and she saw some sign of hope. Mark was a novelty, a handsome, motivated, polished, polite young man who was interested in her as someone who had something to offer. With no special effort, he treated her like a lady, and once she got over her initial suspicion, she responded like a woman in love.

For Mark, the first big payoff from developing Susan as an informant came in September. Susan told him that Cat Eyes, still living at her house, had brought home a duffel bag containing two sawed-off shotguns and some ski masks. She had found it in the children's room, which Kenneth had given to Cat and Sherri, forcing Miranda and Brady to sleep in the living room. Cat was clearly making big plans, Susan reported to Mark.

"Watch the papers," Cat had told her with a sly wink. "Easy Street is just up the road."

Mark took the information back to his then-partner, Dan Brennan, and the FBI quietly alerted local banks to be on the watch.

Cat had chosen for his next heist a branch of the First National Bank in Ferrells Creek, in the hills fifteen miles south of Pikeville, five miles from the northern Virginia border. The bank, which was near a town called Elkhorn City, population fifteen hundred, usually had plenty of cash on hand. It was housed in a one-story building with a parking lot, beside a used-trailer dealer. In Virginia, the roads were good. Cat had arranged for a getaway van and an accomplice to drive it.

On the morning of September 10, Cat entered the bank and approached the teller's window, waiting patiently for a few seconds while a woman in front finished tucking money into her wallet. The teller looked up with surprise. Cat was wearing a huge pair of lumberjack's coveralls that swathed him from neck to foot, and a black knit ski mask turned around backward, with two eye holes clumsily cut out in front so he would not expose too much of his face, especially his distinctive green eyes. He was holding but not brandishing a sawed-off shotgun. Cat was having some difficulty seeing because the eyeholes in the knit mask shifted when his head moved.

The teller, Rosemary Childers, had been an employee of the bank for eleven years, working her way up to branch administrator. She was filling in at the window that day because the regular teller had called in sick. Cat put a pillowcase down on the counter and said, "Fill it up with money." The teller noted that the pillow-case had a print of pink flowers on it, but it was grimy, as if it had been used to carry fishing tackle.

While she took stacks of bills from her cash drawer, Cat Eyes raised the gun and swung around, ordering the half dozen or so other people in the bank: "Freeze, and put your hands up!" Some were confused at the sequence of the command, but tentatively, hands went up.

Childers took this brief opportunity to drop a dye-pack into the pillowcase along with the money. A dye-pack is a clever security device that looks like a standard bound stack of bank money a hundred bills thick, but with a real ten-dollar bill on top of bill-size newsprint. Once the dye-pack passes through an electronic beam at a bank's door, a timing switch is triggered. The next time it's jostled, the device explodes like a firecracker, splattering red dye on the fleeing culprit and his loot.

"Into the vault!" Cat Eyes shouted to the bewildered employ-ees and customers. There was some commotion while Rosemary Childers went to look for the key. When she found it and opened the vault, Cat ordered her to take the stacks of bills from a shelf and drop them into his pillowcase, which he held open like a trick-or-treater. She managed to drop in a second dye-pack, but this one Cat Eyes spotted. "And no dye-bombs," he ordered. Sheepishly, the woman removed it. The pillowcase now contained $12,807 in bills, 182 two-dollar bills as well as the real ten-dollar note stuck atop the hidden dye-pack.

Cat Eyes closed the vault door, thoughtfully not all the way because there were people inside, and ran to the exit with a joy-ful shout. Just outside, he broke stride to perform a small victory jig like football players do after grabbing a pass in the end zone. At once the dye-pack exploded, initially causing Cat to think he had been shot and was watching his own blood spurt. When he realized what had happened, he dashed for the van, screaming at his accomplice, who had been lying down on the front seat, to get going. As they tore out of the parking lot and turned toward the Virginia border on US 460, a bank employee coming to work sized up the situation, chased after them, got the license number of the van, and stopped at a gas station to phone the state police.

The number was busy.

The van was found ditched on a side road at Ferrells Creek, along with a couple of hundred dollars soaked with red dye.

After this, Cat didn't return to Susan's house, which the authorities were now watching. But a week later, in the Tug Valley branch of Pikeville National Bank in South Williamson, another alert bank teller, Debby White, became suspicious when a very polite but highly nervous dark-haired man with amazing green eyes sauntered in to exchange a wad of two-dollar bills, 182 of them in all—all stained at the edges with red dye. "Usually two-dollar bills come in only in deposits," she told the police. "You never see exchanging of bills like that."

As Cat left the bank, she called the state police, who promptly notified the FBI. Mark was out of town to serve a fugitive warrant, and Dan Brennan finally got through to him on the phone and explained the situation. "Talk to Susan," Mark said. "She'll fill you in."

Brennan went to see Susan, but she refused. "I only talk to Mark," she told him.

When Mark found her the next day, she defended her loyalty to him. "It's your case," she said patronizingly. "I don't want you to give away the credit. You worked on this case very hard."

She told him where Cat was holed up—at his mother's house in West Virginia. When Mark and Dan Brennan arrived there with state police to handcuff the suspect, Cat insisted that he walk beside Mark, for the benefit of a Williamson newspaper photographer who had showed up, alerted by the police scanner. The story in the paper the next day credited Dan Brennan as the FBI man who broke the case, however.

Susan was furious about that. She had her brother Bo drive her to Pikeville the next day where she found Mark at the FBI office. He counted out fifteen one-hundred-dollar bills and gave them to her as payment for informing on Cat Eyes. She tried to hand one back to him, saying, "I want you to have this."

He shrank from it. "I can't take that, Susan!"

She insisted, "You did all the work and you're getting screwed out of any credit."

"You don't understand how this organization works. You're making me a hero. Maybe I didn't get the big write-up in the paper, but my bosses know who did the work, and I get the credit for you."

"I want you to have this. I won't take it back."

She dropped the money on his desk and hurried out. In a panic, he thought, *Is she trying to set me up?*

He immediately phoned Hulse, his distant supervisor at the Covington office, who told him not to worry. He should write a covering memo and put the money in the safe toward the next payment, which would come if and when Susan agreed to expose herself and testify against Cat Eyes.

Later, when Mark broached that subject with her, Susan said she would consider testifying, but that she was afraid for her life. If she testified at the trial, she said, she wanted enough money to move out of the area with her children.

Mark asked, "How much money do you think you'll need?"

"Four thousand dollars."

"No problem," he said.

3

Mark knew enough about what he was up against in eastern Kentucky to regard Susan as more than a source of information. To an outsider anxious to assimilate, she offered the invaluable cachet of acceptance. Being seen with a local girl made him look like one of the boys. It never occurred to him that for her, the opposite was true. To the extent that he found camouflage with her, she was flushed into the open. Susan had known instinctively that once she made her pact with Mark, there would be consequences. As if to ensure that she had some kind of at least implied protection in her newfound status, she had made it a point to tell everyone in Freeburn that she was working for the FBI. In fact, she positively trafficked in it, lavishing on the idea that she was something like a partner of Mark's.

"Like an executive secretary," she told some people back in Freeburn.

Kathy Putnam implicitly understood Susan's dilemma. From the beginning, Kathy approached Susan with a mixture of empathy and wariness that enabled Susan, a woman acutely alert to opportunity, to discover a rapidly blurring zone between Mark's professional and personal life, and to quickly step into it.

In fact, Kathy recognized in Susan a kindred soul. No one else ever really understood that—not her husband, and certainly not Susan herself, who seemed to have drifted into the Putnams' life as aimlessly as a cloud trailing across a mountain.

The unlikely alliance between these two women had developed on the telephone during the summer and fall of 1987 as the Putnams settled more steadily into their new life. Susan had taken her role as an informant seriously, regarding it as a full-time job that required her to be on call and to report in frequently. And Kathy, because Mark was out on the road so much, and the FBI office had no secretary, had stepped in to help as an unpaid receptionist, fielding many of his phone calls from their home. Susan had called the house for the first time about a week after her initial meeting with Mark.

"Kathy? This is Susan Smith," she had begun in a matter-of-fact tone. "I'm working for the government. I don't know if your husband told you about me or not. I'm working as his informer on an important case. Is he there? He was supposed to meet up with me at the office, but I don't know where he is."

Kathy said she'd relay the message when Mark got in. Mark had already told her about his introductory discussions with Susan, including the meeting outside the restaurant in West Virginia. He'd also told her something that they both found amusing and somewhat curious. According to Bert Hatfield, right after the introductory meeting at the restaurant, Kenneth had stormed around Freeburn maintaining that the FBI man had actually "screwed" his ex-wife in the backseat of the car, in broad daylight in the restaurant's parking lot when they went out there to talk.

This alone was intriguing enough to whet Kathy's curiosity about what sort of person would be living with an obvious wild man like Kenneth Smith. Kathy—increasingly lonely and unhappy in Pikeville—was pleasantly surprised to find that she liked her.

She decided that Susan was friendly, smart, refreshingly self-deprecating, engagingly ditsy at times, and, she thought, more than a little bit vulnerable when it came to relationships with men. Her first and abiding impulse was to help Susan.

Kenneth's fabrications aside, it was nevertheless apparent to Kathy that Susan was enthralled by Mark, a situation that she accepted with the practiced equanimity of a faculty wife toward an eager female graduate student with a crush on the professor. Besides, in close-knit Pikeville, where Kathy didn't know many people and her neighbors made it clear that they didn't much welcome outsiders, it was nice to have someone to talk to.

During these increasingly frequent conversations, Susan began to ask Kathy's advice on grooming and etiquette, while probing subtly for personal information about Mark. Susan learned that he ran every night—and she told him that she had started running, too. Did he read? Susan began showing up at their meetings with a paperback in her hand. As they got to know each other better, Mark began noticing odd little changes in Susan, as if she were trying to transform herself to become more like the women he knew, and more specifically his wife. Even her manner of speech changed—Susan would correct herself crossly when she said "heered" instead of "heard," for example.

"The calls got more personal as we got to know each other," Kathy would later recall. "I actually enjoyed her calls at first, but you could sense right off that this was someone with an odd fascination for our personal life. Within a couple of weeks or so, she wanted to know things like, 'What are you making for dinner? What does Mark like to eat? What did Danielle do today?' The more I got to know about the awful life she had, the more I saw this as her attempt to understand our life. And I thought I could maybe show her that she had options, if she would just identify them and work at them."

Before long, Susan was calling at all hours, sometimes several times a day. Every time she picked up the phone, Kathy expected to hear Susan's hillbilly twang. In time, Kathy decided that Susan's attitude toward Mark was in fact akin to that of an executive secretary's toward the boss. "She wanted to know where he was and how he could be reached all the time. She expected him to be available. She always claimed that she had important information for him. It was glamorous for her to be working for the FBI. On the one hand, she seemed to have the idea that it was like a regular job and Mark was her boss; then on the other, I think she saw him and her as Bonnie and Clyde."

Susan was persistent. Soon after she started working as an informant, she began showing up at the courthouse nearly every day looking for Mark. Since he was often out, Susan would pass the time bantering with courthouse employees, especially the officers in the probation and marshal's divisions, where she managed to establish the impression that she and Mark had a close working relationship, and leave behind suspicions that it was a close personal one, too.

Mark's take on Susan was less complicated than his wife's. He had noticed, for example, that Susan tended to boast about sexual relations with men at the courthouse, men he was quite sure had never been involved with her. "She has a big mouth, Kat," he warned his wife. "Watch out."

Susan's dependence on Kathy grew as the friendship deepened. They sometimes spoke for hours, Susan's troubles spilling out one after the other to a receptive ear. The dead-end relationships, money problems, despair, abysmal self-esteem, half-baked aspirations, and chronic ineptitude—Kathy readily recognized these afflictions because she had overcome them herself. She believed that in time she might be able to help Susan do the same.

Patiently, she would say, "Listen, Susan. I have been there. Believe me, I know where you are coming from. You can get yourself together."

To look at her then, poised and by all appearances self-confident, ensconced in what seemed to be a solid marriage with a spouse who loved her deeply and a bright-eyed young daughter who would be a delight to any parent, it would have been difficult to imagine what similarities in their lives Kathy was alluding to. But they were there under the surface and they were striking.

Kathy Ponticelli and her younger sister, Christine, were daughters of an autocratic but devoted second-generation Italian-American father and a mother who offered quiet, unassuming encouragement to her girls. The household had strict rules: no chatter at the dinner table, help out around the house, be home by curfew and not a minute later, get good grades, go to Mass on Sunday, and don't get in trouble with the nuns.

A smart and perceptive girl who felt that there was probably more to life than the tedium of Manchester, Connecticut, a small town aspiring mightily to become nothing more ambitious than a suburb, Kathy managed to break all of the rules except the one about good grades. Kathy coasted through St. James parish school and then East Catholic High School, sullen and bored. Unable, she thought, to do anything right other than study, she compensated for her lack of self-confidence with a brashness that some would misconstrue as effrontery. Her high school misdeeds, still painful for her to recall even after she'd grown into a well-adjusted young woman, had begun innocently enough, with hemline-length violations and back talk. If social acceptance meant dating the loutish captain of the football team, opening a purse to brandish a stash of joints, talking street-tough, copping cigarettes in the girls' bathroom, flouting the rules—in general, courting the fires of hell in the next life, and detention, threats of expulsion, and inclusion on lists of suspected school troublemakers in this one—then so be it. On the other hand, not many of her female classmates pointedly carried, as she did, a well-worn paperback of *Catcher in the Rye*. At East Catholic High, such an attitude led right down the slippery slope to what her devout parents saw as the worst of all ignominies: public school, to which Kathy was banished in her junior year, and from which she dropped out a few months later, days after she turned eighteen.

She was one of those skinny, fresh-faced girls who would grow up to become a winsome beauty, yet never quite appreciate the fact that the transformation had actually occurred. Nearly two decades later, she continued to see herself through a murky lens as a gawky, self-conscious kid holding back tears of rage as she was mocked for her appearance. *"Ponticelli, your ears are sticking out! Look at her ears! Look at her ears!"*

After Kathy dropped out of high school, the similarities to Susan's life became more pronounced. She had a boyfriend who in retrospect reminded her of Kenneth. She horrified her parents by moving into an apartment in a run-down, crime-ridden part of East Hartford with that boyfriend who drank heavily and had a propensity to punch any man who glanced more than casually at his girlfriend. The young man's mother tended bar in a club that featured go-go dancers, where Kathy took a job as a waitress and bartender. Keeping her shirt on didn't make her feel any more virtuous than her friends who danced with their shirts off, some of them young mothers trapped in the gritty economy of divorce on the fringe of postindustrial America.

"There are ways to get better tips than tending bar," one of the girls told her. "You know about the massage parlors, right?"

Things got worse for her. The boyfriend was thrown into jail after a fight with a man who had flirted with Kathy in another bar. Then a man who followed her home and forced his way into the apartment.

In one of those long late-night phone conversations, she told Susan about this.

"I'm no blushing maiden, but I really didn't know what was going on in those massage parlors, and I was too embarrassed to ask questions. I thought you put on makeup and dressed sexy and you go rub these guys' backs and you get tips for that."

Susan inhaled a cigarette loudly and said skeptically, "Really?"

"Really, Susan. I talked to a couple of different people who told me you could make really good money. I was busting my ass bartending till two in the morning, and then waitressing for breakfast at the Holiday Inn. I was living in a housing project and basically just getting through the week. So I went and got a job at this massage parlor, and the manager guy who hired me had a quick look and said, 'OK, talk to Erin. But you know the drill.'"

"Did you?"

"Hell no!"

"Who's Erin?"

"The boss of the girls, I guess. She kept the schedule, anyway."

"She told you what was going on?"

"Not really, because I was too naïve to get what Erin was saying. 'Basically, what goes on in there—' she pointed down a little hallway where there were some little private rooms with dim lighting and a single bed for the back rubs."

Susan snorted.

Kathy went on, "'—What goes on in there is between you and the client.' I remember that she used the word 'client.' Now that I think of it, I wonder if she was being indirect because they were worried about cops, and maybe there was a worry about an undercover cop with a tape recorder. I have no idea. This place was basically a storefront with rooms in the back, definitely seedy, but really, Susan, I thought prostitution was illegal."

"Well it is, honey. Did you do it?"

"I worked there a couple of days, a week or so maybe, I wasn't catching on. OK, I took my shirt off—"

"Come on! That's it?"

"I got the idea. I had this black nightgown? So, yeah, I would put on this nightgown and rub these guys' backs, and they'd then ask for, you know, a hand-job, but I told them 'You need to do that yourself.' I was shaking so bad I actually scared the clients. They were probably afraid to complain, but the word got around that I was absolutely no good at that shit. There were things I drew the line at, is all."

Kathy had been sipping wine through this long conversation, which occurred when Mark was out of town on a case. It was now after one o'clock in the morning.

"I turned a trick or two when I was down on my luck," Susan said. "No big deal, really."

"And?"

"Between you and me and the hitchin' post?"

"Absolutely."

"Up in Chicago a few years ago, I was introduced to this gentleman who ran an escort service for businessmen in town at hotels near the airport."

"Not high class, then."

"Well, all of them had folding money, let's call it that."

"What did you have to do?"

"What was necessary."

"Was it ever any fun?" Kathy asked, giggling inquisitively.

"Hardly never."

"But sometimes?"

Kathy could almost hear Susan shrug.

The nighttime phone conversations between the two women orbiting around Mark Putnam became regular occurrences. There was another story that Kathy had vowed never to tell, which came spilling out one night, lubricated by wine.

"When I was working at that place—"

"The massage parlor?"

"Yeah. I had gone shopping in Hartford one day and I bought myself a pair of jeans, and a man followed me home and pushed his way into my apartment. I recognized the guy from work, and I even knew his first name and that he was from the neighborhood. So I thought I could handle it."

"Big mistake, honey."

"Yeah, tell me about it. He raped me."

"Shit."

"I went to work and told them what happened and they were like, 'Whoa!' The guy was a regular. They were worried about the cops. And I'm just crouched in the corner, crying. And the manager goes to me, 'You can just get your ass out of here!'"

"Scum," Susan said.

"So I went to the police station and told them what happened, and they went and picked the guy up. I had lied to them that the guy had had a knife, because I didn't know how I was going to explain how he got into my apartment without me screaming. Then they said they had the guy and they wanted me to testify—"

"'Course they did," Susan interjected.

"And I said, these are rough people. I'm going to get hurt if I testify against them. They kept asking me all these questions about the massage parlor, about the things that went on there, and I said, 'I don't know!' The only thing I know is they have red lights in the rooms, and if a cop would come in, the manager at the desk flips the thing and the lights come on and then you're supposed to quick get your clothes back on. I told them everything I knew about the place, but I hadn't been working there that long. I couldn't stop crying. There were two cops at a desk facing me, firing questions. And then the door opened and I turned my head and the guy who raped me was there with another cop, and he wasn't even handcuffed, and the cop said, 'It's your word against him, Miss. I just wanted to see your reaction.' All I could say was, 'Get him out of here, and get me out of here!'"

"Don't cry, it's in the past," Susan said.

"Nothing is ever in the past, Susan," Kathy said softly and went on, "so what they did was they put me in protective custody in a hotel for a week while they worked on closing the massage parlor and issuing a citation. And that night, the guy did come back to my apartment with three or four other guys and they trashed the whole place. Which is when they got arrested."

"Guy wasn't charged with rape?"

"No. I was too afraid to press it. I knew I would get hurt. All they cared about was busting the massage parlor. They didn't care about me in the least. It really left a sour taste in my mouth about the police."

"But you married an agent of the law."

"That's different, Susan. I am a different person now."

All of her life, Susan had a way of getting people to talk, which was the skill that made her such a good informant. But as she laid out her own pitiful stories to Kathy, she was genuinely touched by the way Kathy responded to let her know that, current impressions of a poised, well-adjusted woman aside, they shared some hard times.

After she was raped and her apartment destroyed, Kathy sought refuge with her ex-boyfriend and together they moved to a trailer in Jacksonville, North Carolina, where he said he could find work painting houses near the sprawling Marine Corps advanced-training base at Camp Lejeune.

Kathy told Susan, "I got a job tending bar, and I saved up a little money, a few hundred dollars. But I'm working all the time and I'm not meeting my bills. I just wanted to just go back home even if it meant living with my father's rules. I'd do whatever it took. So I set up a street hustle."

"You? What kind of a hustle?" Susan was laughing at the incongruity of Kathy, who she had seen as so elegant, contriving something as rough as a street scam.

"It was my idea. I thought up what you'd call a 'dry hustle' to do on the Strip in Jacksonville, this military town. So we went down to the Strip and I more or less propositioned five guys—you know, young Marines with money burning a hole in their pockets. I said we had five girls at the hotel, and if they'd give me money up front I would take them up there to have fun. I had my boyfriend waiting in a car and I'd told him, I'll get the money, break into a sprint, get in the car with you, and we're gone."

"How'd that work out?" Susan asked skeptically.

"Not good. I got less than two hundred dollars. As we were driving away, a cruiser pulled up with the lights flashing. It turned out that one of the guys I hustled was an undercover cop. They arrested us both. I couldn't believe this was happening! I was eighteen! I tried to explain to the cop, because they were charging me with prostitution, they were asking me about these girls supposedly in the hotel. I said 'There are no girls at a hotel!' I poured my heart out. I told them about the rape and handwrote out a long statement, but I could tell that the cops thought that I was hiding something bigger. I said all I wanted to do was go home to my parents and have enough money to see a doctor. I had been very worried that I had got some infection from the guy that raped me. But they threw me into jail for a few days. I got home and my parents did get an attorney for me and they eventually dropped the charges."

"Mark knows about this?"

Memory floodgates fully open, Kathy couldn't stop talking to the only person she knew in the world who would fully understand.

"I told Mark after we were married and he applied to the bureau, when I was really scared that this was going to come up.

The FBI does a background check on you. But it didn't come up, as far as I know. Maybe because it was a misdemeanor and the records weren't kept."

"Adjournment with contemplation of dismissal. ACD," Susan said knowingly.

"What?"

"That's what your lawyer got you, to settle some piddly misdemeanor charge. It means the record is wiped clean if you don't do it again."

"Really?"

"So don't be dry-humping no Marines, Kathy."

"Dry *hustle*, Susan, for Christ's sake!"

"Whatever," Susan said, and both women dissolved in throaty laughter and mutual cigarette coughing.

Kathy's parents had been very clear about their conditions for her coming back to live with them in Manchester, Connecticut. If you're going to come home, you're going to live by our rules, her father had said, and when she returned, she did her best to comply, and to accommodate herself to their diminished expectations.

Then a man ten years her senior, who had a steady job in a gravel factory, entered her life. She married him virtually on impulse. Her father gave her a job managing an apartment complex that he and his father had built in Manchester; she got her high school equivalency diploma and enrolled in community college. It looked like things were working out at last.

But there was a dark side to her new husband that Kathy hadn't anticipated. He deeply resented the "airs" he said she was putting on by insisting on continuing college. He was also intensely jealous. The marriage, which lasted four months, ended one night when, in a drunken rage, he smacked her around in the car and pushed her out, bruised, mortified, and half-naked, onto her parents' well-groomed front lawn.

Not at all sure that she was getting through, Kathy tried to make Susan see the parallels in their lives, by way of showing her that it wasn't too late.

"Susan and I both had lifelong feelings of inadequacy," Kathy would explain later. "We got involved with the wrong people, looking for love wherever we could get it, always looking for easy answers. We both got involved with impossible men. We both had a history of running away. We never felt we were good enough. We didn't face reality and just assumed it would somehow magically work out."

Susan confided to Kathy that she was a regular drug user, "Pills, to help me relax." Though she definitely liked to drink, especially as her unhappiness with being alone in Pikeville grew, Kathy herself had never abused drugs, but she'd spent enough of her life with people who did to understand the predicament involved in being around them. "I was scared by cocaine, but I was pulled into that world. It was the same thing as Susan's life, basically—the people around the kitchen table, people coming and going all day, strangers asleep on the couch when you got up in the morning," she said later, describing her late teen years.

However, by the age of twenty-one, Kathy was on track at last. She recalled, "My overriding resolution was not to have to crawl back to my father. I was determined by then. I was no longer married, and I got my associate degree. I had a decent job managing the apartments; I was living in a nice apartment that I'd furnished beautifully from secondhand shops. I even had a new Datsun 280ZX. Then I saw Mark and he changed my entire life."

They met serendipitously on a Friday night in July of 1982, two days before Mark's twenty-third birthday. In the apartment next door to her lived an avuncular, hard-drinking elderly man, who had asked Kathy to join him for dinner at a local restaurant where a woman he was dating would be singing. At dinner, however, he drank so excessively that he was listing severely by the time the singer came on. At an adjacent table, a sprightly middle-aged widow sitting with a male friend noticed Kathy's plight and caught her attention.

"Men," the older woman commiserated, rolling her eyes.

Kathy smiled back. "What are you going to do with them?"

The woman looked Kathy over appraisingly and asked a few tentative questions about her age and marital status. "You know," she said, pulling her chair closer, "my son would be perfect for you. He's a good-looking guy. He just graduated from the University of Tampa, and he's going to be an FBI agent. I can call him and ask him to come over."

Sure, Kathy thought. *Some guy sitting at home on a Friday night while his mother hustles dates for him? And what kind of guy wants to be an FBI agent?* But the woman was engagingly persistent. "Come on," she said, getting up. "*Come on!* We're going to call him."

"Listen, we need to leave," Kathy protested, noticing that her companion's elbows were sliding off the table. "I have to get him home." But the man got unsteadily to his feet and wobbled across the dance floor to join his friend the singer between sets, announcing that he was going home with her.

On her way to the ladies' room, Kathy passed the older woman at the pay phone. "You've got to meet this girl," the woman was saying into the phone. "She's beautiful." She grabbed Kathy by the elbow and thrust the receiver into her hand. "Talk!"

Flustered, Kathy mumbled, "Hello?"

There was embarrassed laughter on the other end, and a deep voice said, "I have to apologize to you for my mother putting you on the spot. The woman is incorrigible."

Kathy was intrigued by the sound of his voice. They talked for a while and seemed to have things in common. She liked his sense of humor. She heard herself saying, "Well, why don't you come down here then, if you want to talk?"

"Would it be worth my while?" He didn't sound arrogant, just assertive enough to be worth a look.

"Yeah, it would be worth it."

Twenty minutes later, a dark-haired young man with flashing eyes and a dazzling smile walked in. He shook her hand, held her chair, made her laugh, and treated her like the most important person in his life. By the end of the night, she was hopelessly in love.

"We connected right away," she recalled. "We talked all night long. He told me about his plans to get into the FBI as a special agent by working his way up from clerk. I told him about my own hopes to have a husband and a family, a good, working marriage, security, and simple happiness. It was very clear very fast that this was the man I really wanted in my life, and he felt the same way about me. We talked and laughed, and we made love for the first time in the morning, in my apartment, as the sun came up."

When he met Kathy, Mark was two months out of the University of Tampa, where he had been the captain of the championship soccer team and from which he had graduated with a degree in criminology. In September, he was to start work as a clerk at the FBI office in New Haven.

Mark, his younger brother, Tim, and his sister, Cindy, had spent part of their early childhood in a public housing project in East Hartford, while their father worked hard to provide a better home. A burly, soft-spoken man who always had another job or two to do after his regular workday driving a truck for Sears, Walter Putnam soon put together the down payment for a comfortable house in middle-class Coventry. Walter had dropped out of high school to enlist in the Navy, and he and his wife, Barbara, placed great value on their children's education—although it was

Tim, not Mark, who was considered to be the brains of the family. Tim was "college material." Mark was the jock.

However, in his freshman year of high school, Mark was offered an athletic scholarship to the prestigious Pomfret School in Pomfret, Connecticut, fifty miles away. Going off to prep school posed a tough decision for a boy who stayed close to home and was already a star soccer and baseball player in high school. His mother opposed it, advising him, "Stay at home. You're going to be all-American." Characteristically, his father's response was to throw the question back at him. "Think it out. I know the answer, but think it out."

In time, Mark knew, too. He recognized the opportunity and welcomed the chance to prove himself to his father. He knew that he wouldn't be able to coast through Pomfret on a soccer ball and a smile, as he had so far through public high school. His teachers had been padding his grades and told him so. Mark had already decided that he wanted to be an FBI agent, although he hadn't told anybody yet, and he was aware that the FBI was fussy about accepting only college graduates with good academic records. His father, delighted that Mark opted for Pomfret, told him, "If you want to go, you go. I'll handle your mother." Despite the scholarship, it would cost Mark's parents about $1,000 a year to send him. They'd make do, his father said.

Later, Mark would recall his apprehension about leaving home for an expensive school like Pomfret. "For the first time, I had to study. I had to prove myself in a group of people who I knew were intellectually superior. I was so intimidated by that. I absolutely hated the place when I got there. It was such a totally alien environment. My initial impression was that I was surrounded by these prissy rich kids who had it made all their lives.

"I was never comfortable having people know much about my private life, so it took me a while to acclimate. But then I began to realize that some of these kids, their parents had just shipped them off to get them out of the house. And others I got to know and found out they were in the same boat as me—working-class kids who were there on grants or scholarships. I began to relax."

The summer before he went to Pomfret, Mark broke his leg in a soccer scrimmage. The cast came off only a week before classes began, but he started anyway on the team, playing through the pain, never mentioning the injury to any of his teammates. He rapidly assimilated. "The soccer team was going great—we were winning games right and left. Friends started coming, girls started coming around. My grades were good, and this time I worked hard for them. And boom, before I knew it, I was back in a fold again, a nest."

Meanwhile, his relationship with his father, who had overcome a drinking problem a few years earlier, underwent a significant change. The man who had been distant figure through much of his childhood became a confidant. Mark sensed that through him, his father was vicariously living out a part of life that he had never been able to experience.

"We began to have meaningful talks on the phone after I went to prep school, which was odd because the man usually hated the phone. He wanted to know what people were doing, what I was studying, what the rich kids were like, what the girls were like. I was dumbfounded. I had never heard the guy talk that way. He had left school at sixteen, so I guess it was a world he had always wondered about." Mark's father and mother made the trip to watch him on the athletic field on weekends. Mark maintained a B average, played baseball, and captained Pomfret's undefeated soccer team in his senior year. He graduated in 1978 and enrolled at the University of Tampa.

The relationship between father and son grew even closer during the summer between prep school and his freshman year in college, when Mark frequently went out on the road with his father.

"On the road at night, we would come into a truck stop and my father pointed out, many times, where guys would come up and offer him like twenty thousand or thirty thousand dollars for his load. You know, the deal was he could leave the truck, go in for a cup of coffee, and come back and report the cargo was hijacked. He told me, 'It would have been no skin off my teeth, and man, there were times when we really could have used that money. It was easy money. But it would have been wrong. And there's no two ways about it. You be honest in life, Mark. That's it.'"

Mark never forgot. At the start of his sophomore year, he decided to major in criminology; in his earnest way, he told his father that he intended to become an FBI agent because he believed in what he had learned about honesty and justice, as corny as it might sound. "My old man was the one person I knew I could talk to about the FBI and not get laughed at," Mark remembered.

During Mark's sophomore year, his father died of lung cancer. The broken relationship would leave him with a powerful, nearly overwhelming sense of incompleteness. At the funeral, he told his mother, "If I could be half the man that he was, I will be happy. I'll have made it."

He returned to school an even more serious young man, with goals firmly in place. Mark had developed a reputation as a heart-breaker among campus women, and he was chagrined by it now. He began dating a chemistry major, independent, self-sufficient, and assertive. He liked that in a woman. He liked someone who would stand up to him, who knew what she wanted, who could goad him and keep him laughing at himself, and who would share his values without question.

When his mother introduced them in the summer of 1982, smiling, beautiful Kathy Ponticelli, it appeared, was just such a woman. He fell in love with her with the same force that she did with him. From the first night, they were inseparable.

"We were like teenagers dating," Kathy recalled. "We played, we talked—it was just us, there wasn't room for anyone else in our lives. By the end of the summer, we moved together to a tiny apartment in Middletown, about halfway between New Haven, where he was going to start work in the FBI office in late August, and Hartford, where I had just got a job as a paralegal at an insurance company."

Many weekends, they drove down to New York City, to explore, to have dinner and see Broadway shows like *A Chorus Line* and *Dream Girls*. They did the tourist things, rode a horse-drawn carriage in Central Park, had their portrait sketched in charcoal on Times Square, went to the top of the Empire State Building to watch the lights of Manhattan twinkle at twilight. One night on a Rhode Island beach, they made love in the sand and skinny-dipped in the cold ocean. He took her to Fenway Park in Boston for her first baseball game. Her parents liked him enormously. The summer seemed endless.

"I was already pretty well straightened out, but this was the icing on the cake," Kathy said many years later. "I loved hearing about his life—things like prep school, senior proms, college pranks, graduation day—things that I had missed. Mark had done everything the right way, always.

"God, we were a perfect fit. For everything I learned from him, he learned something from me. He was more or less attracted to the self-assurance I had developed by then. I'd gotten all As in community college, and by now I wasn't ashamed of who I was or what I had done. I taught him how to manage money and balance a checkbook. He was so naïve about some things—like he'd never count his change. He was an impossible sucker for garage mechanics. I showed him life: you shop around for a garage; the bills come due; the rent has to be paid; the oil has to be changed in the car. We seemed to fill in each other's blanks."

They lived together for almost two years, putting aside money for marriage and a baby. When they agreed it was time to get married, Kathy decided that it was important to tell him every detail of her past, including the parts that were difficult to tell. He listened in stony silence—then walked out without a word. She didn't see him for three days, during which time she thought she would never see him again. When he came back, he said only, "I don't ever want to talk about that again. Any of it." And except for when they were worried about her misdemeanor arrest coming up in the FBI background check, they never did.

After he was promoted to night clerk at the New Haven FBI Bureau, where he fielded agents' after-hours phone tips and edited their investigative reports as part of his duties, Mark took a second job during the daytime as a clerk at a liquor store. On Easter weekend of 1984, without alerting either of their families they drove to New York City to get married. They'd chosen New York for the wedding because they thought it would look more romantic than Hartford on their marriage certificate The only objection came not from their families but from the bureau, where Mark's supervisor let him know that the FBI frowned on elopements, even by clerks.

But they had other things on their mind than the FBI. They wanted to have a baby.

Kathy would always remember the night Danielle was conceived. "My doctor had told me I should go off the pill a few months before we planned to conceive. Mark had come home from his night job; we were lying in bed, and he kissed me in that way. I reached for my diaphragm, but he put his hand on mine and said, 'It's time. I want you to have my baby.' We made love. This is difficult to say, but our lovemaking was always intense. This time it was so different—even the way he looked at me was different. He was making love to me as the mother of his baby, and I remember that as the most perfect moment in my life."

She remembered something else. "As soon as I started to show, he would not make love to me. He was petrified that he would hurt the baby. He treated me as though I was a queen."

Danielle was born on New Year's Day of 1985. Eighteen months later, after years of work and a long period of anxiety awaiting the results of his application interviews and tests, Mark was finally accepted into the FBI Academy to begin training as a special agent They both would later recall this period as the happiest time of their lives, happier even than their first summer together. Kathy's most enduring impression of her husband comes from the days right before they left for Pikeville, when Danielle was just two. She simply remembers Mark sitting, at Danielle's insistence, on her Fisher-Price toddler's chair, a friendly giant at a little girl's tea party.

4

Federal agents have been paying informants to provide information on illegal activities in Appalachia since the days of the bloody "moonshine wars" of the Prohibition era, when the Cumberland Plateau was one of the chief sources of bootleg alcohol for Midwestern cities such as Chicago and Cincinnati. Heavily armed teams of government agents were so diligent in their crusade against the prosperous hillbilly moonshine industry that railroad cars had to be chartered to haul thousands of natives off to overcrowded federal penitentiaries. To the mountaineer, already seething under the tyranny of outside agents hired by coal companies to thwart union activity, the invasion of "foreign" law enforcement officials, operating with the assistance of local authorities, left what Harry M. Caudill called "the deep-seated conviction that he is governed not by just laws but by corrupt and venal men—men who would betray him when it was to their purpose and reward him when it was to their gain."

This paradigm was still firmly in place two generations later when a wild man barged into the FBI office in Pikeville late in the summer of 1987 filling the doorway with his bulk.

"I'm telling you, gentlemen, it's a million-dollar operation!" Charlie Trotter boomed without any preliminaries. The two agents' first impulse was to reach for their guns. But Charlie held up his palms and motioned for them to relax, settling himself into a chair and saying, "I want to give you guys the biggest case you are ever going to work."

Not impressed, Dan Brennan said, "Yeah, what's that?"

"Stolen trucks, gentlemen!" Charlie replied, folding his arms and looking from Brennan to Mark to see who was looking back hardest.

Mark thought the man resembled Prof. Harold Hill, the flim-flam salesman from the musical *The Music Man.*

"A goddamned Sears catalog of them!" Charlie declared.

Brennan tightened his lips and found something to read.

Charlie leaned forward to scrutinize Mark, who scrutinized him back. Charlie flashed a grizzled grin under his Fu Manchu mustache. At six feet and 190 pounds, wearing a tight muscle shirt over arms festooned with prison tattoos, Charlie adjusted the little leather cap that sat jauntily on his shaved head. Mark had never seen anything quite like him.

Brennan excused himself and went home. Then over the next four hours, as Mark made notes and encouraged him to go on, Charlie spun out his tale of betrayal and indignation. At the heart of Charlie's tale of woe was a willingness to sell information, and perhaps to testify if the price was right, about what he described as a huge multistate operation in stolen vehicles, truck parts, and construction and mining equipment—an elaborate "chop shop" located on a secluded mountain somewhere near the town of McRoberts, just over the Letcher County border twenty miles southwest of Pikeville. Since he was a member of the ring that ran the operation, Charlie had details. He identified the "brains" of the operation as one Vernon Mullins, who over the past several years had recruited a gang of thieves who stole the trucks and other equipment throughout several states and towed it back to the Letcher County site, from where it was being sold.

"It's going to cost you, but it'll be worth the price," Charlie promised. Was the FBI interested?

Mark didn't commit himself. He thanked Charlie for his time, took a number where he could be reached, and said he'd be in touch.

When Charlie left, Mark called a local cop he knew in Letcher County and asked him what he'd heard about the operation. "Yeah, we've been after that son of a bitch Vernon Mullins for a long time," the cop replied, "but you can't get near him. He supposedly runs a big chop shop somewheres."

Mark then checked Charlie's criminal record. He was a certified desperado, a hardened criminal involved in drugs and robbery, who had also done time for attempted murder. Such a résumé was not necessarily a bad thing in a potential informant, assuming you could keep him on your side.

Brennan, looking forward to his transfer to another office within months, tried to discourage his young partner's obvious enthusiasm. "Mark, you don't want to mess with that," he warned.

"Why not?"

Brennan whistled. "Stolen parts, man oh man. You're overwhelmed with paperwork. It's a real hassle. The reporting requirements are unbelievable." He pulled out the bureau's procedural manual to illustrate the complications ahead: Every part, every vehicle, would need to be thoroughly documented and traced to its source, which could be anywhere in the country. Fingerprints would have to be matched, owners of the stolen equipment notified and assuaged. It would require tracking down original police theft reports from every jurisdiction involved, not to mention insurance reports and claims documents. If the operation were as major as Charlie was maintaining, it would be a full-time job.

As always, Mark considered Brennan's advice. But he knew that if Charlie's information was good and if the investigation were thoroughly professional, such a case would break new ground in the territory. It wouldn't be just another bank heist, fugitive arrest, or drug bust. This—sophisticated data-based investigative procedure—was what made the FBI, at its best, the finest law enforcement organization in the world, Mark believed. This, he understood, could be a career-maker.

"I'll give it a shot," he told Brennan, who shrugged and replied, "Suit yourself."

Obviously, the first question was, what was Charlie's motive? The answer appeared to be fairly simple—money and a desire for revenge. The chop-shop operation employed teams of spotters, hot-wire artists, and mechanics to steal the equipment, transport it, and then disassemble it into parts. The way Charlie described it, his specialty—stealing trucks and delivering them to the site—was worth $300 to $500 a vehicle, with an extra commission on each individual part subsequently sold. Charlie was angry because he hadn't been paid for the last truck he'd brought in, and he figured that if Vernon Mullins and his boys weren't going to pay, the FBI was. It was no secret in the hills that the FBI paid well for the right information. Charlie figured he could become a rich man and settle a score at the same time.

Money talked, but not all at once. Mark realized that Charlie was impetuous; like most outlaws, his plans rarely extended more than a week or so into the future. Charlie was mad, but he was wily, and before he got himself killed by spoon-feeding the FBI, the anger would have passed. Mark knew he would have to work him carefully, step by step, over the weeks and months. Eager to get going, he called him back and set up a meeting.

It helped a lot that Mark came to genuinely like Charlie. As their alliance evolved, they met once or twice a week. Usually, Charlie would stop by the office, and they would get in the car and drive off into the hills, where they would be able to talk without being observed. Snapping open a can of beer from the six-pack he invariably brought along, Charlie was curious, laconic, and, Mark thought, hilarious when he went into his hillbilly act: "They done me wrong, Mark boy!" he would wail. "The varmints done me wrong, *and they will pay!*"

Mark also realized that Charlie was working both sides of the fence, maintaining his activities with the chop-shop gang in a perilous balance between conflicting demands. While Charlie claimed that he had returned to the good graces of the gang only to facilitate the gathering of information, Mark knew that he couldn't drop his guard against the possibility of a double-cross. Once, when Mark caught him in a lie, Charlie responded with a gravely injured look.

"You're a ruthless bastard, Mark. A shabby bastard, and I thought you was my friend."

"I am, Charlie. But I have a little bit of smarts and I know when somebody is trying to screw me over. I check things out, Charlie. Always remember that."

"What was them college girls like, Mark?" Charlie said, abruptly resuming their friendly conversation. "I'll bet they wasn't like a good wild mountain woman."

Bit by bit, Mark built his case. Charlie liked not only the money, but, it appeared, he also liked the attention. And Charlie delivered.

In the fall, not long after Cat Eyes was arrested, Charlie had ridden along for the hijacking of three trucks in Maryland. They were coming down the mountains toward Kentucky when Charlie realized he had forgotten to call Mark, as arranged, to let him know when the convoy was on its way. It wasn't time to make arrests yet, but Mark insisted on knowing what Charlie was up to. At the Putnam house on Honeysuckle Lane, the phone rang around ten o'clock.

"Charlie, where are you?"

"Pay phone, man. We're coming in around midnight."

"Charlie, aren't they wondering who you're calling? Aren't they suspicious?"

"The other two trucks went on ahead. It's just me and this old boy. I coldcocked him, punched his lights out. He's out."

"Why the hell did you do that?"

"So I could call, man," Charlie reasoned.

"Is he all right?"

"He'll be okay."

"What are you going to tell him when he wakes up?"

"I'll just say I didn't like the way he was a-looking at me. He'll understand."

Already well accustomed to telephone intrusions, Kathy herself merely added Charlie Trotter to the growing list of people—Susan most prominent among them—who called at odd hours, usually with an air of urgency, wanting to talk to Mark. As she had when he was a clerk, Kathy happily pitched in to help with the official work, fielding the calls and even spending hours some nights going over his laboriously handwritten interview reports, known in the bureau as 302s. That sometimes involved interviewing Mark to clarify the account. As she edited and neatly typed the 302s for him to send on to his supervisor in Covington—well aware that an agent was judged by his paperwork—she herself became fascinated with the quirky outlaw world of eastern Kentucky.

As a chilly autumn arrived, the Putnams were looking forward to the birth of their second child. Kathy had become pregnant a month after they moved to Pikeville. They'd planned on having two children, and as in everything else Kathy supervised, they were right on schedule. In late October, six weeks before she was due, Kathy intended to take Danielle with her to Connecticut, where they would stay with her parents until Mark joined them for what they hoped would be a three-week Christmas vacation centered around the birth of a son.

Life in Pikeville had settled into a pleasant routine, Mark's long working hours and the incessant phone calls notwithstanding. Sam Smith had been transferred out of the office, allowing Mark to finally have his own desk, and enabling Dan Brennan, now the senior agent, to claim the Bronco. Since Kathy needed the family car at home, Mark made do with the wheezing old Dodge left behind by Sam, consoled by the fact that the car's decrepitude at least provided cover, since no one would have guessed that such a sorry vehicle belonged to the FBI.

His initial apprehension about being a rookie in an unsupervised environment had abated. Mark's superiors made it clear that his work was appreciated—suddenly, with his presence, the office seemed to be bustling with action; the paperwork was humming back and forth between Pikeville and Covington, where his nominal supervisor was an agent named Terry Hulse. His success in cultivating Susan and Charlie as informants was impressive; so, too, were the reports that he had significantly improved relations between the bureau and the Kentucky State Police, whose Pikeville post was one of the busiest in their department. Before Mark arrived with good cheer and law-enforcement collegiality, state cops had resented the FBI as exceedingly glory-conscious and aloof, but the word filtering through the overworked Pikeville post was that Putnam was different. Veteran state police officers there had never before come in contact with an FBI agent who made it a part of his routine to stop by the post and shoot the breeze, trading information, offering to help out even on minor criminal investigations of the sort that the FBI often disdained. Mark established himself as someone who showed up even for the scut work, the excruciating night-long surveillances in mountain backwaters, the down-in-the-mud searching for physical evidence at a crime scene, the interminable routine interviewing, the warrant-serving in places that required a hike into the woods. Hungry for the camaraderie of police work and anxious to learn what he could from experienced state cops who understood the region, Putnam worked, as one of the state cops would later recall, not entirely complimentarily, "like a damn rented mule."

"I was basically a sponge, soaking up everything I possibly could," Mark would later concede. "Maybe I was overeager. Work was all I wanted to do."

When he wasn't working, he applied the same fervor to his family life. For a young couple just starting out in a new home, on a salary of just over $30,000 a year, money was adequate but not plentiful. Mark and Kathy seldom went out, preferring to have intimate late-night dinners at home on weekends. He always tried to get out of the office at a reasonable hour on Friday nights, which was designated "date night" with Danielle, who wore her prettiest dress to accompany her father to the Dairy Queen or the McDonald's out on Route 23. Mark also volunteered to coach a boys' soccer team at the YMCA in Pikeville.

Kathy regarded their family routine, happy as it was, as fairly mundane, and she was baffled by the deep curiosity Susan exhibited about small personal details between her and Mark. She realized that Mark was somewhat concerned about the intense nature of Susan's interest, which he couldn't easily defuse because he needed to maintain his relationship with her at least long enough to ensure that she would testify at the bank robbery trial of Cat Eyes, now scheduled for January. Furthermore, the bureau was encouraging him to maintain Susan as an active, productive informant, since she was promising to develop and pass on information about other, as yet unspecified, criminal matters in the Tug Valley.

This meant that Mark met with Susan regularly. Unbidden, she continued calling the Putnam home almost daily. For Kathy, who sensed that Susan felt neglected, empathy overcame prudence. She shrugged off a disquieting sense that Susan's inquisitiveness about both her husband and her family might be drifting into an obsessive attraction.

The initial evidence of this was innocent enough to be vaguely flattering. By the end of the summer, Kathy, now five months pregnant, had decided that she was tired of having shoulder-length hair, which had lost its bouncy curl. She went to a beauty salon in Pikeville and had it styled and layered shorter and told Susan that night how pleased she was with it.

"I guess Mark likes short hair, huh?" Susan asked.

Kathy replied, "Mark likes women who take care of themselves."

A few days later, Mark mentioned that Susan had cut her long hair short and had asked if it was like Kathy's.

Not that Mark had much time to ponder Susan's hairdo. By late October, after months of painstaking detail work and hand-holding with an increasingly skittish Charlie Trotter, Mark decided that the groundwork was well enough laid to move to the next stage on the chop-shop case. He had brought Brennan up to date on the investigation and alerted the Covington and Lexington offices, as well as the state police in Pikeville and the sheriff's department in Letcher County. The next step necessary before a full-scale raid was to photograph the operation itself. After Charlie drew him a map, Mark persuaded a pilot from the state Department of Mines and Minerals to fly him over the site in a small plane. Through gaps in the thinning autumn foliage they saw it—an expanse the size of two football fields littered with trucks, bulldozers, radiators, axles, engines, coal scoops, end loaders, and hundreds of other pieces of equipment—a veritable supermarket of stolen parts, displayed for sale to the right buyers on graded shelves cut into a mountain.

The raid was scheduled for the last week of October, which would be right after Kathy and Danielle were due to leave for Connecticut. The timing was excellent for Mark, who knew that the real work would come following the raid and the arrests. He would have to spend weeks on the scene, painstakingly creating an inventory of thousands of pieces of evidence that would be needed to assemble a major federal case of interstate theft. With his family out of town, he could work at it around the clock, and without guilt.

After work on Friday night, the Putnams drove to Lexington, where they spent the night in a motel so Kathy and Danielle could catch an early flight the next morning. When they checked in, there was a message to call the office.

Kathy saw that something was wrong. "The raid is going down tomorrow," Mark told her disconsolately. "There was some kind of glitch with the search warrants and they had to move fast."

The next day, after seeing Kathy and Danielle off at the airport, Mark drove the three hours directly to the site, but he was already too late. Dan Brennan was on hand supervising the dozen or so officers who had conducted the raid and were crawling over the location, marveling at the extent of the operation. The news was not good. There had been no arrests; someone had apparently tipped off Vernon Mullins and his men, who were nowhere to be seen when the police stormed up the hollow. The only living creatures anywhere in the vicinity were a pack of menacing Dobermans, who weren't impressed by badges and guns.

As Brennan briefed Mark, a heavy downpour erupted from black clouds over the mountains. Most of the officers fled to their cars, and Brennan departed, saying he'd see Mark back at the office. Furious at what he regarded as an operation that had been botched despite all of his careful preparations, bewildered that someone could have tipped off the suspects, Mark stood ankle deep in cold mud on the hillside and took out a notebook. He crawled under a bulldozer to look for its vehicle identification number.

For three weeks afterward, he stayed at a tiny motel in Whitesburg and spent the daylight hours at the muddy chop-shop site, often accompanied by sheriff's deputies, a state cop who had helped to prepare the case, and a technician from the National Auto Theft Bureau that represented the interests of various insurance companies. They photographed hundreds of vehicles and parts, recording whatever identification numbers they could find. As Charlie had promised, it was a haul. Mark was conservative about placing a dollar value on the cache of stolen material, but after the preliminary inventory, he estimated that they had recovered $2.2 million in stolen equipment that was traceable directly through serial numbers to its owners.

Regional newspaper accounts of the raid, quoting state police estimates, put the total value of all the equipment at $6 million and called it the biggest single recovery of stolen vehicles and parts in recent memory. But, the newspapers also pointed out, no arrests had been made. Police were still looking for the thieves.

The trucks and other equipment were moved into a fenced-in area nearby for safekeeping. It was almost Thanksgiving when Mark was able to get back to the office to continue his statistical work, which involved entering the mass of serial numbers and other data into the National Crime Information Center computer. When numbers matched, the next step was to locate and notify the owners, who were spread out over a five-state area. The owners then had to be interviewed, one by one.

Brennan had been right. The detail work was daunting.

But Mark, who had begun police work as a clerk, had been prepared. What he didn't expect, when he returned to the site one

Saturday, was to be confronted by a man named Charlie Tackett, whom Charlie Trotter had named as a ringleader in the operation. Tackett, aware that no arrest warrants had been prepared and that no evidence yet linked him to the crime, strode right up to Mark with a broad grin and held out his hand. Mark had spoken with him once in the initial phase of the investigation and was left with the strong impression that Tackett felt he had protection.

"Mark, how you doing, son?" he said, clearly amused at his own audacity.

Mark narrowed his eyes. "Hey, Charlie, where have you been?"

"Now, I don't want to be telling you that."

"Where's your boss Vernon these days?"

Tackett laughed. "Let me tell you something: Vernon and I have a lot of friends in this area. We're businessmen, son. A lot of people depend on us for parts. I don't know how many people have come up to me—"

Mark lost his cool. "Charlie, is that some kind of threat? Because if it is, you can just shove it up your ass. If they want to shoot me, go ahead and let them. But I guarantee you, there'll be about eight thousand agents who'll come down and bust every fucking thing that's going on down here, every business you got going, and every business your partners got going. So I don't think that would be a very good move."

"Oh, man, nobody's threatening nobody," Charlie said, kicking at the dirt and chuckling. "I'm just fucking with you, man. No threats! This is a game with us—a game. They're not going to get us. You don't even have enough to make an arrest warrant."

So far, that was true. Mark was depending on Charlie Trotter to supply that. "Charlie, this isn't state court where you can buy your way out of it."

"Time will tell. Time will tell. You'll come around. We got a lot of people that we know, a lot of people on the payroll."

"I know you do."

Both men's gazes drifted to where a local cop was walking around with a clipboard, looking down at some parts.

"Like I said, there are a lot of people on our payroll."

"Shove it, Charlie. It isn't going to work."

But Mark had reason to worry as the case wore on.

Twice, the site where the parts were stored was broken into by thieves, who carted things off at night. Angry and frustrated, Mark moved back to the motel after Thanksgiving and even spent several nights on the site in a sleeping bag. When he went back to Pikeville, he had a call.

"Bad news," said a local cop who was also on the case.

"We got broken into last night. They got all the CB radios."

In all, there were four burglaries within seven nights.

Mark was in the area one morning when a battered pickup truck pulled up. "You Putnam?" the driver called through the open window.

"Yeah," he said, approaching the pickup. "Who are you?"

"Well, I ain't going to say. But they say you're a good boy, and I hate to see you wasting your time."

"What do you mean?"

"Well, you know that guy you been working with?" He named one of the cops.

"What about him?" Mark said.

"I hear he's been selling CBs," the driver said, and rumbled off.

The next morning, Charlie Trotter came by the office with more unnerving news for Mark. He looked nervous. "I had a problem last night. I was a little drunk and some of the boys jumped me and took me aside. He lifted his shirt and turned around. From shoulder to belt line, a crude X had been carved in his back.

5

Though she hated being away from Mark, Kathy was glad that she had chosen to go back to Connecticut, which she thought of as home, to have the baby. She had developed some minor complications late in the pregnancy and felt more confident knowing that she would deliver in a hospital in Connecticut. In December, Mark managed to get the time off to fly back east. He was with her on December 9 when Mark Jr. was born, the image of his father.

In the baby book Kathy bought to match the one they'd kept for Danielle, the new father wrote:

Who would have thought that your mom and I were capable of producing a son? From the moment I saw you, healthy and strong, I realized you were going to be special. Your mom and I have been through so much during the pregnancy, and the fact that you made it through unscathed meant only one thing—your sister and I won't be calling you Looie Loser. Seriously, every man needs a son to do things with. I only hope you know how to fix cars and machinery so you can teach me. I would like to take this opportunity to welcome you to our family and wish you luck—you will need it in

*dealing with your mom and sister. Right now you appear to
be your mama's boy, but that will change in time. Ever hear
of the Sox?*

Your old pop

It was reinvigorating to leave the problems of Pikeville behind for
a few weeks, but Kathy could see Mark's distress, barely masked
by the glow of the new baby and the holidays. The botched raid
at the chop-shop site had bolstered his conviction that he needed
to do everything himself, instead of depending on others. Side-
lined in Connecticut, he fretted about the implications of what
had happened. Recovering stolen goods was only half of the job,
and even with the material in hand, that aspect of the case still
needed months of hard work. The other half was bringing criminal charges against thieves brazen enough to laugh in his face
and claim that they had "protection." His key informant had obviously blown his cover—that *X* on Charlie's back was a bloody
message not only to its victim but to his supposed protector as
well. Mark brooded over the possibility that he wouldn't be able
to come up with criminal indictments of the Mullins gang as
easily as he had come up with the stolen trucks and bulldozers.
There was also the problem of Cat Eyes, whose trial was coming
up right after New Year's, with no guarantees that a mountain
jury was going to return a guilty verdict on an amusing local
boy. Susan's testimony would be crucial—but there were no guarantees that she would actually go through with it and publicly
expose herself as the accuser. He wondered if he was in over his
head.

With a sense of foreboding mixed with impatience to get back
on the job, he returned to Pikeville with Kathy, Danielle, and the
baby a few days after Christmas.

Susan was in the office waiting for him with a big smile. She startled him with a kiss on the lips and said brightly, "I got you a couple of things for Christmas. I'm sorry I didn't wrap it but you know how it is."

He was bewildered. "Susan, don't buy me anything."

She took out a pair of expensive running shoes and a Nike T-shirt and set them proudly on his desk. "Well, you wear those ratty old sneakers all the time, and I think you could use these."

"I can't take these, Susan!"

Her face clouded like a scolded child's. "I will be very insulted if you don't take these. You've been very good to me this year. This is just between us."

Not wanting to hurt her feelings, he muttered thanks clumsily. But as soon as she was gone, he got on the phone to Terry Hulse in Covington and asked him for advice on what to do with a gift from an informant. Again Hulse told him not to worry, just to write a memo about it and put the stuff in the safe. But he also wondered whether Mark was worried about more than a pair of sneakers and a shirt. "Hey, is there anything going on with this girl?" he asked.

Mark considered his response for a moment before replying, "Well, she has made her intentions known if that's what you mean."

His supervisor didn't seem overly concerned. "Just be careful," Hulse told him. "And do good work. See that she testifies."

Ensuring that she testified was the main reason he had been going to the trouble of sustaining his relationship with Susan, who required high maintenance, not only from him but also from Kathy. Susan, he had come to believe over the fall, was a loose cannon. She continued to shoot her mouth off about working for the FBI. What little information she had managed to pass on since the Cat Eyes arrest—mostly tips on small-scale criminal activities in the Tug Valley—wasn't worth the effort. Partly thanks to connections he'd developed through her, and partly thanks to his own hard work, he now had a growing network of informants. For that, he was grateful to Susan, and his feelings for her complicated things. She had been among the first people to accept him in his new post. But she'd been paid, regularly. It was time to move on. Mark was looking forward to putting an end to his work with Susan as soon as the trial was over. Because she had, indeed, made her intentions known.

It was during their last meeting, in December, before he'd gone to Connecticut. He had been driving Susan home to Freeburn and as was their routine they pulled off on a mountain siding to talk. She seemed unusually pleased with herself. "I lost ten pounds, you know."

He hadn't noticed, but he told her, "Jeez, you look terrific."

"I started running every night, just like you."

"That's great, Susan."

"Just in case you're interested."

"Interested in what?"

"Oh, like a little fling."

"A *what?*"

She gave him a look. "A fling, Mark. You know?"

"Jesus, Susan, I'm a married man. I got a new kid on the way. I can't be doing stuff like that."

She persisted, "Come on I like you, you like me, right? I'll tell you right now, whatever you want, we'll do it."

"What? What about Kathy, Susan? She's your friend, for God's sake."

"Why's she have to know?"

He started the car and tried to make light of the situation, and Susan found other things to talk about as he drove her home.

Not that propositions were especially startling to a good-looking young man new to the region. In his first month on the job, for example, a bank teller had passed him a note with her phone number on it and the message, "Call me anytime." Some women in Pikeville and in the mountain belt made clear enough signals of availability to any polite young guy who had all of his teeth, he had thought unkindly. As for Susan, Mark realized that his relationship with her, which evolved partly through a social process that almost necessarily involved elements of flirting, had become confused in her mind, if not in his. Susan's attentions had been on his list of things to worry about over the holidays, as he came to wonder whether he really knew what he was doing in Pikeville. Keeping all things under control was Mark's singular impulse. In dark reflective moments, especially when he woke up with a start in the middle of the night, he wondered anxiously about whether he was losing it.

In the interim, he had to work closely with Susan as the Cat Eyes trial date approached. She was apprehensive about testifying—she said that Kenneth was making her life more miserable than usual, raging about her "ratting on a friend"—but she seemed to take comfort in the implicit protection offered by her alliance with Mark, who felt that he could not risk doing anything to shake her confidence. Sometimes, Susan managed to talk her younger brother, Billy Joe Daniels, known as Bo, into driving her the thirty-five miles from Freeburn to Pikeville, a chore that he resented. Bo had already decided, with circumstantial evidence bolstered by his sister's uncharacteristically girlish prattling about her close relationship with the FBI man, that Susan and Mark Putnam were sexually involved.

Susan came through valiantly in court. At the trial of Cat Eyes Lockhart, the fact that a local woman was actually taking the stand to testify was the talk of the courthouse. Informing for pay was one thing. Standing up to admit it in front of everybody was something else entirely. For Mark, it was a coup; for Susan, it was exposure.

At the trial, Cat Eyes maintained his innocence with a sense of injured pride, though he did so with the rococo lexicon that any parent recognizes as a sure sign a child is spinning a whopper. According to him, he had been arrested and unjustly accused by authorities who would never let him live down his past as a bank robber.

"It seemed like, wherever my personal being was, they would always be law enforcement agencies such as FBI, local authorities, whatever, because when the circumstances of a bank robbery would occur, in specifically speaking in the areas, which was a number of bank robberies, I would be the first individual they came to, regardless of my whereabouts," Cat explained earnestly, if confusingly.

Susan was more direct when she took the stand, avoiding the glares of Kenneth and her brother, who had come to court with her.

"Mrs. Smith, do you know a person who is 'Cat Eyes' Lockhart?" the prosecutor asked.

"Yes, I do."

"Is that person in court today?"

"Yes, he is. He is on the left in a plaid shirt."

"During the summer of 1987, did you have any occasion to see Mr. Lockhart with any firearms?"

"Yes, I did. He stayed in my guest bedroom, with Sherri, and he had this green duffel bag—it looked like an army bag, you know, and a pillowcase that he had a lot of stuff in. And he had two guns . . ."

"They were both shotguns?"

"Yes."

"Were they both sawed off?"

"Sawed off," Susan said.

"Did there come a time that you were aware that a bank at Belcher in Pike County had been robbed in early September of 1987?"

"Yes."

"Turn your attention to the few days before that, and I want to ask you if you had the occasion to see Mr. Lockhart and Ms. Justice a few days before that robbery."

"Yes, I did," Susan said as Cat Eyes's girlfriend, Sherri Justice, looked daggers at her. "It was at my home on a Friday night a week before the bank was robbed, about eleven o'clock. They came to my house. They were very nervous, upset . . ."

"Was there any discussion by Mr. Lockhart and/or Ms. Justice in your presence of robbing a bank?"

"Yes, both of them was speaking at the time to me."

"What did they say?"

"About robbing a bank. They didn't say what bank, they just said a bank in Pike County."

Susan's testimony, with her positive identification of the shotgun, clinched the prosecution's case. Cat Eyes was found guilty and sent back to the penitentiary, but even as he was going to prison once again, he refused to believe that little Susie Smith, a girl he said he loved, had done it to him of her own free will.

"That Kenneth, he done put her up to it," Cat Eyes said sadly.

A few weeks after the trial, Dan Brennan was due to be transferred out, and Mark considered the possibility that his replacement, Ronald Gene Poole, a thirty-seven-year-old agent coming down from the Chicago office with a reputation as a good undercover investigator who liked to handle drug cases, might be the man to shoulder some of the growing burden of carrying Susan as an informant. Most of Susan's tips lately had to do with drug cases, which Mark himself had little interest in, since he thought they were too easy and accomplished little even if you broke one. He hoped that if his new partner were interested, he'd be able to pass Susan on to him, neatly solving one looming problem with a gracious gesture of welcome besides.

Brennan asked Mark to accompany him to the Landmark, the most prominent of only a handful of motels in Pikeville, to meet Poole, who was staying there while he found a place to live.

Brennan had already met Poole, and he had a word of caution on their short drive across town. "This guy's a little, uh, different from what you would expect in an agent," Brennan said tentatively.

"How so?"

"Well, you'll see."

Mark soon understood. At over three hundred pounds, with shaggy hair and perspiring heavily, Ron Poole looked like an overweight school crossing guard with a patronage job from a town school board. *Holy shit*, Mark thought when he saw Poole shambling toward them. *Maybe this guy does such great undercover work because the last thing you'd take him for is an agent.*

Not only Poole's appearance, but his attitude as well, offended Mark's idealized sense of what an FBI agent should be. It was clear from the start that this was going to be an uneasy relationship.

Poole invited them into his room for a get-acquainted chat and looked over his new partner sharply. "I don't care who I work with," he told Dan in a cool tone, "as long as it's not a goddamn Yankee."

"Surprise," Mark replied curtly, holding out his hand.

Poole cultivated his unruly image and let Mark know right away that he had no intention of "carrying" a rookie. Staking out his position clearly, he said that he worked alone and without interference—which suited Mark fine. Poole let it be known immediately that he had been transferred out of the Chicago office after drug dealers threatened his life. He was also known, during eight years in the bureau, as an agent who delivered the goods. As Mark initially guessed, Poole did, in fact, manage to infiltrate criminal activities because he was persistent and because he looked like anything but a cop. He delivered, but his superiors apparently preferred to keep him at arm's length, which meant teaming him with a rookie in a remote office like Pikeville without on-site supervision. Poole had been an accountant before he joined the FBI. Using Poole to fill the vacancy opened by Brennan's departure seemed eminently logical on paper—in Pikeville, the former accountant could be paired, with perfect bureaucratic logic and expedience, with an ex-clerk.

Mark, who had hoped for a new partner from whom he could actually learn things, quickly understood that Poole would not be that man. A few days after Poole arrived, Terry Hulse phoned Mark from the Covington office to check in. Terry extolled Poole for his record of investigative expertise and bravery. Mark's impression was that he was laying it on a bit thick.

Does he want me to cover for this character? Mark asked himself as Hulse went on. But all he said was, "I'll do anything I can to help."

It didn't help matters much when, a few weeks after Poole began work, he met a young Pikeville woman named Myra Chico. Myra, who worked as a part-time reporter for the local radio station, made it a point to know all of the local cops, whose cooperation was always useful when a story broke. "If you wanted something out, you called Myra and hoped she got it right," one cop said later.

When she introduced herself to Poole, she tried to break the ice by complimenting him—on his partner. "To me, Mark Putnam is the epitome of what an FBI agent should be," Myra chirped. Poole glowered at her.

Still, however skeptical Poole was about being teamed with an agent who he thought looked like a magazine model, not a cop, and a goddamn Yankee to boot, Poole had to concede that Mark had obviously managed to put together sources, not the least interesting of whom to him was pretty little Susan Smith, the sassy girl from that coal-mine town. Even his wife, Kathy, had made a real effort to make Poole feel welcome in Pikeville.

Shortly after Poole arrived in town, Kathy suggested to Mark that he invite him to the house for dinner. Poole eagerly accepted. Kathy recalled that he spent much of the time regaling them with war stories about his undercover work in Chicago and, before that, in the mountains of North Carolina, from the bureau in Charlotte. He also disarmed her by candidly discussing his weight problem, which, he said his previous supervisor had humiliated him over, going so far as to bring a bathroom scale into the office and making him publicly weigh in each day. Immediately sympathetic and characteristically empathetic, Kathy described to Poole the diet and exercise regimen she was using to firm up after having the baby.

"I can see it's been very successful," Poole told her, looking her over. Mark made a mental note how his new partner seemed to leer at his wife.

A few nights later, when Mark was working late and on the road, Kathy was surprised to get a phone call from Poole. Danielle and the baby were in bed; she'd been doing aerobic exercises and answered the phone out of breath.

"Breathing heavy?" Poole said in a manner that struck her as oddly suggestive. But she brushed it off, and Poole said he was calling to see if he could borrow a diet book she had mentioned at dinner. They talked for about a half hour, mostly about diets, but also about the long hours Mark put in. Innocently, she mentioned that she was looking forward to the day when they would get out of Pikeville.

Poole recounted his experience in Chicago when he'd been transferred after receiving threats. Given how miserable life in Pikeville had become for her, she was very interested to hear what he had to say about getting out. "That's all you need," he told her, in a tone that she thought sounded almost hopeful about seeing Mark, at least, get out of town. "Guaranteed. You'd be out the next day."

It occurred to her then, and she would become deadly certain of it later, that Poole might be jealous of Mark, and she wondered whether she should warn her husband. But she decided that Mark would think she was being silly. She could handle Poole herself. When he phoned back a few nights later to thank her for the diet book, she commiserated with him about the difficulties of staying in shape. He told her that he appreciated the help and added that he'd make it a practice to check in on her when Mark was working late "since you're there by yourself with the kids." And in very short order, Ron Poole had joined Kathy's little assembly of regular nighttime callers. Kathy was lonely enough to welcome the acquaintance and canny enough to realize that Poole might become useful to her at some point, though she was repulsed by his sexual intentions.

In fact, a quarter century later, Mark's early cop buddy in Freeburn, Bert Hatfield, laughed when he remembered Ron Poole, who died in 2000 at the age of fifty. "Poole, that boy was a pussyhound first and foremost, and an FBI agent, maybe second," Hatfield said from his car lot in Freeburn. "Being a big-shot FBI guy, he managed to get plenty of women, but Susie would have nothing to do with him that way. She played him like a fiddle. It drove him nuts that he couldn't get in her pants."

As Poole insinuated himself into the new region and began developing his own cases, almost exclusively those involving drugs, Mark was hoping for the opportunity to pass Susan along to his new partner—but his supervisor cautioned him to think long and hard about her proven value to his own career. Good sources like that, Terry Hulse told him, didn't grow on trees in eastern Kentucky.

"Listen, you started out with a bang down there," Hulse told him when Mark broached the subject during one of his infrequent trips to Covington to review case files. "You were there a few months and you got this informant. And she actually *testified*. Keep on this woman, Mark. Look at the potential."

Mark agreed about the potential; he just didn't want to be the one to develop it any further himself. He was worried that he was stretched too thin already. But he felt his resistance weakening in the face of his supervisor's blandishments. "She can mix in with anybody, that's for sure," Mark had to concede. "She can talk to politicians, she can talk to drug dealers—anybody. I know we should keep her on, but I'm not sure I can get much more out of her. Poole thinks he can work with her on his investigations."

"Do you think she's blown her cover for you?"

"Maybe. Maybe not. With her, it's hard to say. She's full of surprises, that one."

On the long drive back to Pikeville, annoyed with himself for not standing his ground, Mark tried to assess his position. As fond as he had become of her, he was uneasy about Susan, professionally and personally. On the other hand, every time he decided she had outlived her usefulness to him, she managed to come up with something new to make him reconsider. For example, after his impressive first year in Pikeville, he had decided that once the chop-shop case was finished it would be time to shift gears and move aggressively into what he regarded as the big time: political corruption. Through the bureau grapevine, he had heard that the US Attorney's office in Lexington was starting work on a major, top-secret investigation into interlocking networks of corrupt politicians, judges, and sheriffs in the region. A web of kickbacks, shakedowns, extortion—the essence of official corruption—lay like a drying fishnet over eastern Kentucky. Once the investigation got going, there was no telling where the trail would lead in a place like that.

With uncanny prescience, Susan showed up in the office at primary election time carrying a bag of red, black, and white pills. She held them up to Mark's face.

"Where'd you get that stuff?" he asked anxiously.

She named a politician who she said had given them to her in Freeburn, "to pass out for votes."

Thinking it incredible that anyone in her hometown would trust her enough to give her illegal drugs, Mark took the pills away and flushed them down the toilet. While he couldn't be sure where she'd got them, the last thing he wanted was to have a sack of drugs on hand. He knew by now that Susan's stories only checked out about half the time.

But the problem was, he never really could tell which half. One day that spring, Susan sauntered in with new information. She named two men who she said were planning to rob a bank in Phelps, a town on the way to Freeburn. Overwhelmed with work on the chop-shop case, worried about Charlie Trotter wavering as an informant, Mark didn't want to encourage her. He knew that Susan felt neglected and had been crying on the phone to Kathy about how miserable her life was, especially with Kenneth on her back all the time about her work with the FBI. She was broke again and desperate to get back into action. But Charlie Trotter had also started crying on the phone about feeling abandoned. By this point, Mark didn't have either the time or the energy to coddle Susan, a task he more and more often left to the far more patient and sympathetic Kathy.

"Susan, how do you know they're going to rob the bank?" he asked her doubtfully.

She insisted that she had heard it directly from one of the would-be robbers himself. She identified the man as an uncle of Cat Eyes who lived near Freeburn.

This sounded even more preposterous to Mark. "Susan, he knows you *testified* against Cat Eyes. Why would his uncle trust you?"

"Well, he wants to get in my pants."

Everybody wants to get in her drawers, he thought dismissively. "Susan, I can't believe this, that he would tell you something like that," he said.

She insisted it was true. She said she had driven the man to the bank herself to look it over. To prove to him that she was not working for the FBI anymore, she had even given him the gun that he planned to use in the robbery. She had teed the whole thing up.

"No way," Mark told Poole, who had been listening intently, when she left. He wrote up a standard note to the miscellaneous file summarizing what she had said, and promptly forgot about it.

A week later, Mark went to FBI headquarters in Washington, DC, for a few days of work on a case involving a fugitive terrorist. He was in the office of the FBI Technical Services Division when an urgent phone call from Poole interrupted him.

"The bank in Phelps just got robbed!" Poole cried. "What the hell do I do? I don't even know where this place is!"

Mark groaned and suggested, "Call Susan."

Poole was of course happy for that suggestion. In his conversations with Kathy, he'd made his interest in Susan very clear. He'd also said that he believed Susan was still in love with her husband, which came as no surprise to Kathy, since Susan herself had confided the same thing. Kathy thought it pathetic. She also was worried about Susan's increasing drug use. She despaired of ever being able to help her straighten out her chaotic life. Kathy warned Poole, who was separated from his wife, not to get involved.

"I can take care of myself," Poole replied angrily, and he startled Kathy by hanging up.

For her part, Susan realized that Mark was shunting her aside. That knowledge made her more miserable, her drug use worsened, and her need for money increased.

She turned to Mark's wife as usual. "Poole wants me to work with him on these drug cases, but I need to work with Mark," Susan told Kathy through angry tears.

The bureau money was available for a productive informant, of course—and Susan was desperate to put enough together to move out of the house she shared with Kenneth into an apartment with her two children. So with few other options, she began working small drug cases with Poole. She complained, however, that more often than not, these were investigative trips where they always ended up alone at a bar or a restaurant. Steadfastly, she rebuffed Poole's overtures, but she worried how long it would be before he would cut her off financially if she didn't give in.

By the summer, Kathy decided unilaterally that it was time for a real vacation. Except for the Christmas trip back home when little Mark was born, they hadn't been away together since before Mark went into the academy, which now seemed like ages ago. Kathy had squirreled away enough money to do it right. She announced to Mark that she had already made the arrangements. Like it or not, they were going to a place they had visited once and loved: Myrtle Beach, a resort on the coast of South Carolina. At first, he resisted mightily, insisting that his workload was too staggering even to think about getting away. She was adamant.

"We're going," she said. "You'd better go find your bathing suit."

She prevailed. In August, they packed up the car and the kids and drove across the Appalachians and the coastal plain beyond to the sandy sweep of Myrtle Beach, where they spent ten days. It was a sun-drenched island of peace, serenity, and intense joy in their still-young marriage. It would be their last truly happy time together.

6

The vacation reverie faded fast. The night after they returned, Poole was on the phone, telling Kathy the last thing she needed to hear, which was that the bureau was cutting back on spending and that "first-office agents" such as Mark, who could usually expect to be routinely transferred after two years or so in one place, were now likely to spend four or five years before being relocated to one of the offices of their choice.

She was crying when Mark came home. He didn't want to talk about transfers. Instead, he read Danielle her bedtime story and without a word went out for a longer run than usual. While he was out, the phone rang.

"Is this the FBI's wife?" a gruff voice said.

"Who's calling?"

"Just this: Your old man's fooling around with a girl named Susan Smith. That's all." The caller hung up.

When Mark came back, she tried to talk to him about Susan. But all he would say, was, "Don't be ridiculous."

Mark, in fact, was furious over the rumors about him and Susan that were circulating, not only because they weren't true, but because they confirmed that he had allowed the situation to get out of control. Out of his depth, stretched to his psychological limit, he felt himself sinking under the weight of his inexperience. At the same time, at home with two small children, in a place she had come to despise, besieged by an increasingly distraught Susan, annoyed by constant calls from Poole and Trotter, Kathy had fixed her hopes on getting out—soon. Now, with the bureau's policy change, she plunged into a depression that deepened as the sunlight began its steady fade into fall and that mountain looming over the back of their house grew darker.

Three mountains away, in Freeburn, Susan, herself dejected about Mark's indifference, depending on pills to lift her spirits in the morning and to put her to sleep at night, threw off any semblance of discretion. Desperate to recover emotional ground and persuade herself that there was hope, she told anyone who would listen that Mark Putnam was in love with her and was planning to leave his wife. She openly described herself as being under FBI "protection."

In Pikeville as well, she did everything she could to encourage the notion, now widespread in the courthouse, that she and Mark were having an affair. It was as if she were on a campaign to make it all come true.

Whenever she managed to cajole her brother into driving her to town, she'd drop into the FBI office unannounced, and when she didn't find Mark there, she would poke her head into one of the nearby offices, put on a long face for the marshals and probation officers, and say, "Where's Mark? He promised to meet me."

When Mark would get back, they'd say, "You're in trouble, buddy. You done stood her up." Mark refused to get drawn in the teasing. He'd just force a grin.

Once he stopped to chat with a small group of courthouse workers.

"That girl is nuts," one said.

"Today she come in looking for you. She had a tank top on, no bra," another put in. "Somebody made a remark about her chest, you know, and she said 'Well, you want to see?'"

"She pulled up her shirt! She's flat!" the courthouse worker said gleefully.

Later, Susan told her own version of the incident. It was obvious that she believed she could make Mark jealous by flashing the courthouse workers.

Mark understood that some of this situation was his own fault. For a time before the Cat Eyes trial, he had thought it helpful to keep certain people with their eyes on courthouse comings and goings from thinking that Susan was acting strictly as an informant, that their relationship was somehow more personal, if only by way of ensuring her some protection. But he sensed that it was more complicated than that. In ways he did not care to explore, he was possessive of Susan. The unhappier his wife became, the more pliant Susan seemed. He looked forward to her smile and coquettishness. In painful moments of introspection as he ran long laps alone in the night around the high school track near his home, he also wondered whether he was exploiting Susan's unconditional trust just to prove that he had, in fact, managed to fit in as an outsider in this alien place.

Susan, running sprints on her own mental track, gave him no room to maneuver. Kathy, meanwhile, had begun to take Susan's pitiful nighttime calls less with the attitude of a concerned friend and more with that of worker for a crisis hot line.

Susan's family was furious with her because of her testimony, which had sent a local rogue to prison. As she became brazen in her insistence that she would continue her work as an informant for the FBI, the abuse from Kenneth intensified. She made no attempt to put on a brave front with Mark. "My family doesn't like

this at all," she told him. "They don't talk to me anymore. Somebody gives me a hard time in a bar, they won't come to my rescue.
Shelby doesn't agree with me working with a Yankee cop."

Shelby Jean Ward was Susan's older, more responsible sister;
often, during her battles with Kenneth, Susan stayed at Shelby's
house in Freeburn. Mark had only spoken to Shelby on the phone
a few times when he needed to reach Susan. He was well aware of
her antipathy.

Years later, Mark tried to sort out how and why the experience
in Pikeville deteriorated so drastically.

"Both Kathy and I would talk about her at home," he remembered. "Kathy would say, 'That girl has it so hard. Kenneth beats
her up; the other people are threatening her for testifying for you.
Social Services are trying to take her kids away. She's doing a lot of
coke and pills.'

"The first thing they teach you at the FBI Academy is don't get
involved with your informants. That's rule number one. I knew I
was already over the boundary with Susan. I thought, 'This girl
had really helped me out. She's put me on the map with the bureau,
and because of my association with her, more and more people are
helping me out. And she has this incredibly shitty life.'

"Man, I was starting to go over the edge. I was feeling sorry for
Susan, but the truth is, I was feeling sorry for myself, too. I knew
the invitation was there with Susan. At home, things between
Kathy and me were sporadic. We'd hook up, we wouldn't. I was
always working. We weren't communicating at all. Kathy was miserable—I would come home from work, and she'd be crying. And
I just didn't want to hear it because I heard so much crying from
people all day long. I just wanted to come home and relax without
any problems, but there she was, laying problems on me: 'I hate
this place and these people; we've got to get out of here; you're
working too much; you don't care about me; all you care about is

that job.' I'd go out for a run, or I'd drive back to the office and do paperwork until Kathy was asleep. I just abandoned her."

Meanwhile, Susan's calls to Kathy became more frantic. Kathy hardly even mentioned them to her husband anymore. Sometimes when they were together nights at home the phone would ring.

"Mark and I would look at each other, and I'd pick up. Sure enough: 'Kathy? Is Mark there?' And I'd say no."

Susan's intrusions became so frequent that Kathy paid less attention even when they did speak. But she did listen raptly when Susan told her in one call how "close" she had become to her husband. "I like to feel him near me," Susan said dreamily, and there was no denying what she meant. Kathy discounted it as drug induced fantasy, but still she warned Mark, "Don't you ever get involved with this woman."

He looked insulted. "Kat—"

She was furious at him, for the same naïveté that she had once found so charming. "You *know* what I'm saying, Mark. She will get pregnant and she will ruin you."

"Kathy, I'm not stupid. I love you."

As winter approached, with the sun behind the mountains for much of the day, shacks clustered on the ridges and far up into dark hollows were exposed under bare trees, with wisps of chimney smoke curling into a gray sky. Kathy resented even the season. Susan's calls persisted like a cold drizzle. Fielding them at night, Kathy would tell Susan that Mark was out when he wasn't, using hand signals to convey to him how drugged and agitated Susan sounded. Yet she maintained her sympathy, even when the drugs and despair turned a conversation with Susan into an emotional ordeal.

"What's the matter, Susan?" Kathy said, hearing her familiar sniffles one night.

"Oh, Kathy, I don't know what I'm going to do. Kenneth, he just makes everything so hard. I know I got to get out of here, but he'll come after me, Kathy. He won't never let me go."

"Susan—"

"It's always about the money, and Mark. He knows about my working with Mark, and he won't let me just do what I need to do and get paid for it. He wants it all. He's saying I should give him the money."

"Listen, Susan, calm down. We can work this out."

Sniffles became sobs. "I keep telling him, I'm the one that's in danger, Kenneth! I can't even think straight no more!"

"Susan, you have to calm down and tell me what happened. Are you listening to me?"

"Kathy is Mark there? Is Mark listening?"

"No." She caught Mark's eye as he lay on the living room rug playing with the kids. "Why?"

Mark retreated upstairs with the children.

"I don't want him thinking I'm crazy or nothing, Kathy. If he thinks I'm crazy, he won't work with me. My work is important, Kathy. I don't do it just for the money. Mark needs me, God's truth. I just keep getting stuck in these horrible situations."

"Mark isn't here, Susan."

Susan laughed derisively. "You sure that son of a bitch ain't home?" she said with rueful chortle: "You're alone just like me— we're by ourselves while the big man is out making a name for hisself—himself." Kathy sighed, lit a cigarette, and settled in for the duration.

"I know he just wants to forget all about me. Mark thinks I can't do nothing for him anymore, I know he does. It don't matter to him about the danger I was in, it don't matter that I could have got killed, just as long as he's got his reputation and his big government job. I'm the one has to worry about these people up here. They all know that I'm an informer. I tell you one thing, Kathy. Mark, he don't know the information I could give still. And I might not help him again, ever. All he cares about is that job; he don't even care about me getting hurt, or you stuck at home with the babies. You know, you're the stupid one!"

Kathy stiffened and said, "Susan, where's Kenneth?"

"Gone. He hit me and took the car. I don't even have a car!"

"All right. What about the kids? Susan, are the kids okay?"

Susan mumbled that they were. "Brady's in bed. Miranda was running when I called you, but she'll tire out and curl up somewhere. Kathy, he's started to hit me in front of the kids and they cry. I just can't deal with this no more."

"The first thing is, you have to calm down, Susan. Are you messed up now, or can you listen?"

Susan insisted that she was straight.

"Tell me what happened, Susan."

"He hit me in front of the kids."

"Did he hit the kids?"

"No."

"Are you hurt badly? Do you need to go to a hospital?"

"No, I'm okay."

"Why did he hit you?"

"Oh, Lord, he was all fucked up and accusing me of having money. Money that he didn't know about. And why wasn't he getting any of the money. He said that I was spending too much time with Mark and not getting anything out of it. I told him Mark and me has to spend a lot of time together, it's my work. I told him you knew all about it. You don't object so why should someone who's my ex-husband? When I talk about Mark, it gets him furious. He just loses it. And I told him I said sometimes me and Mark go to motel rooms and all—"

"You told him *what*?"

"I told him that, about motels—" Quickly, she added, "— Which ain't true. You know I ain't sleeping with Kenneth no more, and he's real jealous. I tell him about my feelings for Mark, what a gentleman Mark is. I said, Mark cares about me as a person. I can't help my feelings for Mark, Kathy! Mark would never do me like Kenneth does. He's just like the devil, Kenneth is. He started slapping me and hitting me, and Miranda was crying—"

"Susan, you have to realize, when Kenneth is like that and the two of you start fighting, you can't antagonize him, Susan. It only makes matters worse for yourself—"

"I know, I know. I don't want to make things worse. I'm so sick, Kathy. I don't want him hurting me; I just want him out of here. I wish I never knew him."

Kathy stubbed out one cigarette and lit another, and pulled the phone over to the counter where she could pour herself a drink. "Susan, how many times do I have to tell you? You are better than this, Susan! You have to take charge of your own life. You know that you're smart enough to get you and those kids away from this! But you have to care enough about yourself first. All those children have is you. Do you want them growing up like this? You have got to give those children a chance at a decent life, Susan, by getting yourself and those kids out of there."

Calculating her position, Susan said, "There's something I didn't tell you about. I signed custody of Miranda to Kenneth. I had left and I signed her to Kenneth. I don't have rights where she is concerned. If I left, he could get her back. I think about what happens if I leave, and I can't. The kids all dirty and without shoes—not like your kids. Mark don't care about anything that's happened to me—"

"Susan, you have got to start taking responsibility for yourself."

"I *have* decided, Kathy."

"If you're sure you really want to do something I will try to help you. But you have to take charge of yourself."

"I want that, Kathy. You're a friend to me; I can't talk to no one else."

Kathy sensed this was going nowhere. She said, "What are you going to do now?"

"I don't know. I did look at a couple of apartments, though. One was real nice. I got to be far away from where he is."

"You can do anything you set your mind to, Susan."

"Why couldn't Mark just tell the court to fix it for me? He can do stuff like that if he wants to."

"No, he can't, Susan. That has absolutely nothing to do with Mark or the FBI."

"It don't matter because Mark won't fix nothing for me anyway because there's nothing in it for him, no big case for him to show off to his supervisor."

Exasperated, Kathy said, "Susan, that's the point. You can't expect everybody to fix things for you. You have to take responsibility—"

Then Susan, or Kenneth, slammed the phone down.

Whatever its social risks, informing for the FBI at least paid well, especially for people, such as Susan and Charlie Trotter, who were otherwise unemployed.

Shortly after the raid on the chop-shop site, Mark had counted out $5,000 in hundred-dollar bills for Charlie's work—bringing his total to $11,000 to date—with more to come after indictments and a trial. Yet Charlie was already broke and calling regularly, clamoring for more. He told Mark he had spent most of the money on prostitutes and cocaine.

Susan, however, had yielded hers to Kenneth, with whom she was still trying to live. In the fall, Mark had given her another

$4,000, which he said was payment for assisting Poole on his drug cases, as well as for the work on the Phelps bank robbery. In reality, the $4,000 was more of a charity payment. Kathy had been pleading Susan's case—Susan was afraid of Kenneth, she needed to find a place to live—and Mark knew there would be no problem getting the bureau to approve another $4,000. But Susan didn't use the money to move out. Instead, soon after she got it, she phoned Kathy to say that Kenneth had claimed half for drug debts he said she owed. The other half had gone to a used car—Kathy thought it was interesting that the car was a Dodge Diplomat, similar to Mark's bureau-issue vehicle. Kenneth had promptly taken possession of that, too.

"I bought that car as an investment," Susan told her.

Shaking her head, Kathy wondered if this was hopeless. An *investment?*

Mark insisted that it was pretty much hopeless. Yet he had no stomach for the scene that Susan would undoubtedly make if he tried to break the connection entirely. For a cop, Mark had an unusual aversion to confrontation. Trying to foist her off on Poole wasn't going to solve the problem, either. Poole was obviously interested in continuing to work with Susan—in fact, she'd told Kathy that he had expressed his interest in a "long-term relationship with benefits for the both of us." But she hated working with him. On paper, Susan's cooperation as an informant continued to look good—but Mark was seriously worried about the lengths to which she would go to ensure her continued employment. The Phelps bank robbery was a case in point. Susan had helped solve the case for the FBI, but the fact was, she had also helped to plan the robbery, entrapping Cat Eyes's uncle. The entrapment had been clever, almost brilliant. What, Mark worried, would this girl come up with next?

Mark kept busy elsewhere, mostly over in Letcher County. While working the chop-shop investigation, he was trying to position himself to make inroads into official corruption that would dovetail with the secret corruption investigation he'd learned about. Letcher County, where anything (and, it was said, anyone) could be bought, was an excellent place to do that.

He wasn't aware of the fanciful stories Susan had been circulating in the Tug Valley. Unable so far to interest him in her sexually—and Susan was a woman for whom sexual attention was crucial—she had simply wished it to be true, as she had wished so many other things in her life. And characteristically, her wishes were grand. To hear Susan tell it—and her sister Shelby was hearing all of the details now, as Susan spent many nights at her house—Mark had fallen deeply in love with her. They had gone to motels, even to his house (Kathy, she said, was often away with the kids in Connecticut), where they had wild sexual romps that lasted until dawn. Susan told people that she had already become pregnant by Mark, but lost the baby in a miscarriage. Still, there was plenty of time for more! There was a lifetime, in fact, since Susan maintained that he assured her he was going to divorce Kathy to marry her. Furthermore, Mark had appointed her, Susan Smith, to a special position as a US informant, fully protected from assault by federal law, she said—"just the same as a clerk in the post office."

People in Freeburn knew Susan well enough to assume that only about half of what she said was true. But there was at least a suspicion that *some* of it was true. Shelby was furious at Susan's imprudence and warned her to forget about the FBI man and stay away from Pikeville. Kenneth also showed his disapproval, but more bluntly. As Susan made clear to Kathy, without fully explaining why, he roughed her up regularly, though Kenneth always denied it.

Unable to turn her back on Susan, Kathy championed her cause more urgently to Mark, importuning him to do whatever he could.

Late one afternoon at the end of October, Susan called Kathy to tell her she was in the hospital. At first, Kathy was afraid she'd been beaten up, but Susan assured her she was in only "for tests" for a few days because she was "run-down" and exhausted and needed to "build myself up because I lost too much weight." Kathy was considering telling her what she really thought, which was that she needed to cut out the pills and cocaine, when Susan burst into tears. "Nobody has been out to see me since I got here," she sobbed. "I haven't even heard from my family."

Kathy bought a get-well card, signed it, had Danielle write her name on it in her child's loping scrawl, and handed it to Mark when he got in that night. He didn't want to sign it. He was even less happy when Kathy suggested that he deliver it personally. Kathy insisted, "That girl has led a tough life, and you owe her, Mark. Aren't you going to go visit her?"

"Absolutely not. No way. That's personal, not business."

"Well, I think you should, Mark. That girl has helped you out. You've kind of put her out front with those people where she lives. A lot of them won't even speak to her now because of what she did for you. I think you owe it to her to at least go see her."

He acquiesced, not wanting to get into it more with Kathy, but her interference in his business with Susan annoyed him. Sure, he felt sorry for Susan. Yes, her work had put a feather in his cap—she had delivered, no argument. She had also been paid well. As far as he was concerned, it was well past time to move on.

Susan was in a hospital in Williamson. Unhappily, Mark drove out there and found her alone in a double room, pale and thin, but animated. She giggled over the card when he gave it to her. Then she put it on the nightstand. Tugging at his hand, she said, "Why don't you climb into bed with me? Ain't nobody else in this room. The door shuts."

"Susan, cut it out."

She stuck her chin out raffishly. "Right here, right now. Nobody would ever know. What do you say, Mark?" She pulled the sheet back. She was naked underneath.

"Come on, cut the crap," he protested.

She just smiled innocently.

"Susan, that would be a major mistake. You know that."

She knew no such thing. "Not if nobody ever found out," she insisted. "And they won't."

He changed the subject and left within a few minutes. But on the drive back home, he found himself reflecting on the offer. She made it sound so simple. *Pure submission*, he thought. In his cranky, beleaguered frame of mind, it had a certain appealing lack of ambiguity. In the days ahead he put Susan out of his mind and forced himself to think about his other mounting troubles, as if by way of penance.

He had come to comprehend, with some bitterness, that the career potential in the chop-shop case could cut both ways. The US attorney's office in Lexington, exercising particular caution in assembling the case because of its possible use as a springboard for bigger things down the road, hadn't yet come up with the indictments of the Mullins gang. In Letcher County, the delay was being read differently. On the one-year anniversary of the raid, noting that no suspects had been charged, although everyone knew who they were, a Letcher County newspaper had even printed a story suggesting that not only certain local police officers, but the "federal boys" as well, had been paid off by the criminals. There was no doubt in anyone's mind, least of all Mark's, who the "federal boys" were. He was infuriated by the story, and he took it very personally, since it was the first time in his life that he had ever been accused, however elliptically, of wrongdoing. He was convinced that the insinuation had compromised his reputation in the area. Yet he never mentioned it to anyone, not even his wife.

The pilfering of material from the site had become so routine that it had become a local joke that the stolen goods were cheaper now than they were back when Vernon Mullins and the boys were selling them. Mark was convinced, though he had no evidence, that at least one of the local cops was working with the thieves. This gnawed at him constantly. He didn't know whom he could trust, and so he trusted no one.

He left the house early one morning and saw that all four tires of the Olds had been flattened in the driveway. That was the first warning that the line between work and home had been erased. Others lie ahead like a boulder on a hairpin mountain road.

Another came when he was working in the driveway one Sunday afternoon, furiously chopping firewood for the stove, working up a comforting sweat. He was interrupted by the light tapping of a car horn. At the curb, Poole had pulled up in the Bronco, with Susan beside him in the front seat. They waved and looked as if they were going to get out to visit, but after Mark turned his back and strode into the house, they drove off.

He confronted Poole in the office the next morning.

"Why in hell did you bring her to my house, Ron?"

Poole showed innocent surprise. "We were out for a drive and she only wanted to see where you live, old buddy. That's all."

Mark's face was so red that Poole thought for a second that he might throw a punch. "Don't you *ever* bring a fucking informant to my house! Do you hear me, Ron? Don't ever do that again." Poole muttered that he'd meant no harm.

That night, Mark angrily warned Kathy to be more careful. He wasn't the only one she was hearing such warnings from, however. One day she was out front picking up Danielle's toys in the driveway when a woman who lived across the street, and who hadn't been particularly friendly in the past, came over.

"I know your husband's got that case in Letcher," the neighbor said, crossing her arms against a chilly wind knifing down through the hills. "You should tell him to be very careful up there, that's probably the worst county there is." As she left, she added, "My brother was shot and killed up there."

At the end of the day, Kathy was standing at the kitchen sink pouring milk into the baby's bottle when she happened to glance at the window. She was startled to see a man looking directly at her. He grinned, showing missing front teeth. He wore a knit cap over stringy, greasy hair. She dropped the milk carton into the sink and in a panic grabbed the .357 that Mark kept on the top pantry shelf. She glanced at eleven-month-old Mark Jr., smiling in the playpen, then checked to see that the gun was loaded.

Feeling her throat constrict, she moved toward the front door and yelled up at Danielle, "Stay in your room, okay, honey?"

A small voice came down. "I'm just playing. I'm the mommy and Amanda is the baby."

"Just stay in your room!"

Kathy slipped outside trying to remember what Mark had taught her about the gun—defensive tactics, how to round a corner, confront a suspect. You keep the gun down, not up by your head like the goddamn cop shows. Try to stay sideways to your opponent to present a smaller target. She took a breath and edged around the corner of the house—and promptly forgot everything Mark had shown her. She faced the intruder clutching the gun with both hands in front of her face, just like on the cop shows.

"Don't you move!" she ordered.

Terrified, the stranger raised his hands as high as he could, just as he himself had seen on the cop shows. "Okay, lady! Okay!" he said, practically choking on the words. From the corner of her eye, she saw another figure dash behind the bushes next door.

"What are you doing looking in my window? You're in my backyard looking in my window!" Kathy shrieked.

His eyes were wide. "Okay, okay, lady! We was just a-fixing the cable wire, putting in new wire. The cable TV?" His hands fell to his side and he turned to look for his partner, who was peeking from an azalea bush at the corner of the house.

"I said don't move!" Kathy screamed. But then she saw the spool of heavy wire on the ground beside the patio.

Seeing that she wasn't going to shoot, the cable man forced a nonthreatening smile that had the effect of making her angrier. "I was just looking in to see was anybody home," he said in a high-pitched voice. "Let you know we was working back here."

She lowered the gun to her side. On the man's shirt was the logo of the local cable television company. She felt more foolish than she ever had, but she let loose on him in anger. "You dumb fucking hillbilly!"

He shrugged and looked askance.

"Why didn't you simply ring the doorbell and let me know you were out here? Looking into windows. How stupid can you be?" She felt like a bully, which only made her madder. "I almost shot your ass, do you know that?"

"Yes, ma'am," he said meekly, glad for the opportunity to provide an answer this madwoman might accept.

Just then, Mark's car pulled into the driveway. They watched him approach with a quick alarmed stride.

"What's going on here, Kat?"

"This idiot. I almost shot him. He was looking in the window!" Her heart was thumping; she felt like a frightened child. She also realized how easily she could have pulled the trigger if the man had made even one careless move.

Scowling, Mark realized that his wife had almost shot an innocent laborer. He thought fast. The best way to diffuse the situation—he didn't want Kathy to have to explain herself to the local police—was with an effective offense. No point in letting the guy see himself as a victim, he decided. Pikeville was a litigious place, always had been. Let him think he's getting off easily. Mark flashed his badge at the stranger, who looked it over carefully and nodded in acknowledgment. "What's going on here friend?" Mark asked in an accusatory tone, while casually taking the gun out of his wife's hands.

The cable man yammered like a schoolboy to a teacher breaking up a fight, "I'm just a-fixing the wires, officer, and she comes out wanting to shoot me! I didn't do nothing!"

Mark demanded some identification, which the man dug nervously out of his pants pocket, and said, "Don't you think it might be a little better to go the front door and knock instead of looking in the window?"

"Yes, sir, buddy. We should of thought of that."

"Next time you will, right?"

"Sure will, sir." Mark handed him his identification card back like a state trooper letting a speeder off with a warning.

After the cable truck pulled away, Mark marched Kathy into the house and sat her down at the kitchen table. She felt her face burning. He tried to make a joke out of it while admonishing her at the same time: "Hey, Kat—I know they raised the rates, but you can't be holding the cable company at gunpoint, you know."

She was not amused. "You bastard!"

"Me? Hey, you're the one who almost shot the guy for Christ's sake! What the hell did you think you were doing?"

He went upstairs, pointedly taking the .357 with him. Hearing him laughing with Danielle as if nothing had happened, she banged around in the kitchen in a fury. How could her marriage come to this? Had the power shifted so decisively? How had she become so ridiculously afraid?

He trotted back downstairs and stood there stretching, cocky and smug in his gray sweats, ready for his run before dinner. Outside, the mountain in back of the house loomed dark against the twilight sky.

She snapped on the kitchen light and fumed, unwilling to speak. "Come on, don't you think you're overreacting a little?" he said with an attempt at cool reassurance, patting her behind and trying to hug her. But she pushed him away and said sharply, "Don't patronize me, goddammit!"

His expression darkened. "You knew what we were getting into from the beginning, Kat. I thought you had what it takes. You took this on, Kathy."

"I didn't take *this* on," she said, flinging a gesture toward the window. "I was always there for you. I did my best, Mark. But I didn't bargain for this. This, Mark, is too much to ask!"

"*What* is? Pull yourself together, Kathy." He was shouting. Mark never shouted in the house.

That did it. She threw down the fork she'd been using to fix Danielle's plate and brushed past her daughter, ignored the baby's wailing, grabbed her coat and her keys, and stormed out the door in tears. As she backed out of the driveway, she screamed at the face of the woman next door peering from her window.

"Mind your own fucking business!"

A few miles out of town on Route 23, she acknowledged that she had nowhere to go. She stopped at a convenience store for cigarettes. On her way back home, she pulled off in the dark near the sway bridge over the Levisa and sat there furiously smoking, waiting for her heart to stop pounding. She forced herself to think of the last really happy time she could remember, in Myrtle Beach: sunlight on the faces of her husband and children, a startling blue sky, the surf breaking in clean white curls at their backs. Amusement-park lights twinkling on black, dinner, walks in cool night sand. When the kids were in bed in the next room, she'd put on a silky teddy and they'd nibbled cheese and crackers and sipped red wine while they talked. She'd given him a massage with lotion heated in the baby's bottle warmer. They'd made love in the dark, smelling of the sea and suntan oil.

As she calmed down, she ordered herself to stop overreacting. She remembered the lectures they gave for agents' spouses who came to the orientation session at the academy before their partners started training. *Know what you are getting into: The pressures of a cop's life are intense. Marriages fail. Keeping them working requires constant vigilance.* For some reason she thought of a much earlier time in their life together. He was still a clerk waiting to get into the FBI; she'd had six FBI most-wanted posters framed and hung them in the hall as a joke. He loved them. The "Putnam collection," he'd called them when showing them to friends.

A car rattling over the bridge made her look up. Feeling the chill, she turned on the engine and went home.

But the warmth of the house seemed artificial, the colors too bright. In her cotton Strawberry Shortcake nightgown, Danielle bared tiny white teeth to show that she'd brushed them; Mark played with the baby, who tottered into a castle of plastic blocks his father had built. "Okay, buddy, knock it down, go ahead." And young Mark kicked the castle blocks down. "Okay, buddy, you want to play, you got to pay, help to pick it up." The children and their father lay on the floor.

"Gonna get you!" she heard him say with a laugh, pretending to chase the kids up the steps.

Breathing shallowly, she sat back. The phone rang.

"Hello, Susan, how are you?" Kathy said in a monotone.

Mark caught her eye, shaking his head.

"Sure, Susan, he's right here. Just a minute." She slammed the phone into his chest. Wordlessly, she went upstairs to check on the kids.

Mark was still on the phone when she came down, speaking in the intimate tone a man uses with his wife. "I know that Susan . . . I know. I *know*. Susan, don't say that. You know that's not true."

When Kathy stepped into his sight, his tone became firmer. "Susan, if you don't want to work with Ron, just tell him. It's that simple, just tell him."

Mark put the phone down with a shrug. "She hung up," he said, coming into the kitchen where Kathy was busy with the dishes.

"What's wrong with her now?" she asked in a flat voice.

"You know, I really feel sorry for her, really bad for her. She's a good kid. She's just so screwed up. If she'd get the hell out of here, she'd be okay."

"Wouldn't we all."

He went on about Susan's problems and was surprised to see disgust on wife's face.

"You are too close to her," she snapped, as if she herself hadn't been encouraging Susan's persistence. "What's she doing for you now? You're finished with her, Mark! I thought you wanted to get her off the books. She doesn't want to let go, I can see the way she's working you. Everybody knows her game. You know how naïve you can be."

"Naïve? Hey, who almost shot off the cable television man's ass today?"

"Shit!" she shouted.

Calmly, he picked up the leather billfold with his badge from the counter and tossed it onto the kitchen table in front of her.

"Hey, you know so fucking much, the job's yours. Put on the badge. Why don't you show me how it's done?"

He slammed the door and went out for his run.

While he was gone, the phone rang again. This time it was Ron Poole, who registered her sniffles and asked what was wrong. Grateful for some sympathy, she blurted out her misery.

Poole lectured her sternly. "How many times have I told you? You guys don't have to put up with this. What are you waiting for, shots through the window? You've had threats. Those boys in Letcher County play hardball. Who do you think let the air out of your tires? That was just a little warning."

"Mark says—"

"*Listen to me!* All that husband of yours has to do is talk to Terry Hulse about the threats. Tell them you're scared. They'll get you out. I mean it. I'll back you up. I'm telling you, you'll be gone in a heartbeat."

"Mark says there's not enough of a real threat—"

"Fuck what Mark says! What the fuck does he know, a rookie scared of his boss? *You're* smart. You do not have to stay here. You know how it works!"

When Mark came back he found his wife taking a hot bath, deep in thought. She asked him to close the door and leave her alone.

7

Kathy had come to the conclusion that Poole was right, even if his intentions were wrong. The threat she felt to the safety of her family was genuine, no matter how amplified it was by her personal anguish about having to remain in Pikeville, perhaps indefinitely, as her marriage drifted away from its moorings.

Mark didn't see it that way at all. Yet he himself, deeply disturbed by the insidious way his work had penetrated into his home, had felt strongly enough about it to warn her repeatedly about the calls from Charlie Trotter, some of which—like Poole's—she hadn't even told him about. "Just don't mess with him," he said flatly. "Take a message and hang up. I'm the one that went to the academy, Kathy. I mean it, don't get involved. These are dangerous people."

Her position on that was, if they're so damn dangerous and the family's safety was being compromised, why not ask for a transfer? She knew the answer without asking. Mark thought he could handle it without endangering anyone. And besides, he was adamant about not wanting to look like a quitter.

So Poole's advice to take matters into her own hands made sense, even though she was savvy enough to see that it was offered mostly to serve his own agenda. Poole disliked Mark, which figured. Mark was intensely competitive and determined to shine in the eyes of his superiors, which couldn't help but make Poole look bad. Furthermore, Poole's interest in Susan was obvious—he'd made that clear not just to Susan, but to Kathy as well. Meanwhile, poor misguided Susan was in love with Mark, as she had told both Kathy and Poole on several occasions. As time went on, she became obsessed.

The situation was crazy, Kathy thought. They had paid their dues. She had intervened previously, when her husband was mired in inertia and doubt about even getting a job with the FBI. It was time to do so again, for the sake of her husband, their children, and their marriage. It was time to find a way to get them out of town. The problem was that she didn't know how to do it without driving her husband farther away.

An odd opportunity to force the issue presented itself quite un-expectedly in the second week of November, when Kathy's sister, Chris, flew up from Florida to visit for a week and offered to baby-sit to allow Kathy and Mark a rare Saturday night out. They were delighted for the chance to be together somewhere other than at home. They went to dinner at a restaurant called the Showboat. Afterward, they stopped for a drink at the cocktail lounge of the Landmark motel, which was the most popular of the very limited nightspots in Pikeville.

As they entered the crowded lounge, they edged through a small group of people dancing woodenly to a blaring rock band. Through a haze of cigarette smoke clinging to the room, Mark saw a familiar face at a nearby table.

"That's the guy I pointed out on television," he whispered, try-ing to ignore the man's wave.

Kathy squinted to recognize a local politician from a forlorn coal town in Letcher County. Mark knew him through one of his informants. When the official had been interviewed on television about a minor story out of Letcher County, Mark had pointed him out to Kathy as a man involved in cocaine dealing, saying, "That's one of the guys I'd like to get talking."

There were no vacant tables in sight, and the man kept beckoning. "We'll stop for a minute and leave," Mark muttered.

"What's up?" he said as the politician scraped to his feet and swept Kathy onto a stool with a broad gesture of hospitality. Kathy was wearing a low-cut sweater and a skirt that was shorter than most people in Pikeville were used to seeing on a wife. She was uncomfortably aware that their new companion was staring at her thighs.

The man seemed delighted by the new company. "Why don't you relax and let me buy you a drink?" he offered, flashing Mark a quizzical look that said, *Wife or girlfriend?*

Mark explained, "This is my wife, Kathy."

The official was planning to go home soon and suggested they take the table when he left. But first, they should have that drink. A round was ordered. The two men spoke for a few minutes about something of more than passing interest to them both, the delay in making arrests in the chop-shop case. Everybody in Letcher County was talking about it. Their companion pursed his lips. "Well, you ain't come up with any indictments yet. I hear some of the property is disappearing. Problems?"

This was a sore point, and Mark tried not to show his concern. He sipped a beer and said in a measured tone, knowing that the conversation would be repeated, "We're very methodical. We always get our guy." Looking his companion in the eye Mark said, "Why don't you tell me something about the case that I don't already know?"

This elicited a boisterous laugh. The politician wiped some beer from his chin. "I don't know anything about that, man. Nothing."

As they talked, Mark had spotted a local businessman he wanted to talk to at the bar and excused himself for a few minutes. He kept an eye on the table, though, and noticed with some amusement that the official had edged closer to Kathy. She nodded cordially at her companion. Watching him light his cigarette with a practiced flourish, she reconsidered Poole's advice: *Get involved in something. I'll help get you all out of here.* She wondered if she was looking at opportunity leering at her across the table, trying to get a peek down the front of her sweater. His voice was oddly high-pitched. "And what about you, little lady? Do you just sit there looking pretty or do you say something?"

She hated being patronized, but batted her eyelashes and replied, "When I have something to say I say it," she said glancing pointedly across the room to show that she could see that her husband was out of earshot.

He had moved close enough on the high stool to press his thigh against her. She flinched, but covered by saying quickly, "You know, I saw you on television."

This had its effect. "And did you like what you saw?"

"Actually, yes. I remember telling my husband, now this man is a *politician*. You had on just a casual shirt. Not like the windbags in fancy suits that we have back East."

He exhaled cigarette smoke in a leisurely curl. His leg rubbed against hers. "Why do you sleep with a cop?" he said, not wasting any time.

"I married him." She had her swizzle stick between her lips and ran her tongue around its tip, not quite believing her own nerve. He watched, transfixed. "Honey, I don't get much from my wife either," he said.

At that point, Kathy pressed her leg against his, which caused him to reappraise things. Now he looked startled. Boldly, he said,

"Honey, your husband don't know what he's got, does he? You're a hot little bitch, ain't you?"

The music was loud. Many people in the room were drunk. She smiled brightly and led him on, telling him at length that she was bored, miserable, lonely, and never had any fun. "It's been a long time," she said, and watched his reaction. "My husband is always working, and I think he finds what he needs somewhere else, if you know what I mean."

He did. This went on for a few minutes until Kathy deftly brought the subject around to the virtues of cocaine and sex together. "It's a lot better when you do coke first," she said with a small sigh.

"Hell, you didn't never touch no coke."

"Sure I did, back East. But now I'm an agent's wife. There aren't many chances to make a connection these days."

"Hell, that ain't no problem around here."

They stopped talking and looked up innocently as Mark approached the table with another round of beers. Kathy had a gleam in her eye. When the politician got up to go to the men's room, she had a mischievous look. "Mark, this guy is doing a lot of talking. I could find out anything I want from this guy."

"What the hell are you talking about, Kat?" he said. Mark wasn't quite sure what she had been up to, but he knew she was pumping the politician for information. Knowing Kathy, he also guessed that she would get some. The prospect was enticing, but he was cautious. He said, "Don't say a word to him. If he wants to talk, let him talk." She winked.

"Believe me, Kat," Mark added, whispering in her ear over the noise of the music. "He's smarter than he looks. When he comes back from the john, I'll walk away again. Let him talk. But watch yourself. Just listen, OK?"

Kathy shot him an angry scowl and said, "Just get out of my goddamned face, Mark!" He stiffened, but then felt their companion looming behind his shoulder. Frowning, Mark made another excuse to leave. Walking away, feigning drunkenness, he placed himself in a group of people almost out of sight of the table, but still where he could keep a discerning watch on the man, who was grinning with the look of someone who thought his ship was about to come in. After a few minutes, Mark watched him get up and leave Kathy alone at the table. Then he came back. In a moment, Kathy sat bolt upright and the two shook hands. With a quick glance around the room, the Letcher County politician walked out.

Mark hurried back to his wife. She was already pulling her coat on and handed him his. "What's going on?" he said, following her out the door in a hurry. It was well after midnight, and time to go home anyway.

"We got talking about drugs," Kathy said when they got in the car.

"I kind of thought you would."

"Well, I kind of told him that I like to party a little bit, but I can't because of my husband being who he is. I told him everything has to be discreet."

"What did he say?"

"He said, 'Well, you can do coke anywhere,' and I said, 'Yeah, that's true, but I don't know anybody, and I can't trust anybody.'"

"And he said?"

She took a gulp and giggled, imitating the official's twang. "'You can trust me, sweet thang. You sit tight for a minute, and I'll be raht back.'"

"And?"

"And this." Eyes wide, she opened her pocketbook and showed him a wrinkled plastic bag on top. "Mark, he put a gram of coke in my pocketbook. He said there was more, anytime I was interested."

"What! Are you sure? Jesus, do you know how bad we want this guy?" He glanced furtively around the darkened parking lot, suddenly afraid that she had been set up. How would he explain this if he and Kathy got busted then and there with a gram of coke in her purse?

"Don't touch it!" he ordered. "Let's get out of here!"

Despite the hour, they drove to the office a few blocks away, where Mark got on the phone, and woke up Terry Hulse in Covington. Hulse took it in stride, if a bit groggily. His instructions were to phone Poole and have him come down immediately to witness Mark securing the cocaine in the office safe. Mark offered to take Kathy to the emergency room for blood and urine tests to show that she had not used any of it, "just for the record."

That wasn't necessary, Hulse assured him. "Just make sure the stuff is locked up." Hulse said that he would want to interview Kathy himself "to see if this leads us anywhere."

When Poole finally arrived, unhappy to have been called out of bed to witness something so trivial as a packet of drugs, Mark locked up the cocaine, which was in fact two grams, along with a cocktail napkin on which the Letcher County politician had written his phone number for Kathy.

It was after three by the time they got home. They talked a little about the implications of her stunt, with Mark bristling at her insistence on following up on the politician's offer to supply more coke. Mark wanted no part of that. Entrapping a local politician certainly had allure, sure. Once a man with connections and declining options started talking, there was no telling where the lines could lead in the tangle of coalfield politics. Although he had at first encouraged her, and was in fact proud of her, he was also irritated by his wife's impetuous intervention in what would be a criminal matter. This was a dangerous game, and he wanted her out of it immediately. He figured that Kathy could make her statement for the record, but beyond that, he wasn't prepared for any further involvement by his wife. He made himself clear and drifted off to sleep.

Kathy stayed awake, her mind churning. She relished her success in inducing a presumably crafty politician to pass two grams of coke to an FBI agent's wife, with the agent himself not twenty-five feet away. Now *that* was undercover work! Additionally, the encounter had shown her what she recognized as an opening—there was enough danger involved, that, if she were part of the actual police sting, it might be enough to transfer them out of town. She figured she knew what she was doing. All she needed was the chance to work it out.

It appeared as if she was going to get that chance, too. On Monday morning, energized by possibilities, Hulse and another agent from Covington drove all the way down to Pikeville to take her statement. They came right to the house, without Mark, who was instructed to wait in the office. Kathy supposed they were there as a formality; but she saw their interest sharpen as she described what she had done—and insisted that she could do it again.

"I can get this guy," she told them, quite sure of herself. "He told me he would get together whenever I want. I know you guys want this man, and I can get him without any problem." Encouraged by their receptiveness, she plunged ahead, telling them, "The only thing is, I have to call my shot soon, one way or the other, so he doesn't smell a setup. I'm already in this, you know." They didn't chuckle condescendingly, as she had feared they would. Instead, they discussed with her the wisdom of allowing an agent's wife to participate in what would be a significant drug bust. Could she manage this? Would she be able to get away with wearing a wire? She concluded that she could and would.

Seeing that she had them, Kathy offered to take a drug test to establish for the record that she was not a user herself. That wouldn't be necessary, Hulse repeated with a smile and a nod toward Danielle and little Mark playing in the next room. Saying he would be back in touch, Hulse left with his colleague.

Mark was furious when Hulse told him about the conversation with Kathy. He said, in a sharp tone that he never thought he would take with his boss, "We've got two small kids, for Christ's sake. I'm not letting my wife get involved in this kind of thing. Would you let your wife get involved in something like this?"

Hulse shook his head understandingly. "Yeah, I see your point."

But Kathy kept at it until Mark finally relented and called Hulse to say that he had changed his mind, that she was available to take the next step, which would be to make what the bureau called a "controlled call" to the official from their home, to set up a meeting, with Mark and Poole on hand as witnesses. Under bureau orders, Poole came to their house a few days later with a tape recorder to supervise the call, which was made from the upstairs telephone in the hall outside their bedroom.

"That coke was really good," Kathy said during the short conversation, practically purring into the phone. The man was smart enough not to incriminate himself on the phone. But he did say he would be glad to meet her somewhere. She told him she'd call when she knew she could get away.

The ball was in the bureau's court. Hulse told them he would have to notify the US attorney's office in Lexington before the next step was taken. Meanwhile, Kathy was instructed to avoid any contact with the target. The long Thanksgiving weekend was coming up, and a decision about pursuing the matter had to wait.

Kathy was feeling a lot better now that she had at least taken some initiative, no matter what might come of this wacky scheme, and she found herself looking forward to the holiday. She always liked to cook a big dinner for Thanksgiving, which posed something of a problem in Pikeville because their social circle was so small. The men Mark knew at the courthouse and state police post all had their own family obligations, and none of them had been anything more than casual work-acquaintances anyway. The Putnams really hadn't had much time to develop friends. But Kathy had a thought. She hadn't spoken to Susan for several days, and she was hoping Susan had made some progress in her so-far futile attempts to leave Kenneth and start looking for a new place to live. When Mark came home from work, she suggested, "Why don't we invite Susan and her kids for Thanksgiving dinner?"

Mark felt the hair on the back of his neck bristle. "Wait a minute," he said; "I do not want an informant in this house. Do you understand? All I want is a day off to be with my family. I don't even want the phone to ring."

As it happened, Susan called that night, but the talk wasn't about Thanksgiving or finding a place to live. It was about the encounter with the same man from Letcher County who had slipped Kathy the cocaine. Kathy was further alarmed to hear her rattling off most of the details of the possible sting operation, including the controlled call from their home and the fact that Kathy had agreed to wear a listening device during the sting.

"Susan, how did you find out about that?" Kathy demanded.

"Oh," Susan said off-hand. "Ron Poole told me."

Kathy was flabbergasted. Without alerting Mark, she called Poole at home and demanded to know why he had given such sensitive information to a woman who had the biggest mouth in eastern Kentucky. Poole was in no mood to be challenged; he was a mumbler, but this time he spoke with clear intent and vitriol. "I didn't tell her anything. Your fucking *husband* probably did. You listen to me: Nobody fucks with me like that! Don't you *ever* fucking talk to me like that. I'll tell you something else, Kathy; your fucking husband has been fucking me over on two of my cases. Tell him he better smarten up or else."

Kathy didn't know what to say. It was obvious to her that *Mark* wouldn't have told Susan, who had no reason to lie about that, at least. But she was stunned to hear what sounded very much like a threat from Poole, her husband's partner. She was shaking when she hung up the phone.

Then she had another disturbing phone call on a night when Mark was working late. "The boys in Letcher understand that you like to party," said a man obviously disguising his voice. If so, the caller said, Vernon Mullins would be happy to arrange that party. All he wanted in return was a look at Mark's investigative file on the chop-shop case. Shaking, Kathy had a sudden suspicion that the anonymous caller was Charlie Trotter. Brashly, she said, "Vernon has to deal directly with me, Charlie. Got that?"

There was an appreciative chuckle on the phone. "You really are one holy bitch, ain't you? You just be careful not to screw me over. Just remember, I got the FBI behind me anytime I need it." The caller cackled uproariously and hung up.

The week after Thanksgiving, Mark got a call from the US attorney's office in Lexington asking him and Kathy to come to a meeting to discuss the talk of the drug sting. They argued about it on the drive all the way to Lexington, where they met with US Attorney Louis DeFalaise, and two of his assistants. Terry Hulse was also there. It was readily apparent that the men had discussed the idea thoroughly—and liked it. Mark was appalled and especially peeved at the way Kathy kept addressing her comments and appeals directly to DeFalaise.

"You guys are nuts," Mark said with distaste when they asked him if he would leave the room for a moment so they could talk to Kathy alone. In the receptionist's office, he thought, *That woman is going to sell them on this! They're going to deputize her ass right in there.*

He was right. When he was asked to come back in, it was apparent from their faces that she had persuaded them. "I know you guys want this man," Kathy was saying, "and I can get him."

Mark tried to suggest that, rather than Kathy, they use a more conventional informant; he mentioned Susan, but even he knew that wouldn't work. Everybody knew Susan. Finally, when it was decided that Kathy would be authorized to call and arrange a buy, he threw up his hands in disgust. Extraordinary precautions would be in place. The meeting was to be in a car in the Kmart parking lot in Pikeville, a safe, logical place for a drug dealer to meet a housewife. There would be agents and cops hiding in cars. When the cocaine got passed, dozens of cops would leap out and make the arrest before the perpetrator knew what hit him. Full details were to be worked out in the coming week.

After the meeting, Hulse, who had quietly begun to share Mark's misgivings but was reluctant to dampen the enthusiasm in the federal prosecutor's office, sent a Teletype message to FBI headquarters in Washington outlining the plan and requesting official authorization for an agent's wife to go undercover. The Drug Enforcement Administration was also notified.

The Putnams were hardly back home when they got the word. A reply to Hulse's Teletype message had rocketed back from Washington practically with flames coming off it. No one in Washington had ever heard of such a lamebrained idea! Not approved! Chastised but also somewhat relieved, Hulse ordered it called off immediately.

Out of the hospital and back with Kenneth, Susan needed money. More than that, she needed attention from Mark. Sadly aware that she had exhausted—or alienated—most of the sources of information she had used in the Tug, where no one trusted her after she double-crossed Cat Eyes's uncle, she knew that she had to develop a new forte to rejuvenate her career as an informant for Mark.

Poole suggested that if nothing in Pike County was working, she might look to her past, specifically her drug connections up north. She'd mentioned a cop she and Kenneth had gotten to know when they lived in Cicero, Illinois, a cop heavily into drug traffic who could line up a fairly big deal if the money was there. That was worth considering, Poole said appraisingly, while also envisioning a few nights in Chicago in the company of Susan.

Susan figured it was worth a try since she didn't know what else to do. First she made a call to Cicero to ascertain from an old contact that the crooked cop was still active. He was. She then called Mark, not Poole, to tell him she had important information on a new case. She met him at McDonald's, where he said he didn't have time to take her for a ride. They sat in the car in the parking lot while she described the scenario she had in mind, which involved infiltrating a major urban cocaine and crack operation and drawing its connections to the Tug Valley. Yet Mark looked bored.

"The guy that runs it?" she continued, moving in for the close.

Impatiently he said, "Yeah?"

"Well, he's a cop."

Now he was interested. He took out a notebook.

It was apparent, however, that she didn't have a lot to offer yet. Susan hadn't had much contact with the Cicero crowd since well before Cat Eyes showed up at the house. Actually, on those increasingly infrequent occasions when Susan would manage to put together enough cash to make a drug deal, she and Kenneth usually scored out of Cincinnati, closer to home.

Susan told him that she had already discussed the situation with Poole. That was fine, Mark said. You can work it out with him. Poole knew the Chicago drug scene. When Mark mentioned to his partner what Susan was considering, Poole brightened. They decided it could work—if Susan was able to back up what she said and deliver a crooked cop engaged in interstate drug trafficking. It would involve undercover activity—Poole figured he could pose as her boyfriend and help her to infiltrate the operation. Crooked cops seldom worked alone—it was likely other officers were involved, if one was. What's more, cracking this kind of a drug operation out of Pikeville had a special appeal; the bureau brass would love to see the imperious Chicago office tweaked by two agents out of the hills of Kentucky. Poole, in particular, savored the prospect of a triumph over his former colleagues. This was, he maintained, a "win-win situation."

There was a problem, however. Susan still didn't want to work with Poole, who physically repelled her and, as her instincts flashed alerts, even frightened her. She only wanted to work with Mark. Poole took this personally, as an insult from Mark as well as Susan. A week before Christmas, Mark drove Susan into the hills north of Pikeville to a place where they had stopped to talk often in the past, a clearing just off an abandoned coal-mine road, twenty minutes out of town. The name of the road was Harmon Branch, and he would drive her to this mountaintop once more, about six months from then. Mark had been brooding about his difficulties, professional and personal. Nothing was working out; nothing was being resolved, and his marriage was on the rocks.

It was late afternoon, not yet dusk, but the sun had dropped behind the mountains and the air was cold. He let the engine run, scribbling notes disconsolately while Susan talked. Then he felt Susan's hand resting lightly on his shoulder.

"Is there something wrong? You seem way out in left field, honey."

She had not called him that before.

"Oh, you know, everybody's got problems, Susan."

"I know there's problems at home because Kathy tells me about them."

He was not happy to hear that. How often did Kathy and Susan talk about personal affairs? He had no idea.

"She's feeling as bad as you are, honey, but there isn't anything you can do about that right now. You have got to have somebody, and maybe for right now I'm that person for you. Whatever I can do to help you feel better about yourself, I intend to do. Like I always say, you are real different. You care about people. You listen to me. You helped me a lot. A lot. Now it's your turn for attention."

As she leaned toward him, he noticed the gold chain with a tiny cross she wore. She was rubbing his neck now, and he leaned in to enjoy it.

"God, are you tense."

"I just need some time off. That or a good ten-mile run to sort everything out."

"Well, you can't run here. Look at me, Mark. You know how I feel about you."

"Yeah, I know."

"Any time you need a release, I'm around."

"I appreciate that, Susan. But I don't think that would accomplish anything. It would just dig me in deeper, you know? I'm already in pretty deep." He was not sure exactly what he was trying to tell her.

"Mark, sometimes you have got to look past that and take care of yourself. You've been looking terrible lately. Real ragged."

She moved close to him, kissed him, stroked the inside of his thigh, studied his face with a smile. "I think you should make love to me right now, Mark."

"I don't think that would be a good idea, Susan"

"I think it's too late for that, honey. Just relax." *Jesus*, he thought. *Why the hell not? Why the holy hell not?*

In the car on that mountaintop they made love for the first time.

He didn't see her for a few days afterward. He told himself it had been nothing. Quick, passionless, detached, as if he weren't even a part of it. He told himself, *It's like a pickup in a bar at college. You see a girl you know will do it. It's over and forgotten before you know it. No sweat. That's the last you think of it.*

Of course, that wasn't true.

And he knew what a fraud he was a few days after that when he drove her up to the same place again, like a horny teenager. Afterward, he said he would take her home to Freeburn.

"You seem pretty upset," she said as they drove back onto the main road.

"I am. I'm pissed off at myself, not at you." He stroked her hair lightly, caught his reflection momentarily in the rearview mirror, and said, "I betrayed myself, my wife, my kids, and my job."

She laughed at his gloom. "Mark, honey, you take yourself entirely too seriously. It wasn't no—any—big deal, baby. It was just a fuck in a car."

Years later, Mark would insist that, rumors in Pikeville and Freeburn aside, they had sex no more than five times over a two-week period, always in his car. Then, aghast at his recklessness, disgusted with himself as he had never been before, he broke off the relationship.

Characteristically, instead of confronting Susan, he chose to avoid her. He shut her out of his life. Now, more abjectly than ever before, Susan felt abandoned, but she was determined not to show it. She doubled down; became energized and even agitated with her fantasies. She countered suicidal thoughts by telling herself, and others who would listen, that she and Mark Putnam planned a wonderful life together, once the details could be ironed out. As on TV, a happy ending was coming.

Kathy had never really suspected that her husband was having an affair. But around Christmastime, she detected a palpable change in Susan's demeanor. She wasn't calling as much as before, and when she did call, she chattered on about things other than Mark or her own wretchedness in Freeburn. She seemed happy and more confident in herself than Kathy had ever known her to be. In some ways, she even seemed manic. "She seemed like she was on top of the world, for once," Kathy would later recall. Kathy was heartened to think that her self-esteem seemed to have undergone repair. Maybe Susan was finding ways to take responsibility for her own destiny. At least, Kathy thought, *something* seemed to be getting better for *someone.*

She wished she could say the same about her own situation, which had deteriorated alarmingly. She was constantly, vaguely afraid. Later, she would struggle to analyze the breakdown and sort out its causes. What parts were depression and paranoia, and what was a reasonable psychological response to real threats? How much fault lay in unreasonable expectations, Mark's overbearing pride, the bureau's indifference and ineptitude, the infernal manipulations by Poole, Susan, Trotter, and others who might have agendas she could not quite see?

This much was for sure: Free-floating anxiety aside, there were deliberate attempts to frighten her. The worst came in the middle of January, with Mark out of town for the night on a bureau training session. The phone rang around midnight. Picking it up tentatively, Kathy heard a voice growl, "We ain't sure whose side you on no more. We think you been sleeping with cops too long. You're alone with them babies tonight, ain't you?" Frantically, she grabbed the .357 from the shelf and stormed around the house snapping off lights. She spent the night on the living room floor in the dark, back against the couch, gun pointed at the door.

On February 2, there was another frightening call, this one at four-thirty in the morning with Mark at home. Kathy would remember the date because she always had a notepad by the phone and she'd learned a form of shorthand when she managed her father's apartments. She always, almost obsessively, took good and copious notes, even in the middle of the night. She also kept monthly calendars, and on this date, next to the notation *Kids portrait Sears 9 A.M.*, she'd scrawled, *Kenneth called A.M. ???* She remembered it because the exuberant Susan she had experienced so recently had now plunged back into despair.

She had never spoken to Kenneth before. All she knew about him was what Susan had told her. Kenneth, who sounded drunk, wasted no time on social preliminaries.

"Kathy, this is Kenneth. You listening?"

"Kenneth?" she said huskily, standing in the dark upstairs hallway in her nightgown. For some reason, the previous owners of their house had installed only one upstairs phone jack—in the hallway on the second floor. Mark had been promising to run one into their bedroom for over a year. It was one of the chores he hadn't got around to yet.

"Do you know what's going on with yer husband and Susan?" he demanded. In the background, Susan cried, "Kenneth, quit it!"

"What's going on Kenneth?"

"Mark and Susan, that's what's goin' on. Been goin' on. They been fuckin' in motel rooms. You think that's right? You care about that?"

"Kenneth—"

Susan grabbed the phone crying. "Kathy, I am so sorry!" There was a crash as something hit a wall.

"I'm so sorry, Kathy! Kenneth is just wild. See, he found out that, well, see I was pregnant and I lost it, but he's saying that the baby was Mark's and I told him it wasn't true. You know what I been going through with him. He just doesn't understand that Mark and I, we have to meet sometimes in private places and all, for work."

There was a scuffle. She heard Kenneth: "Your fucking *work*? That's what you call it?"

"Kenneth no!"

Susan was tiny but she knew how to fight. She managed to grab the phone as Kenneth screamed, "Tell her if she wants to see the pictures I got of you two goin' to them motels—"

"Kathy, I swear there ain't nothing going on with me and Mark."

The phone dropped again and Susan yelled, "Fuck you, Kenneth!"

Now Kenneth was back: "Is that all right with you, Kathy? Them fucking is all right with you?"

Mark had gotten out of bed and was standing beside his wife, who was sitting cross-legged on the floor, incongruously scrawling notes in the dim predawn light.

"Who is it?" Mark said anxiously.

"Kenneth and Susan."

Mark grabbed the phone. "Kenneth, why don't you just calm down. Get your shit together, Kenneth. There's no point in raving over the phone, OK, Kenneth?"

Kenneth suddenly hung up.

When they got back into bed, Kathy said, "She's so alone, Mark. I'm afraid he's going to hurt her. Should we call the state police?"

"Kathy, don't do this! Go back to sleep. They're always fighting. Susan should know better, Kathy. She instigates this. When it comes to Kenneth she says all the wrong things. Can you blame him for getting all pissed off?"

Kathy's anger flashed at her husband for his insensitivity in crudely blaming Susan. *What kind of a cop are you, really?* she thought. Fighting back tears, she stammered, "You can't say that, Mark!"

He turned his back to her in the bed. "Look, I'm not Susan's babysitter. I'm tired of this shit and tired of the games Susan wants to play. I just can't deal with her anymore."

They were silent for a full minute while she listened to him breathe.

"Mark?" she said. "I thought she said she couldn't have any more kids."

He exhaled heavily and leaned on an elbow to glower at her. "What are you talking about?"

"She told me that when she had Brady there were complications. That she couldn't have any more."

"She told me that too. What's your point?"

"She said on the phone that she was pregnant and lost it, and Kenneth said it was your baby. That's why they were fighting."

Mark was silent.

"Mark? Kenneth said it was your baby."

"Jesus Christ!" he said, exasperated. "Kathy, you should know by now that you can believe only about a tenth of what that girl says. It isn't worth discussing. Leave it alone. Can we go back to sleep for the fucking hour that's left before I have to get to work?"

She did not sleep. For the first time, she felt doubt about her husband. She had already considered the possibility that Mark might have slept with Susan, but she dismissed it as ridiculous. *Mark and Susan?* So what if Susan said that she loved him. Lots of women found Mark attractive and some of them let him—and her—know it. She had asked him in the fall, point-blank, "You didn't have sex with this woman, did you?" His reply had made her feel both foolish and slightly disloyal. "Of course not, Kathy. How well do you know me?" She didn't see a need to ask him again. She knew him that well.

Kathy had tried to contact Susan after that harrowing predawn phone call from Kenneth, but she didn't answer the phone. When she did call back a week or so later, the happy Susan, brimming with self-assurance, was back. They talked of the weather and kids, but Kathy found it remarkable how little interest Susan expressed in Mark, to the point where Kathy herself brought her husband up.

"I know Mark's been out of touch," she told Susan. "You wouldn't believe how busy he's been."

"Oh I know. He hardly ever even gets a chance to have dinner at home," Susan said. "Poor baby."

That caught Kathy short. "You saw him?"

"Oh, you know Mark!" Susan said but then flitted off to a new subject, her plans to go to the country-western bar on Route 23 that night to see the featured singer and owner, Marlow Tackett.

"Marlow says he wants to audition me," Susan said.

Kathy shook her head as if to clear it. "For what?"

"For my singing, 'course. He thinks I might have a recording career ahead."

"I didn't know you sang, Susan. What do you sing?"

"Well Marlow, he says that when I sing 'Stand By Your Man,' I do it even better'n Tammy Wynette does. Can you believe that? That's such a mournful song, ain't it, Kathy? If it's done right, there ain't a dried eye in the place." In a thin off-pitch voice, Susan sang a line of that song into the phone, "*Give him two arms to cling to . . .*"

In your dreams, Kathy thought, wondering what stimulant Susan was on this time. Actually, it was news to her that Susan even thought of herself as a singer. Clearly the girl could not sing. She dismissed that as another pitiful dream of a lost country girl. She was instead interested in what Susan had implied about seeing her husband, which she also doubted.

"Listen, exactly when did you see Mark, Susan?" Kathy managed to ask as Susan prattled on.

"Mark? I can't say much because I'm working on an important case. You know how he is!"

"Susan—"

"Gotta go, Kathy dear. Guess who just pulled up out front!" The call ended.

Shocked, Kathy immediately dialed the FBI office in downtown Pikeville. The call was picked up on the third ring.

"FBI Pikeville, Special Agent Putnam," Mark said.

An early spring came to the Appalachians. The narrow streams in the hollows tumbled with runoff from the melted snow, and the wildflowers bloomed on scarred hills—but not on the mountain that loomed behind the Putnam house, where the runoff merely left muddy stripes that Kathy thought looked like great claw marks.

After well over a year, the indictments in the chop-shop case had finally been handed up in February. Vernon Andrew Mullins, his nephew Charles Edward Tackett, his son, Michael, and four other Letcher County men had been charged with conspiracy to violate federal law by receiving, possessing, concealing, storing, and altering the identification numbers on stolen motor vehicles and equipment that had crossed interstate boundaries. They all pleaded not guilty.

In early March, a detention hearing was held in the federal courthouse in Pikeville. Tom Self, the assistant United States attorney who would prosecute the case, asked that the men be held without bail and specified that Vernon and Charles Tackett presented a threat to the community.

Almost frantically, with Poole whispering encouragement in phone calls that Mark still didn't know about, Kathy began to pressure her husband to make his case for a transfer as quickly as possible. With less reluctance now than he would have had before the indictments were in place, but still uneasy because he believed that he was stretching the facts, Mark testified at the detention hearing that the defendants presented a danger to his family. He alluded to information from Charlie Trotter that some of the defendants had made veiled threats against him, his wife, and his children.

"I do not feel safe," he told federal magistrate Joe Hood. "I have a gut feeling that given the opportunity, some harm could come to myself or my family."

The judge allowed the men to go free on bail after warning them not to have any contact with Mark or his family.

But the implied threat was enough for Hulse, who had become deeply sympathetic to the Putnams' plight in Pikeville. After the hearing Hulse sent a memo to his own supervisor in the Lexington office to request that Mark and his family be transferred. It was clear from what Hulse wrote that the situation had become severely tangled not only for the Putnams but also for the bureau itself. Hulse described Mullins as "a very arrogant individual," previously convicted for other stolen-vehicles operations, who "has allegedly been paying off state and local law enforcement personnel to protect his operation over the past years."

Noting the threats that had been made to Mark, Hulse added in his message to the Lexington supervisors that Judge Hood had told the defendants in court "that they better pray to God that nothing happens to any potential witness" and specifically ordered them to stay away from the Putnams. Hulse said that Trotter had been working "both sides of the fence" and had told Mark that Mullins knew "where Putnam lives and what bedroom Mark and his wife sleep in, as well as his daughter." Hulse said that Trotter had been threatening to take back information about payoffs of state and local cops and threats to the Putnams "unless we pay him more money." Hulse noted, "We have paid the source approximately eleven thousand dollars over the past two years."

Moreover, Hulse pointed out, a Kentucky state police officer whom Mullins claimed to have paid off had potentially embarrassing information. Along with Trotter and Mullins, the dishonest cop was fully aware of the drug transaction with Kathy Putnam and the politician from Letcher County.

Hulse added that a local newspaper had run an article on the hearing that mentioned the threats to Putnam, and that "the neighbors on Putnam's street told them that they did not want their children at the Putnams' house for fear of something happening to them." Hulse said he had spoken with Mark and believed it to be "in his and his family's best interest to move him as soon as reasonably possible. You and I have previously talked about a Miami transfer, but Putnam understands that he can go anywhere."

In a follow-up memo, explaining the requested transfer to the FBI director's office in Washington, a supervisor in Louisville referred to Mark as a "highly motivated, dedicated, competent, and aggressive agent who has spent over the last two years in an area that borders on qualifying as a hardship assignment, and at best could be described as undesirable."

That memo argued that Pikeville "is recognized as an area of extensive criminal activity where individuals, groups, and entire families accept violence as a way of life, routinely carry firearms, and have little regard for law and order." Because of that, the memo recommended "an agent with previous law-enforcement experience be selected" to replace Mark.

The transfer orders arrived within days, and Kathy was stunned. It was over at last. It was the middle of April 1989. Springtime.

She barely had time to pack. The bureau sent the movers in and ordered her and the children to leave, with Mark to follow in a few weeks. They were going to Miami! And this time, unlike when they had come to Pikeville from Connecticut, the bureau was even paying for the move. She and the children left Pikeville on March 25 when the moving van pulled away. Mark stayed behind to ready the house for sale and planned to join his family in a week at a temporary two-bedroom apartment in Fort Lauderdale that the bureau had arranged until the Putnams could sell their Pikeville house and Kathy could find a new one in Florida.

8

Mark vowed to keep a very low profile during that week alone in the house on Honeysuckle Lane. He avoided the office, stopping by only a few nights when the courthouse was more or less deserted. With Mark out of the way, Susan was exposed to the persistent attentions of Ron Poole, much to Poole's satisfaction. And as an informant for Poole, Susan had some income, and she could at least work in rural areas farther from the knowing eyes around Freeburn. Poole relished having an attractive young woman at his side, which he believed helped his undercover operations, including the planned sting in Cicero, Illinois, his old turf.

Mark had warned Poole not to underestimate Susan, and as Poole himself had discovered, sometimes she actually did deliver. If the drug operation in Cicero panned out, all the better. Even if it didn't, it would be an adventure, with expense-account dinners in Chicago and ballgames at Wrigley Field, instead of Big Macs out on the Pikeville four-lane. After a year and a half in Pikeville, a break in the monotony would be welcome. And maneuvering Susan into a sexual relationship—one that she manifestly did not want but would probably eventually accept—would be the bonus.

At the prospect of wooing Susan and taking their relationship from a working one to a romantic one, Poole felt not like a grossly overweight man approaching middle age, but more like a young college student. "There's just something about that girl," he told Mark in a phone call shortly after Mark arrived in Florida. Weary of Poole's previous jealous needling about his own relationship with the infatuated Susan, Mark replied with encouragement, "Go for it buddy."

Susan's agenda fit into Poole's well enough. She was lonely, afraid, destitute, confused, and defiant. She had told Mark that she did not want to work with Poole, but her options were few. Poole at least offered protection, a status of sorts, and most importantly, income. She understood the game well enough to know that she needed to provide useable information to keep Poole happy. It was a delicate balance that she desperately needed to maintain. She couldn't imagine kissing Poole, let alone sleeping with him. In her mind, she truly believed that if she could not handle Poole at any point, Mark would somehow arrive from Miami to set things right.

Within weeks, Poole was calling Mark in Miami, complaining that Susan was difficult to handle and asking him to intervene. Reluctantly, he complied.

"When I contacted her she started crying and told me that I was leaving her out in the cold," Mark said. She told him that Sherri Justice had beaten her up. "I asked her what I could do to help and she said, 'Fuck you. You don't give a shit. You're happy in Florida with your family and you don't give a shit about me.'"

Breaking drug cases was no easy task deep in the remote hills of southern Appalachia. The serious drug business was city-based. Marijuana was just a mountain-grown weed, a modest crop scarcely more subject to outside market forces than turnips. Cocaine was another matter, a complicated industry involving financing, manufacture, import, wholesale distribution, and retailing. Only the end of the process, small-time sales, had any appreciable base in a sparsely populated rural area; the Tug Valley was not exactly prime territory. And it had been a long time since Susan and Kenneth ran with the city crowd; most of their friends had forgotten her. Susan tried to rewire her connections. But in the urban drug business, perky little Susan Smith of Freeburn, Kentucky, wasn't a top candidate for doing business with. Still, Susan and Poole were quite a sight, the sassy girl and the fat agent with the mangy hair whom Susan brazenly referred to as "Jethro," behind his back.

Susan was often tormented with the cold reality of Mark's rejection, but just as often buoyed by the fantasies with which she measured her days, supported by whatever drugs she could obtain. Her sister, Shelby, had taken her in, and while she appreciated the sanctuary, she also had to live under Shelby's watchful eye. One or two nights a week, saying that her children needed her, she drove across the river to stay with Kenneth. Usually, she slept on the couch. She and Kenneth fought constantly, and she always got the worst of it. But she always went back. With Kathy gone, Susan had no one to call who would at least listen.

Living with Shelby and her husband, Troy, in Freeburn, the three formed a tense triangle in the little house alongside the Tug. Susan watched television incessantly, while guarding the telephone like a jilted teenager. Shelby was distressed that Susan's favorite television program was now *Miami Vice*, the police drama about brave young cops fighting crime in a stylized subtropical Florida.

Susan's brothers were no happier with her. They had welcomed Mark's departure as a way to erase the stigma, not to mention the peril, of having a government informant within the family. But now, laughing off their warnings, Susan was determined to make a go of it with Ron Poole, even if it meant, as Poole insisted it did, being seen with him in public.

In late April, Poole picked Susan up in Freeburn, handed her a Wal-Mart bag, and told her he had a present. She pulled out a t-shirt and looked at it with a frown. On the front it said, "I HAVE A HILLBILLY BONE DEEP INSIDE." Grinning stupidly, Poole told her, "Get your short-shorts ready. You and me are going to Hillbilly Days." He then let out a rebel yell, spraying spittle her way.

Susan definitely was not going to attend the Hillbilly Days in Pikeville wearing a tight vulgar t-shirt like some coalfield slut, nor would she put on a hillbilly clown costume the way the well-heeled town Shriners and lawyers and shopkeepers and their wives did. "Hillbilly" tourists were even starting to come to southern Appalachia for the commercial hillbilly experience, parading around town dressed like cartoons in celebration of what they liked to think of as their heritage. Susan may have dropped out of school after seventh grade, but she was smart and perceptive enough to resent this ridiculing of *her kind*, no matter how culturally affirmative it was said to be, even if the hurtful words "white trash" were never uttered during the carnival festivities. So when Poole picked her up one midafternoon at their usual meeting spot in front of Bert Hatfield's car lot by the river in Freeburn, she wore a knee-length blue cotton dress, with small earrings and her favorite necklace, a gold chain on which dangled a tiny cross.

Poole was transfixed. "You sure do clean up purty," he said, clumsy as usual, but she smiled despite herself.

Susan did not even think of herself as a hillbilly except during Hillbilly Days, when it was made so clear that she and her people were exactly that. On Saturday afternoon was the hillbilly parade, in which participants, with the occasional front tooth blackened with greasepaint, wear big, comic straw hats and bib overalls and behave the way hillbillies are thought to behave. Hooting and hollering, they parade through town in "hillbilly mobiles," cars tricked out as jalopies, pickup trucks with rickety faux outhouses wobbling in the back, all festooned with signs, washboards, and other claptrap. Meanwhile, the real mountain people like Susan would come into town to ride the Ferris wheel on Courthouse Square and take in the sights.

There was a murmur of curiosity as Poole, sweating profusely in a yellowed golf shirt, his great belly hanging over his belt like a mudslide waiting to happen, threaded his way through a crowd with a pretty girl in a blue dress in tow. Poole kept reaching for Susan's hand, which she moved away from his sweaty grip as politely as she could. He gallantly held her back with his arm as a line of men in a footrace chugged by, part of the "Cornhole Tournament" of carnival-like sporting events held during three days of festivities.

He had a greasy pork barbeque sandwich in one hand as his other reached again for hers. "You ever cornholed, sweetheart?" he asked leeringly.

"Excuse me? I'm trying to listen," she replied with some annoyance, straining on tiptoe to watch a bluegrass, country-western band on a brightly lit stage near the Ferris wheel ticket booth. She swayed gently to the song. It was "Blue Kentucky Girl," a plaintive country ballad of yearning and love lost to the lure of the big city.

As the song ended she felt Poole's hand creep down from her waist to pat her ass. Her eyes rimmed with bitter tears.

"Whiney hillbilly shit," Poole said into her ear as she moved free.

Around 11:00 p.m., he brought her back across the mountains to the ramshackle jumble of Freeburn, where she was staying with Shelby and Troy. In the gloom of reality, she slipped into bed and retreated into the fantasies that had begun to sustain her.

Had her romance been no more than five or six tumbles in a car on a strip-mine road with a good-looking man having troubles at home? No! She persuaded herself. She and Mark had been lovers for two long years, despite the obstacles that kept them apart. Why, he had even brought her to his house, where they fucked like teenagers while his wife was away. It was only a matter of time until they would be together; even now, he was down in Miami making the arrangements to leave his wife and marry her! As she elaborated on it in her mind, Susan also shared this fantasy with anyone who would listen.

What's more, she was pregnant with his child, she told people. Why, they even had names for the baby she carried: Mark, if it was a boy, and Markella for a girl. It did not seem to matter, and no one really had the heart to point out, that Mark already had a namesake. In Florida, it would all work out. It might be complicated, though, given her activities as an undercover informant on major drug cases. Susan even suggested to a few people that they should not worry if she disappeared without a trace. That was how the federal witness protection program worked, after all.

Just how embroidered her tales were not even those who knew her well could say. Among her vivid repertoire of stories of her glamorous life as an informant was one that would later be repeated as gospel by some, about Mark Putnam's parrot. A woman who had known Susan for many years in Freeburn remembered the story clearly years later because she had never heard of such a thing in Pike County.

"A parrot? What's he doing with a parrot?" the woman asked when Susan told her about it.

"He keeps it in his house, of course. It's in a big old cage in the living room, but sometimes he lets it set on his shoulder like a pirate."

"Does it talk?"

Susan rolled her big brown eyes. "Oh, it don't ever shut up! In fact, I was afraid that stupid parrot was going to get us in terrible trouble back when I was living with him, when his wife was up in Connecticut that time? One morning, a deliveryman come to the door and I had to scrunch down behind the couch so he wouldn't see me in there. I thought that parrot was going to give me away. But all it said was, 'Hello! Hello!'" Susan said, "And do you know what that rascal parrot calls Mark?"

"What?"

"G-Man! It says, hello G-Man!"

Susan laughed and laughed, savoring the tale, firmly fixed in her mind. In reality, however, little Danielle had a pet parakeet, which Kathy had casually mentioned to Susan once in a phone call. The parakeet had metamorphosed into a radiant creature with feathers as red as the stripes on the flag, as blue as the sky in Florida.

Susan told her stories at a beauty shop on the road beside the river in Freeburn not far from the foot of the Barrenshee. Being in a house, the beauty shop offered the informality and camaraderie of a coffee klatch. Many of the customers had known Susan all her life, and overlooked the odd stilted enunciation she had developed to disguise her hillbilly twang as she chattered on about the life she imagined for herself far from the Tug Valley. It did not matter that she had gone away before and come home desperate. Dreams required no plans; they happened haphazardly, like everything else she had ever known in life. All she had to do was be there and hope for the best.

Susan did not know that the older women eventually came to look at her with pity. Once, her girlish chatter and brassy boasts had been amusing, but now she seemed shrill, desperate, and somehow past her prime. Now she insisted on not just attention but deference, which was something a girl from the head of a holler was not about to get in Freeburn, not with that act.

The women talked among themselves about how different she had become with her children, on whom she once doted, seven-year-old Miranda especially. Now they got slaps across the face for interrupting, and they had learned to wait for her silently in the beauty parlor, their eyes watchful.

Susan talked of going to Florida, but instead she went to Kenneth, and that was inevitable, too. "All that boy ever has to do is promise that he is going to straighten out, and Susie gets down and kisses the ground in front of him," one woman said. She had been a teenager when Susan was a little girl and had once thought that Susan's irrepressible nature would let her beat the odds. As she watched Susan in the beauty shop, she was saddened to see the pallor under Susan's tanning-parlor bronze, the dark puffy half-circles under her eyes, the tight lines at the corners of her mouth. She tried to remember the sassy little girl in a white cotton dress, skipping along the road beside the Tug as if she always had someplace to go. What had happened to that child? As if alerted, Susan turned and met the woman's distracted gaze defiantly before resuming her monologue about being a "bonded informant" on a mission for the FBI.

"It's a top-secret operation," Susan said, addressing the room at large.

"If it's top secret, Susie, you probably shouldn't be talking so much about it," someone suggested gently.

"Shoot. It don't matter. It don't have nothing to do with this place," Susan replied, shifting her eyes to the window and the shabby old hamlet outside. "Besides, I'm fully protected. Nobody dares do nothing to me. I could even be placed in the federal Witness Protection Program under a new identity."

When she left, they talked about her, not unkindly, but with general sadness. "That must be some protection," one of them said. "My husband saw the poor thing sleeping in her car the other night."

"Susan was leaving messages on the answering machine," Kathy recalled in their new home in Florida. "In one of them she said she was pregnant. Mark told me she was crazy, and I assumed as usual that that was just Susan being Susan."

Early in May, Susan filed charges with the police against her ex-husband. She said that in one of his rages, Kenneth had tied her up and dragged her through the house in West Virginia. He had accused her of being an informant and betraying her own people, she said. From his car outside Shelby's house, he had shouted that she was a whore, and when she got in to settle him down, he drove off, shoving her out the door a few blocks away. She said he threatened to shoot her.

Kenneth retaliated by reporting her to the West Virginia welfare office for receiving benefits from two states. As a result she lost her West Virginia check and was left with the $249 a month from Kentucky. Meanwhile, Susan was finding it difficult to score cocaine and pills just when she needed them most. Since she had announced all over the valley that she was on a top-secret undercover drug mission for the FBI all of her local sources had dried up. Desperate for cash and drugs, she turned to Pikeville.

Almost every Thursday night she took a room in a motel at the crest of a hill behind a strip mall on the four-lane north out of Pikeville, not far down the highway from Marlow's, the country-western bar where she had once dreamed about the singer who would take her away to Nashville. A clerk who worked nights at the motel would later recall that Susan Smith was working as a prostitute.

"She was annoying, demanding, and arrogant and expected to be treated like a queen," the woman said. "She had this attitude that, no matter what she did, she was untouchable. It was obvious what she was doing—she was always with a different man. You'd be surprised at what goes on in this small town."

Adrift, frightened, strung out on whatever cocaine and amphetamines she could scrounge, Susan saw danger everywhere she looked. Here fantasy collided with paranoia and reality; but to those who knew her, there was a sense that Susan was coming perilously close to the end of the line.

Again, there was public trouble. In the middle of May, Susan ran into Sherri Justice, Cat Eyes Lockhart's girlfriend, who threatened to kill her and commenced to beat her up. Kenneth, Susan's brother Tennis, and Tennis's girlfriend witnessed this thrashing.

Confused and battered, Susan now turned with more desperation to Poole, the FBI man who was still in her life, who encouraged her to focus the blame for her problems on the FBI man who had walked out of it, Mark Putnam.

In April, in a telephone call to Mark in Fort Lauderdale, Susan told him that she was pregnant and asked what he intended to do about it. Stunned, Mark asked her if she was sure. She said she was. He was due to come back to Pikeville to finish up work on the chop-shop trial. They would talk then, he promised.

The call from Susan shattered any illusions he had about leaving Pikeville behind. He had convinced himself that the affair with Susan, disturbing as it was to his notion of himself, was a mistake that he had gotten away with. All he could do, he decided, was keep the trouble to himself and find a way to work it out, alone.

Mark was actually scheduled for two trips back to Pikeville for pretrial hearings on the chop-shop case. During the first, a stay of only a few days, he managed to avoid seeing Susan, who didn't find out he had been back in Kentucky until after he left. When he went back to Florida, Mark concealed his despair. Kathy, annoyed that Susan was still calling, but unaware of why, thought that in time, once the trial was over and they were settled into a new home, he would cut his ties.

Shelby had been pressing her sister to confront Mark about the pregnancy, but Susan had been afraid. After she found out that he had come to town and gone, Susan lied to Shelby, saying that she had seen him. They'd argued and he had tried to push her out of a car, just as Kenneth had done, she told Shelby.

The next time Mark was scheduled to return to Pikeville, this time for a few weeks of work, Ron Poole made sure that Susan was forewarned. He telephoned her at Shelby's house and told her that Mark was due in on June 5. Shelby would later tell investigators that she was relieved that her sister would finally have the opportunity to confront Mark about the baby.

On Tuesday, May 30, Susan went to the public health center in Pikeville to have a pregnancy test and get a report confirming it. She explained to the physician that she needed the confirmation to apply for state welfare benefits, although in fact she was already receiving them. Based on what she said, the doctor who interviewed her gave her an estimated due date of November 19—indicating that the date of conception had been near the end of February. The doctor also noted that Susan had had a miscarriage and a D&C on January 2.

Susan took the report to Poole, who made a photocopy of it. That weekend, Susan visited her children at Kenneth's place. It was the last time they would see her.

On June 4, Mark Putnam, full of dread, boarded a flight in Fort Lauderdale. The chop-shop investigation that had consumed him for eighteen months, and on which he had staked his personal reputation, was nearly ready for trial, and the US Attorney prosecuting the case had conveyed his nervousness to Mark. And waiting for him in Pikeville was a woman threatening to expose him as a fraud and an adulterer. He had no idea how he would control the damage.

On the plane, looking out across the vast dark mat of the Everglades he wondered how he had blown it all so easily and with so little thought to the consequences. He shut his eyes and considered how he had disgraced himself, his family, and his badge, perhaps that most of all.

Years later, he would describe what went through his mind on that flight: "Kathy and I were finally in an environment where we could thrive, in Florida. And I threw it away. What did I swear to? Fidelity, bravery, integrity, character beyond reproach—the things that got me into the bureau. As soon as I had the affair, I knew I wasn't equal to my peers, even if some of them were up to their own things. I wasn't upholding my own standards. Yes, I put a lot of pressure on myself. I had to be the best person I could be. And I failed. In Florida, I was in a new competitive environment now with three hundred smart agents, and I knew they'd see that I was a flash in the pan. The only way I got into the bureau in the first place was pure audacity—and a wife who fought for me. I sure did find a nice way to thank her for that."

In gusts of memory, he denigrated his accomplishments. Soccer star, baseball journeyman, good student working hard to keep up his grades, loyal husband, and devoted father—all now seemed to be thin veneer on cheap wood. He'd always feared his father's disdain, and now he knew why. He wasn't good enough, not then, not now, and the truth was about to come out.

As the airplane leveled out at cruising speed over the Florida panhandle, his mind wandered back to his freshman year in high school, when he was hopelessly in love with a pretty girl. There was a dance at the school; she led him outside on a warm spring night, much like this one, to join some friends who had a private party going near the track—booze and marijuana, people acting sloppy.

In a panic, he fled, leaving the gorgeous new girlfriend behind with a can of beer in her hand. He literally ran the three miles home.

In high school, in college, and later in marriage and parenthood, those closest to him knew that Mark Putnam insisted on having an unsullied record. He had to keep it that way, without ever asking the question, *Who says?*

A man who couldn't tolerate small failings in himself was staggered by a big one. How could he possibly explain it when they came to him with the proof? With a female informant, he had compromised the bureau. There would be a scandal. Was resigning the only way? Could he simply tell the bureau, "Look, guys, I screwed this up. I'm sorry. Give me my punishment. I won't mess up again. But there is nothing you can do to me that would be worse than what I have done to myself. Let me work it out. I promise you I will suffer"? No, he could not.

He did not consider discussing this problem with the person who knew him best and loved him unconditionally, his wife. He was in a terrible jam, but he would face it, and somehow overcome it, alone. Having never, ever, been in trouble before, Mark Putnam simply did not know how to ask for help.

In Huntington, West Virginia, which has the closest commercial airport to Pikeville, a hundred miles away through the mountains, he rented a Ford Tempo, in the standard bureau economy class, and told the clerk that he expected to keep it for about three weeks. It was a long and tedious two-hour trip south through the hills to Pikeville, on a road that narrows to two lanes as it climbs and plunges, with a constant barrage of coal trucks barreling north out of the hills toward the docks on the Ohio River.

As Mark drove gloomily south, Ron Poole hurried out to Freeburn to meet Susan at the post office across the road from Shelby's house. He had already arranged a room for her at the Landmark, which he guaranteed with his American Express card. Another person was already at the motel on the FBI's tab. Charlie Trotter, the nervous star witness in the chop-shop case, had been salted away there for weeks, to keep him out of trouble. Mark knew he was going to see Charlie at the Landmark. Susan would be a surprise.

After a restless night, Mark walked into the FBI office in downtown Pikeville and found Ron Poole on the phone.

"Hey, guess who's here!" Poole boomed into the phone. Mark's heart sank. Winking, Poole handed over the receiver as if he were doing Mark a favor.

Susan's voice had a brittle edge. "We are going to get together, aren't we?"

Mark tried to keep his voice down, though he could see that Poole was listening. "Susan, I'll be here for at least three weeks. We'll hook up, I promise you."

"It'd better be soon, goddammit. I'm sick of this. You fucked me over."

The hostility and crudity surprised him. Susan had always tried to be civil and "proper" in front of Mark, even when she was in a fury about something. That pretense was apparently gone. Watching Poole, who was feigning interest in a file, Mark wondered just what had been going on between the two of them, but he didn't want to get into it any further with her, not now.

"Yes," he said patiently. "We'll talk, Susan."

Poole tossed him a suggestive smile when he hung up and said, "Hey, buddy, look there on the desk, would you? Hand me that piece of yellow paper there?"

Mark picked up the document, which lay next to a pamphlet about prenatal care. It was dated May 30; on the top was Susan's childish signature, and at the bottom, that of a technician at the Pike County Health Center. It read, in part:

*I fully understand that if the pregnancy test reading is NEG-
ATIVE, it does not necessarily mean than I am not pregnant. . . . I also fully understand that if the pregnancy test
reading is POSITIVE, this does not necessarily mean that I
am pregnant. False positive readings can occur for such rea-
sons as misinterpretation of results, undiagnosed medical
problems (Aldomet, marijuana, methadone, aspirin in large
doses, phenothirazine, antidepressants, antiparkinsonian,
and anticonvulsants). . . . I have been informed that in order
to lessen the chance of serious problems it is my responsibility
to have the test results confirmed by a physician before considering myself pregnant or nonpregnant.*

At the bottom was the notation: *TEST RESULTS POSITIVE.*

Mark felt sick. He glared at his ex-partner. Why was Poole
involved in this? How many other people had he shown the report
to? Clearly, this problem was already out of control. She was pregnant, the report seemed to confirm. And he was the father, she
said. That certainly seemed plausible. The sex they had in the
car had been hasty and impulsive. On those occasions, he hadn't
thought ahead to carry a condom, and he had no idea whether she
was on birth control. And if Susan had been sleeping with another
man during the short time they had been involved, he knew she
would have bragged about it to taunt him. No, Susan was faithful,
in her way. If there was a baby, he felt he was very likely the father.

Poole lobbed in a comment that interrupted his thoughts.
"Doing anything this afternoon?" he asked. He invited Mark along
on a drive to Letcher County, where he had to do an interview.
Mark, who wasn't due in Lexington until the next day, agreed to
go, but on the long trip down through the depressing coal towns,
along a mountain highway with road signs that said, like a bad
joke, THE TRAIL OF THE LONESOME PINE, he regretted that

he had. Susan didn't come up in conversation. They gossiped about cases and discussed the possibility of reactivating Charlie Trotter as a working informant once the chop-shop trial was over. It was an awkward trip with a companion he didn't like, and Mark was glad to get back to the motel in the early evening. He went down for something to eat, called Kathy and the kids, and climbed into bed to watch television. After a while the phone rang. Susan.

"Where are you?" he asked. The connection from Freeburn was usually fuzzy; now it sounded as if she were next door.

Which was about right. "I'm in the motel," she said.

"*This* motel? When did you get here?"

"I need to talk to you."

"Susan, I'm beat to hell. I have to get some rest because I have to be up at five to drive up to Lexington. I promise you, we'll talk when I get back tomorrow."

"We are going to talk about this, goddammit. Don't think we're not!" She abruptly ended the conversation.

He was up before dawn. He did not look forward to the three-hour drive westward over the mountains to the federal building in Lexington, where Tom Self, a prosecutor known for being methodical, wanted to conduct intensive reviews of the chop-shop case evidence before the trial, which was scheduled to begin in late June.

Mark was there at nine and felt greatly put out to learn that Self had been called to court. Tired and ornery, he cooled his heels for six hours in the US Attorney's office, brooding about his troubles. When Self came bustling in around three, he only had a few minutes to talk. He asked Mark to come back the next day.

On the endless drive back over the mountains, Mark thought about his ex-partner. "What the hell are you doing putting her up in the motel when *you know I'm going to be there*, Ron?" he said aloud, watching the rearview mirror as an eighteen-wheeler loomed bigger, tailgated menacingly for a few seconds, swerved into the passing lane, and roared on out of sight.

No sooner was he back at the motel, showered and trying to relax, when there was banging on the door. Susan stormed in, and her mood clearly hadn't improved any. Her eyes were bloodshot, and he wondered which chemicals were at work.

"You're avoiding me," she said.

"Hello to you, too, Susan. How are you?"

"Don't give me that shit. We are going to *talk*."

"Listen, I promise I'll set some time aside this weekend. Susan, I'm exhausted. I just can't do it now."

"That's just like you. You put everything before me! I should have killed them all when I had the chance."

He had no idea what she was talking about. "Killed who?"

She shrugged. It didn't matter.

It was obvious that Susan was high. Afraid of a commotion that he wasn't prepared to handle, he asked her if she wanted to go out to McDonald's for something to eat. With that, an amazing transformation occurred—the old Susan came back. They ate in the car and talked. Crying now she poured out her misery. She was afraid someone was going to kill her. She described the beatings by Kenneth, by Sherri Justice. Shelby and Ike were threatening to turn her out. She had no money. Kenneth was keeping her children away from her. Poole was pressuring her to work for him, and she didn't know if she could do it. And he, Mark, a man she had trusted as no other, had gotten her pregnant and abandoned her to all that.

"Would you consider having an abortion?" he asked.

She most certainly would not. The fury came back. He could see no solution. As he took her back to the motel, he glanced at the woman sitting stiffly beside him in shorts and a t-shirt and thought, *If this is my kid, she's five months pregnant. The last time was before January. Shouldn't she be showing? Maybe the drugs keep it small.* But he dismissed the thought as craven and wishful. She went back to her room petulantly, without replying when he said he would find more time to discuss it next week.

Mark found Charlie Trotter sitting by himself in a lawn chair outside the room where Poole had installed him a month earlier. Living temporarily at the Landmark was an arrangement Charlie liked just fine, and not only for the security it offered. Charlie had robbed a motel or two, but he was not in the habit of actually staying in them; he considered it the height of luxury to be able to pick up the phone, order a sirloin and a six-pack, and when it came, sign a piece of paper saying the US government was buying.

But Charlie, the toughest man on the mountain, had gone jittery. He told Mark that he was afraid the "Letcher County boys" had located him and were watching. A couple of them, he thought, had been driving by every night.

"They know where I am, Mark," he said with grave eyes.

"Christ, Charlie, do you want to change rooms with me? We can change motels if you want."

Charlie thought it over and said he would be okay. The FBI payment for his work was to come at the end of the trial. It would be substantial—in fact, it was going to be another $30,000 on top of the $15,000 he'd got to date. Charlie said he would stick it out.

"We've been through a lot on this one, Charlie," Mark said as he left. "We can't let the case go down the tubes now, buddy."

Mark was deeply troubled, not only by the possibility of Charlie's backing out, but by the implications of using this man, who had been a friend, and then leaving him to fend for himself. It did not matter much to Mark that Charlie worked both sides of the fence; that was the way the game was played. In another couple of weeks, assuming he could work his way through all of this, Mark knew he would drive over the hills and drop the rented car at the airport. A few hours later, he'd be back in the sunshine of south Florida, with the loving wife and beautiful children and the three-bedroom town house with beige walls and palmettos out front, with neighbors on either side who did not know each other's names. But Charlie could call nowhere else home. After the trial, if he testified, he would have the big check in his pocket, with a pat on the back for a job well done. Charlie would be flush, though he'd piss that away on women and cocaine soon enough. But always, when he woke up in the morning, Charlie would be in these hills where the boys never forget an insult and always settle a score.

These were the ethical compromises inherent in using informants like Charlie and Susan. Truth to tell, keeping them active, as the bureau insisted, was a monumental headache. God they wore him down. He was exhausted by the months of whining and crying, the nearly infantile dependence. Give them a thousand bucks, and they wanted two thousand more. Cultivating informants, keeping them happy and productive, required a huge and often debilitating personal effort: phone calls at three o'clock in the morning, paranoia, scheming, and double-crossing all came with the territory. He had seen how utterly different the FBI could be in a place like Miami, where the rules were clear-cut, the supervisors were on the scene, the work was dispersed among a large number of agents, and everybody had room to spread out: you weren't looking at the same damn faces everywhere you turned. All he wanted to do was get this case finished, control the damage with Susan, leave these hills for good. Why was that so much to ask?

The next day, he again made the drive to Lexington, wasted more time waiting for a meeting that he thought could just as well have been handled on the phone, and made the long trip back. When he got to his room, it was nearly nine o'clock; the only thing he had eaten all day was a glazed doughnut that a secretary had given him while he waited. But he was too tired to get in the car and drive out to a fast-food joint, or even to go down to the dining room, and room service had even less appeal. Instead, he pulled down the bedspread and lay on the bed studying water stains on the ceiling and wondering idly what would remove them. Finally he fumbled backhanded to snap off the forty-watt bulb in the lamp on the nightstand. His eyelids drooped and closed. His body felt light; at last the weight of trouble fell away and he relaxed.

He had been asleep for about a half hour when the phone went off like a firehouse bell in his ear.

"Hello!" he barked, more forcefully than he had intended.

"Heeeeeey." Oh, sweet Jesus, Mark thought, recognizing his ex-partner's signature greeting. The man had the unique ability to raise Mark's blood pressure just by entering his consciousness. "How's it going, buddy?" Poole asked.

Trying to conceal his annoyance, Mark said evenly, "We're all set to go with the trial, Ron."

But Poole hadn't called for a legal report. "You talked the stuff over with Susan?"

"Stuff?"

"You know what I mean, old buddy."

"No, not really, Ron," Mark replied warily. "I've been too preoccupied with this case."

"Well, I can understand that. I'll bet you can't wait to be done with that and get out of here, huh, buddy?"

"Yeah, I'm anxious to get back to Miami."

"Talk to you later," Poole said abruptly, and hung up.

Mark was annoyed at his own cordiality. Why didn't he just tell Poole to take a hike? They were no longer partners; even given the bureau's insistence on agent-to-agent bonhomie, Mark saw no good reason to extend courtesy to a man who always let you know he had a little something on you, then had the nerve to press for acknowledgment of that fact.

Mark thought back to Kathy's warnings about Poole, which he had largely written off to her desperation to get out of Pikeville. "You're naïve," she had said. "This guy has his eye on Susan, and he thinks you're in his way. This guy will do you harm."

He'd replied, with dismissive assurance, "An FBI agent wouldn't deliberately try to screw another FBI agent." He still had no idea how much Kathy had talked to Poole as she plotted to get them out of Pikeville.

Again Mark had fallen into a deep sleep, this time dreaming of the beach, the happy shrieks of his children over the crash of surf, when the insistent ringing of a telephone again broke through. He ordered himself awake. The voice on the phone was Susan's. It was eleven-thirty, she reported in a slurred voice, and asked, shrilly, "Sleeping? You sleeping son of a bitch."

The vehemence surprised him. "Susan, would you shut up and let me get some sleep?"

She banged the phone down. His anger was raw now with rudely dislocated sleep. He hated Susan, wished he had never recruited her, used her, paid her, encouraged her, comforted her, depended on her, and finally, stupidly, dropped his guard enough to have sex with her on the front seat of a car amid the sorrowful debris of an abandoned strip mine on a Kentucky mountain. That, finally, was where she had him, pregnant with his child or not, and they both knew it.

That was his abject ruin, the mortal sin for which absolution could not be had. And grievous sin was not a simple matter; with its commission came the torture of ambivalence and ambiguity. The fact was, as he knew very well, Susan had been there when he needed her, and Susan cared greatly for him. She had accepted this outsider when a lot of people hadn't. Later, she helped get him on the map. Working cases, she was as patient with Mark as he had to be with her. It was a weird balance. He pitied her circumstances and her upbringing. Like Kathy, he wished he could help her. They had always tacitly maintained the fiction of her unsullied reputation, and in a funny way, between them it was true. She had offered herself not only in desperation and desire, but also out of deep and simple trust. Their passion hadn't been devoid of love, no matter how flickering and transient. Furthermore, she had shown physical and even moral courage, beyond the lure of the money, to turn against people he knew she would have to face for the rest of her life, people who knew her parents, her aunts and uncles, her siblings, and her kids. Susan was brave, she had guts; in her own defiant way she was as loyal as a sister. Susan had put her ass on the line for him. Mark knew that his sacred career had benefited—directly, immediately, and substantially. She was an indelible part of his record.

He thought back on the first time he and Susan had had sex, steaming up the car windows like adolescents, the gearshift knob jabbing at shifting limbs. He had always felt nothing but contempt for cops who kept framed pictures of their wives on their desks and meanwhile screwed anything that didn't resist. And now he had done worse. As a civil matter, becoming sexually involved with an informant was a fireable offense. Morally, it was unforgivable.

Now she was charging hard at him, hostile, impatient, unreasonable, and dangerous. She wouldn't give him time. It was going to be like working the bomb squad; disarming her would be tricky, especially with Poole lurking in the background. It could blow up in his face at any time.

He thought of what she had said the other night: "I'm going to be a thorn in your ass, Mark. I'm coming down to Florida to make sure you don't forget me."

9

He had pulled the motel room curtains tight the night before, but they did not fit the window well and the gloom seeped in with the dawn. When he opened his eyes, he looked at the dingy stains on the ceiling.

At least it was June. By noon, the sun was high enough in the sky that the light came over the hilltops. The trees were full and green on the mountains. People were ashamed when the hills lost their cover, exposing the deep gashes from the strip mines, the giant conveyer machines trellised over stepped ridges of blasted sandstone and slate, the sallow streams and tumbledown shacks. Winter was not a good time to sell a house in Pikeville, although now spring was over and still their place up in Cedar Creek remained unsold. Tending to the house was another of the unwelcome chores Mark had to do before he could go home.

He turned over and pressed his face into the pillow, imagining south Florida, Danielle hopping off her bike to run to him in the front yard when he got in from work, Kathy happy again and making plans to complete her degree, little Mark bright and mischievous, a miniature image of his old man. It had taken a lot to get there; all he wanted now was to get back. The bathroom faucet dislodged another drop of water that hit the sink with a resonant *plonk*. Kicking off the thin blanket and stiff bedspread, Mark sat up naked on the edge of the bed, feeling sore and dizzy. He thought, *I've got to start eating and sleeping better than this. Cut back on the hours, loosen up, work out more.* In a few weeks, he hoped, Ron Poole, Tom Self, the bureau supervisors in Lexington, the Hatfields, McCoys, and everybody else in Pikeville, Susan especially, could then do him a great favor by losing his phone number.

His head rested on his chest. The date was June 8, his father's birthday. His father had been dead for ten years, but he still thought of him without fail every day. If the old man had been around, Mark wondered if he would have gone to him and said, *Look, Dad, I'm jammed up here. I messed this thing up bad, and I don't know how to get out of it.* Mark tried to imagine his father's face when it was strong, but what he recalled instead was a familiar sad photograph of a man in his late forties gaunt and defeated with a month left to live.

Wishing that he had inherited his father's equanimity in the same measure as his introspection, Mark made his way to the bathroom, where he scowled at his face in the mirror and gingerly pressed at the puffiness under his eyes. In the shower, the spray was weak, but at least the water was hot and soothing against the tight muscles of his shoulders. He closed his eyes and let the water beat on his face.

There was a pounding on the door as he was drying off on the tacky blue rug. He wrapped a towel around his waist and had barely pulled back the dime-store bolt when Susan pushed her way in, red-eyed and looking as if she'd slept in her car.

"Don't you look nice," she said smiling broadly and tugging at the towel till it came off. "Is that your new *Miami Vice* outfit?"

"Hello, Susan," Mark said wearily. "You're up early."

She brushed past him and went to the bed, but he continued to face the door not willing to acknowledge her possession of his room. *Christ, not now*, he thought. This was business for tomorrow, maybe. Not now.

"I've got to leave for Lexington in five minutes, Susan. I'm going to be tied up there all day." With resignation, he turned to face her, trying not to show the disgust he felt with himself. She didn't look pregnant in her little shorts and University of Kentucky T-shirt. When had Kathy started to show? He couldn't recall.

"Are you avoiding me again, Mark?" Susan demanded, planting herself on the bed. "We got to talk. How many times do you and those guys need to meet, anyway? Why didn't you just get a room up in Lexington?"

"Because I wanted to straighten out some problems here, Susan," he said pointedly. The shoulder muscles had tightened up again. He felt sweat building under his arms; a rivulet began a jerky path down his back.

"Don't give me that bull, Mark. Don't fuck with me."

"If I didn't do that, we wouldn't be in this mess, would we," he said, but he regretted the juvenile crack immediately. He didn't want her riled. All he wanted was for her to let him get out of there. He walked over to put a hand on her thin shoulder and was surprised to feel her flinch. "We'll talk this weekend, okay?" he said.

"I always take a backseat to the precious FBI, don't I?" she said petulantly. He'd heard that before, of course. And the reply, had he chosen to give it to her, would have been: *Yes, dammit. Everything else takes a backseat.* Why was that so hard for people to understand?

Instead, he said, "I've got to get dressed and get out of here." When he came out of the bathroom, she was still sitting on the edge of the bed.

"I've got to go, Susan."

"Wait, wait. I need to use your phone to call my sister, and I need to borrow a pair of shorts," she said, sounding plaintive.

"For what?"

"I didn't bring enough clothes with me. I just want to borrow them. You'll get them back, Mark."

"But why do you need to use my phone? Use the phone in your room."

"I have to call my sister, and I don't want Ron to know I did because it's about him."

This didn't make any sense, but he wasn't in the mood to argue.

He grabbed his bulging files off the top of the television and caught her injured look in the dingy mirror. "Okay, make your call, grab your shorts, and close the door when you leave," he called back as he left, hooking his thumb at the table where his suitcase lay open.

As he shut the door, he heard her mutter, "Bastard."

In the rented Ford, he wondered for a moment about Susan borrowing his clothes, but she was always borrowing somebody's clothes. He deliberately put her out of his mind as he negotiated the high pass that cut through the mountain north of town.

In Lexington, he was once again kept waiting until well after lunch. He and Tom Self finally met late in the afternoon, spending less than an hour going over details of trial strategy. Though Mark resented having his time wasted, he regarded Self as one of the few mentors he could name during his time in eastern Kentucky. Trying to please Tom Self during a prosecution was like trying to get an A from a particularly exacting teacher. Mark thought of him with grudging respect as a "ball buster" who insisted that every flap in a case be nailed down tight before he took it to trial. Often, he would ask Mark to go back and reinterview people he had already talked to, fill in more detail. Self was never confident and never let investigators relax until the jury adjourned.

The chop-shop case was solid and ready to go, assuming Charlie Trotter didn't bolt. Charlie seemed to have steadied the last time they spoke on the phone. Mark hoped he could keep him that way. Still, it was never a sure thing with a mountain jury. Cases got lost simply because jurors didn't like the idea of outsiders coming down on a local boy living hard, making do. Mark never forgot his first trial, when witness after witness ostentatiously crossed their fingers as they swore on a Bible while the judge pretended not to notice, the jury's eyes widened, and spectators nudged one another.

He also knew that the bureau was watching this case carefully—after all the time and trouble, after the emergency transfer out of town, he knew that he had to bring a clean conviction to the table, especially if Susan persisted with her threat of going to his superiors.

Feeling that he had wasted another day, he started back into the hills around five o'clock, as the afternoon sun edged the ragged mountains and cast deep shadows over the valleys. He realized that he needed a vacation. The past two and a half years had caught up with him—everything, even his nightly three-mile run, seemed to take extra effort. In a month, he would be thirty. He no longer felt young.

Susan, determined to force the confrontation that Poole and Shelby had been insisting she have, waited all afternoon for Mark to return. Every fifteen minutes after four o'clock, she left her room to look for his car. Anyone who glanced at the pretty, brown-haired young woman standing on her tiptoes on the balcony of the motel might have taken her for a mountain bride on a honeymoon waiting for her husband to come back from the store: She would look, see nothing, smile wanly, and with studied dignity return to her room.

Mark saw her at the railing when he turned into the parking lot. She did not acknowledge him except to glance his way, steadily but without apparent interest. At the end of a long drive and a frustrating day, he was furious to know that the next thing he could expect was a confrontation. He turned off the engine, braced his arms against the steering wheel, put his head down, and muttered, "Shit, shit, shit, shit, just leave me alone for five minutes." All he wanted to do was read the paper and have dinner. But he forced a look of nonchalance and went up to his room with Susan hard on his heels.

She followed him inside and stood silently by the door until he came out of the bathroom. She had changed into his gray gym shorts and T-shirt since their encounter that morning.

"Are we going to talk about your baby now?" she said. He could tell she had been drinking, and by this time of the day there would be some pills at work, too.

"Not tonight, Susan. Please. I have some calls to make, and I need to spend some time with Charlie."

She snorted. "Your job again."

But he was surprised when she sauntered out without a commotion.

Alone, Mark made a few local calls and then walked down a floor to talk with Charlie Trotter, again installed in his lawn chair, again wavering. "It's going to be tough looking them boys in the eye when I'm on the stand," Charlie said, reaching for the can of beer at his side. He dragged hard on the nub of a Marlboro that was barely visible under his black mustache, then flipped the butt over the railing and folded his hands on a prodigious belly.

From where the two men sat, they could see the single bulb shining in the gathering twilight from atop the cupola of the Pike County Court House, repository of challenged deeds, ancient threats, and tenuously adjudicated brawls.

Having to look the boys in the eye was the curse of this land, of course. But Charlie's testimony was important, if not crucial. Without it, the case could well collapse.

Mark sighed. Charlie slumped in the lawn chair, his powerful hands now tightly clenched between his knees, as if in combat. He turned slightly away, which Mark recognized as a telling shift in alignment, a sign of inner conflict signaling a potential for deceit. Give empathy, not sympathy, he recalled from his classes on psychological manipulation of informants and suspects.

"Charlie, I'm not going to blow smoke up your ass," he said, choosing his words deliberately. "I won't even try to understand what you're going through right now. Just do the best you can, man. You're a stand-up guy. Remember all the bullshit these clowns put you through. Remember what they did to you, Charlie." He stood up and clapped Charlie on the leg. "What do you say we grab something to eat and have a few beers? Uncle Sam's buying."

"Already et," Charlie said, sitting back to nurse his beer.

A little later, Susan thumped pathetically at Mark's door. She stood at the threshold with her arms crossed over her breasts, smiling unevenly. Again, he knew she was high. She lunged at him the moment he shut the door behind her, slapping him hard across the cheek with her right palm. She was wide-eyed and crying.

"You're avoiding me, you son of a bitch! I'm sick of this, Mark! High-and-mighty FBI—I'll see you burn in hell!"

He knew better than to aggravate Susan when she was having a tantrum. She had never acted this way with him before. Spit flecked the corners of her mouth. Her hair was unkempt; she looked as if she had fallen off the back of a truck. Another fifty pounds and ten or fifteen more years, he thought, and this was a woman framed in defeat in the doorway of a busted mobile home, yelling at the kids.

She screamed at him, "My life has been fucked up since I met you!" He resisted the impulse to point out that it had been that way before she met him as well. At least now she was on the right side of the law more often than not.

"Now you are going to pay for it!" she vowed. Her lips trembled. He wasn't sure what she meant, but he looked around quickly to make sure his gun was in the drawer. He remembered: He had put it in beside the Gideon Bible.

"I'm not having no abortion," she repeated.

He wanted to reason with her, and drug rage was complicating that. He felt shaky. He wished her no harm. All he wanted was for her to be out of his life. "Susan, I understand about the abortion," he said, struggling to control the situation. "If this is my baby, I don't want you to bring up that child. Kathy and I would raise it."

He had not anticipated making that suggestion. Immediately, he regretted the hurt the words caused.

Susan was sobbing. "I am a good mother. This is your baby, Mark. You insinuate that I been fucking everybody in Pikeville, but I have not and this is yours!"

"Susan, I didn't insinuate anything like that. Please keep it down. I don't want the neighbors to know our business."

That let her regain the offensive. She stamped her foot. "The damn neighbors? You're so concerned with your reputation? Your reputation ain't nothing now, *Miami Vice*!"

Her pupils were dilated. Whatever was going on, he wanted to change the physical location and negate her ability to threaten him with a public scene. Exhaling loudly, he suggested, "Look, let's go for a ride and cool off." She surprised him by softly taking his hand, as if he had just asked her on a date. It was almost eleven o'clock at night.

With an extremely agitated Susan beside him, he drove north out of Pikeville on Route 23 where the big coal trucks hit cruising speed at night on the long haul up the valley, and east onto the seclusion of Route 119 through rippled mountains, negotiating treacherous turns on narrow winding roads. It was a long loop around Pikeville and then southeast through plateaus of strip-mined mountains over which a waxing crescent of the moon drifted like a sickle through dark clouds. The headlights stabbed at black mountain walls with cascades of harshly lit kudzu loping ghostlike down over rocky shelves streaked with thin coal seams.

They drove into the mountains when they needed privacy from the prying eyes of Pikeville. Mobility eased conversation and they talked while he sped around the turns effortlessly, thanks to Bert Hatfield's instruction.

Again and again, he asked her what she expected him to do. She was nearly hysterical, but when she managed to connect her sentences, they were mostly in the form of disjointed threats. He realized that she had been saving her emotional ammunition for him for weeks.

He tried to reason with her. "Well, with regard to a pregnancy—"

"—With *regard* to? What are you, a lawyer?" She patted her belly. "This baby is yours!"

"Susan, we can discuss this calmly."

"Your FBI will be interested to hear what I have to say. So will that whore wife of yours and those kids." She pointedly did not speak Kathy's name.

She insisted that the baby was his, and that she would tell the FBI, his wife, and his children about it. But unless it was to renounce everything else and stay with her forever, he could not figure out what she expected him to do. He thought about the two and a half miserable years working grueling hours in Pikeville, the phone calls at three in the morning, the threats, the corruption he saw everywhere he looked, the stress of the impending trial, Kathy's misery, the intimidating phone calls from Poole, Charlie

Trotter wavering in his motel room, the stress of starting a job anew in a high profile bureau like Miami. And now, beside him, Susan shrieking. But then she took a breath and her voice was calm.

"Ron says they'll fire you when they find out."

He bristled at that. "What about Ron, goddammit?"

She backed down. "Nothing. He didn't say nothing. They will fire you, though, Mr. FBI."

At the coal town of Meta, he turned right onto Route 194, a narrow two-lane that winds southeast along Johns Creek into the rugged hills that border the Tug Valley. Once in the hills, the only turnoffs are narrow gravel roads put in by mine companies who then abandoned the roads when they finished blasting out the coal, leaving behind chewed out mountains.

As they drove toward Freeburn and Barrenshee Hollow, Susan sobbed uncontrollably. As they approached the crest of Peter Creek Mountain, she caught her breath and lunged across the seat at him, slapping him with both hands. Fighting to keep control of the car, he made out the contours of one of the coal-road turnoffs in his headlights and turned abruptly onto it, bumping about fifty yards up the road and scattering gravel loudly under the car. He shut off the engine and the lights. Susan's sobs were the only sound in the darkness. Where the sky showed above the ridge, it was filled with stars. Mark rolled the window down and felt the air on his hot cheeks and burning eyes. He listened, as if trying to extract from the gloom any sound other than Susan's short panting.

Placing his hand on her shoulder, he said, "Let's try and work this out instead of acting like a couple of idiots." This was exactly the kind of lonely dark setting that had led to sex on other occasions, but even the intimation of affection now caused Susan to recoil in revulsion and slap his hand away.

"What's gotten into you, Susan?"

The question set her off again. "What do you mean *me*? You're messing with me, Mark! I know that now. I don't know why I didn't see it before. I'll be goddamned if I'm going to let you prance down to Florida with your little wife and your spoiled kids to resume your wonderful life. You owe me, buddy!"

He had the sense that these were lines someone else had given her. *Buddy* wasn't a word she used, and Mark thought he knew where she had picked it up.

"Susan, I've given you everything I could. Leave Kathy and my kids out of this." She looked down with surprise. He realized he had been using his index finger to poke at her chest for emphasis.

"You sure did give me everything you got," Susan said, and patted her belly again. He studied her body, thinking again that she did not look pregnant, but not having any good recollection of how a woman is supposed to look at five months.

"And now I'm going to have a little Mark Jr.," Susan went on, having regained her composure. "I'm going to bring this baby down to Florida and knock on your door and put the little bastard right into your precious daughter's arms. Your son is going to want to know why the baby's name is Mark Jr., the same as him. I can't wait to see the look in your wife's eyes! Then you know what I'm going to do? I'm going right on down to your FBI *Miami Vice* office and tell your new friends there how you solved your cases by fucking an informant and leaving her pregnant and barefoot to look after herself in Kentucky. I own you, Putnam! I own you and your precious job!"

She was determined. "I own you! Own you! Ron says they'll fire you and Kathy will leave you!"

"Ron again?" She laughed in his face.

"Susan, just tell me what you want from me. From day one, all you've done is bitch and feel sorry for yourself. Now please just tell me straight, what do you want from me?" His heart was pounding.

Now she was all business. "We are going to have this baby. You will be there when it's born and sign the birth certificate as its daddy. Second, you will leave that whore Kathy and those spoiled kids and marry me. If you don't, I'll ruin your life." She smiled triumphantly.

Mark, never a negotiator, argued as if a compromise could be reached. Kathy hadn't done any injury to Susan. Far from it. Kathy had been Susan's friend, her confessor, even her role model. When Mark wasn't in the mood, which had been very often during their last months in Pikeville, Kathy had been the stalwart who patiently endured Susan's crying jags on the phone, the one to assure Susan that she had value, that she was better than she believed.

Negotiating wasn't working. "Fuck you and your whore wife!" Susan screamed.

His anger flashed. "Hold it, dammit. If you ever call my wife a whore again I'll smack the shit out of you, Susan." And he realized that he meant it. He jammed his right hand under his leg.

"You don't have the balls to hit me, Mark. You're a pussy with no balls! For someone so smart, we played with you so bad. I don't even know why I let you fuck me—you're no man! I've had real men before, and you're nothing. You can't fuck worth a damn, I told everybody that! You're nothing but a spoiled rich kid."

This floored him. He thought of his father; taking on odd jobs to scrape together the thousand dollars a year that wasn't covered by his scholarship at Pomfret. The insult infuriated him. He smacked Susan across the face with the back of the fingers on his right hand. The blow barely fazed her. As if welcoming it, she let out a yelp of satisfaction.

"Well the little boy has the balls to hit a woman! That's the first real emotion I ever seen in you! I hope I didn't hurt your delicate little hand!"

He was breathing in gulps, close to hyperventilating. Sweat burned his eyes. She kept at him. "The only reason I worked with you in the first place was because I saw how pitiful you really were. Seen how they sent a pretty little Yankee boy down here with real men. Maybe your precious FBI wanted to toughen you up, but it didn't work. All the cops used to make fun of the pretty Yankee boy who wanted to work all the time." Having located the vein, she stabbed it in deep, "They laughed at you behind your back!"

He tried to make out her face in the darkness. Her voice was cold and strange.

"I own you, little boy! Now I'm going to have two little Putnam boys sucking at my tits."

"You're a fucking bitch. Susan, you know that?" he said quietly, desperate to control the quiver in his voice, afraid that he was about to cry.

"Oh, the great one spoke out! My hero *spoke*! Did it hurt to swear, Mr. Perfect?" Her breath was sour on his face. Mockingly, she said, "Your life sure ain't so perfect now, is it, honey?"

He tried reasoning again. "Okay, Susan. This is what I think about our problem—"

"*Our* problem? Oh, no, Mark. *Your* problem. I've never been happier myself. I told all my friends I'm going to have an FBI baby. I can't wait to see Kathy's face when I show her our baby."

He resisted the urge to hit her again. His training told him to stay on track, be professional, avoid emotionalism and direct challenge, summarize frequently, maintain poise. Do not take the bait.

"Since you won't have an abortion, after the baby's born I'll come back and take a blood test to establish paternity," he suggested.

She was livid. "I ain't no whore like your wife! I haven't fucked nobody except you! How dare you say that!"

"Well, that isn't what I heard, Susan. I heard your sister threw you out of her house—"

"That's not true!" Again, she was crying.

Sensing advantage, he bored in, impulsively brandishing an option he had not yet even considered discussing with his wife: "If the baby is mine, Kathy and I will adopt it. We will adopt it. You've proven what kind of a mother you are by signing over custody of your kids to that drunken ex-husband of yours. I'll be damned if I'd let any kid of mine grow up here with a slut like you."

Humiliation overcame her. Shrieking, she slammed into him, slapping and scratching wildly, like a child having a tantrum: Mark realized what Bert Hatfield had meant when he said that Susan could fight like a rained-on rooster.

"I won't let that whore raise my kid!" Susan cried.

"She's a better mother than you'll ever be!" Mark retorted, pushing her away roughly with an exaggerated show of personal disdain in the cramped confines of the car. This made her hysterical. She was on top of him, pounding down with her fists. He couldn't get his arms free to shield his face.

"Susan, cut . . . the . . . shit." He struggled into a dominant position, working to pin her arms. Her screaming horrified him. Fogged by their breath, the windows were as opaque as if covered by snow.

"You used me! You owe me!" she protested.

"I *paid* you," he said with cruel sarcasm.

"You bastard!" Susan screamed, flailing at him. "I should have killed your kids." With a guttural moan, she dug a long fingernail at his eye. Electrified by the sudden pain, he swung at her, this time with a fist and as hard as he could. But he missed. His hand slammed into metal on the dashboard.

"Fuck you to hell!" she cried as the punch flew past. Blood oozed from the gash across his knuckles. She saw the bleeding hand and bit it, with her feet pressed stiffly against the windshield. The pain was astonishing. She hissed through her teeth. He needed quiet. He needed to think. *Shut up!* he thought, wrenching his hand free and grabbing her neck with both hands. He held her that way, pressing for silence for almost two minutes, until her fury and his abated. He let out his breath steadily while she struggled weakly and then submitted to his will. "Relax, Susan, relax," he said, almost as if he were giving her a massage. When his breath was fully exhaled, his grip relaxed. The tension drained from his arms, which fell heavily and painfully to his side.

Susan was quiet. He opened his eyes and inhaled unsteadily, not knowing whether ten minutes or ten seconds had passed. His face stung from the slapping. She was a fighter, all right. But now she was leaning against him, her fight gone. He stroked her damp brown hair, wondering why she was not breathing heavily after she had struggled so hard.

"Susan, are you going to take it easy now?" he said, nudging her gently as if to wake her up. He regretted the insults. His lips brushed the top of her head. His shirt was soaked; his right hand throbbed, the knuckles wet with blood. He'd never felt more physically exhausted. "Susan, let's go."

The night had grown chilly; he thought of starting the car to get the heater going. Freeburn was still ten miles around the mountain. Quietly he said, "I'll drive you home."

She slumped forward when he removed his arm. As he tried to ease her gently off the console and into the passenger seat, her neck craned at a grotesque angle.

He blinked and said, "Oh, my God. Oh, shit. Oh, my God." He shook her. He sat her back and pounded on her chest. "Susan! Susan! Oh, my God!" He tried blowing air into her mouth, but her lips were cool and unyielding. He pounded on her chest and felt frantically for a pulse.

His first thought was that it was a coincidence; she'd had a tragic heart attack exacerbated by the excitement. He certainly hadn't *killed* her, not that easily. There would be some explaining to do, but . . .

Then he knew. She was dead and he had killed her.

He cradled her head and rocked back and forth sobbing, staring in disbelief at her face, very white and composed in the chill glow. *I have killed this person*, he thought. *A mother of two children. This girl in my arms.*

Trembling uncontrollably, he got out of the car as if to walk away. But there was nowhere to go. The door slammed and the sound reverberated from black-faced mountain walls. He screamed. That came back, too, with the same empty echo. He fell against the car, hearing only his breathing and the grunts of bullfrogs in the soggy brush, and in the distance the splash of water spilling off a slate ridge like a broken spigot.

He tried to arrange his thoughts. A steady wind rushed through the trees on the mountaintop, like the roar of a stadium. Foolishly he looked around in the dark, as if for a pay phone. He got back in the car and replayed the scene in his mind, desperate for explanations or excuses—the threats, the insults, the rage, the tears, the blows and flailing arms. He went over the story he would tell to the state police or, better yet, to Bert Hatfield at his place on the Tug beside the bridge.

He would expect no special treatment, beyond a certain professional courtesy, a cop-to-cop understanding that this girl had got run over just as surely as if she stood in the middle of a mountain road shaking her little fist at a twenty-ton coal truck rumbling out of a switchback. It was strictly his fault, of course. He would take his medicine. Bert would be heartsick; Bert would know what to do. He would tell him how to break it to Kathy. Kathy would tell the kids.

Another image crept into his mind, that of Danielle as an infant, three or four weeks old. It was the time of their marriage when he and Kathy were happiest—he was working hellish hours, the day job clerking in a liquor store, nights clerking at the FBI in Hartford, praying for an opening at the academy. When he came home after work at one o'clock one morning, the baby lay curled in her crib. Gently, he woke her and she smiled at him sleepily. He scooped her tiny sweet-smelling body into his arms, held her to his chest, and whispered hoarsely, "I promise you: I am going to be the best father I can be. You will always be proud of me. And you will always be able to come to me, with anything. I promise you that, Danielle."

One life was destroyed. Why destroy others? He was on a lonely mountain road. Not a single car had passed in the time they had been parked there arguing and fighting. Furthermore, they hadn't seen anyone else when they left the motel. Chances were, no one even knew that he and Susan had gone out together.

The chilly night was robbing Susan's body of its warmth. Absurdly, he reached over to roll up the window for her sake. Looking at her blankly, he considered suicide, but he didn't have his gun. Then another thought broke through the guilt and terror: He could fake a car accident. He was hurt, she was dead. This he quickly dismissed, however. People don't get strangled in car wrecks.

He got out and walked around the car several times, as if to encircle the problem and confine it, but he couldn't, no matter how hard he marched. *All of my life,* he thought, *I stayed out of trouble. I was the one who got the other guys out of jams in college! I kept my nose clean.* But he was the one alone now on a mountaintop with the body of a girl he had killed. What would his father say to that?

He stumbled to the passenger door and struggled to lift her out, astonished at how heavy she was. He had eased the body almost out of the car when it abruptly toppled to the ground, the head hitting the gravel with a whack. Mark screamed in horror as if he had injured her anew. He fell to his knees and vomited, bile burning his throat. He cradled her head, rocking on his heels, keening. *She is not dead, she is badly injured, in a terrible coma.* It would be horrible, there would be some jail time, but she would be alive and maybe, someday, she would forgive him.

A light drizzle materialized from the mist. He stared at his hands. A mosquito landed on his arm. He watched it take its fill but was unable to swat it. The rain became heavier; rivulets of water splashed from the high escarpments into crevices and hollows and creeks, the rain beating hard on the rocks and leaves as it fell over the Cumberland Plateau, from the watershed where the Tug starts down from the hills to the flatlands where Susan once thought she had seen her future.

He saw the lights of a vehicle coming up the mountain road from far away, blurred through the rain. He watched, squatting beside his darkened car. A big yellow bulldozer lumbered into sight and passed by, emergency lights throbbing. It emitted an insistent beeping sound that changed pitch as it climbed the mountain and disappeared over the crest of the road.

At some point, the rain stopped. Mark was cold and his clothes were drenched; he had no idea how much time had passed. The sky was full of stars.

It was time to move on. Shakily, his muscles aching, he managed to lift Susan's body into the trunk of the rental car. Now his degradation was total. Laying a hand on her small still breast, he said, "Susan, Susan, how did we ever let this happen?"

10

The headlamps probed the fog that lay in the valley where Johns Creek makes its run off the Pikeville side of the mountain toward the Levisa. Mark drove with both hands locked on top of the steering wheel. Ahead the fog reddened with the lights of the Kentucky Carbon Company's Johns Creek loading site, deserted as he passed the tipples and the lines of conveyors descending down the ridge like the monorails of hell. Beyond, at the base of a hill to the west, the trapezoid-shaped cars of a night coal train rolled along the Norfolk and Western spur line.

Mark had decided to go back to the motel and wait. He wasn't sure what he would wait for, but he needed time to consider whether there were any options beyond the single judgment that blared in his mind: *You are done, pal. You are so done.*

Back in the motel he looked at the nightstand where he had left his service revolver in the drawer beside the Gideon Bible. He diverted himself for a moment with the idea of putting the barrel in his mouth and pulling the trigger, but it was not a realistic consideration. He took inventory, standing at the mirror like a suspect in a lineup. He had wrapped a towel around his damaged hand. The index finger throbbed more than the rest of the hand.

He figured it was broken. Susan had fought hard, and those long nails were deadly. No, not deadly . . . they were effective. There were bloody scratches on his arms, and some on his jaw and neck. He certainly looked as if he had been in a fight.

It was almost three o'clock. He took a shower, dressed, walked across the road to the all-night Super American convenience store and bought some Band-Aids and antiseptic. The checkout clerk barely noticed him. In his room he dressed the cut and got into bed with the light on because he was afraid to turn it off. He stayed awake and alert the rest of the night. He couldn't think of anything to do except to go on with the day and see what happened. He had no idea what he would do about the body.

He was still a federal agent with an important meeting in the morning. When dawn came, he forced himself out of bed, and an hour later was surprised to find himself in the car, dressed and shaved, his briefcase on the seat beside him, holding the steering wheel steady at fifty-five on the Mountain Parkway into Lexington. This was no time to attract a patrol car. The sun was shining brightly through the dirty windshield. For the first time, he noticed the long crack in the windshield on the passenger side. As he changed lanes, easing to the right on one of those stretches where a car can pass, he thought about Susan in the trunk.

This time the meeting with the US attorney was long and detailed. Somehow he got through it. How could people not see how guilty he was? What kind of agents were they? Around lunchtime, Tom Self noticed his hand, and to his amazement, Mark heard himself blurting out a lie: "I was out at our old house in Pikeville taking care of a mess in the garage, and I ripped it on a nail."

He watched Self's reaction carefully, and it didn't show anything other than friendly concern. As a kid, any time he had told a lie, no matter how inconsequential, his red face had always given him away. Now that he was a killer, had lying become that easy? Was this something he had never understood about crime until now?

Self and his assistants kept him occupied all day with the minutiae of the chop-shop case, which Mark knew by heart. If Self noticed the scratches on Mark's neck, he did not mention them. In fact, Self seemed completely comfortable with him, even at a few points when Mark had to choke back the dry heaves. *He thinks I'm hung over*, Mark decided. He stopped worrying about the trembling of his hands until the group when to lunch at a corner restaurant, where ordered a sandwich so he wouldn't have to hold a fork. Self was expansive and optimistic about the trial. Mark realized that people, even those with sharp police instincts, could overlook a lot when their guard is down.

By the time Self turned him loose it was after four o'clock. Mark still had no plan. From the courthouse steps he spotted his car. The courthouse workers had rushed for theirs at the crack of four, leaving his alone on a side street in the deep shadow of a sycamore.

Off and on during the day, he had wondered about the smell, figuring that if someone noticed and called the cops, that would be it. There would be nothing for him to decide. They'd cuff him and it would be done. But that hadn't happened. He approached the car uneasily with his nostrils flared. Amazingly, there was no smell yet; the trunk was tight. He dug in a pocket for his keys, thinking, *something is on my side here*. For an instant, he considered opening the trunk and looking inside to make sure she was still there, but he came to his senses with a quick shudder. Best to drive off for the hills. He wondered how long his heart could pound this hard.

It was not yet seven o'clock when he got back to town. He found himself sitting behind the wheel of the car, engine off, in a parking slot in front of the Pikeville state police barracks, his mind as blank as a man's in a stupor. He had no idea how he'd got there.

For a long time he sat, listening to the hum of traffic on the grade below the cut-through. Numbly he stared at the lighted windows. A dispatcher would be at the switchboard in front to cope with the phones; there would still be a sergeant and a couple of troopers from the day shift at their desks in back. Someone he knew would be on duty, laboriously typing a report. Lt. Paul Maynard, the supervisor of the post's overworked detective squad, usually stayed late. Maynard was a friend. Maynard would hear him out, at least, and maybe he'd have some advice to offer before he had to put the cuffs on.

Mark's head was wracked with pain, but the shock had diminished and he could see things more clearly now. He forced himself to think past the self-loathing. *Okay, hotshot, here you are with a body in the trunk. Now what?* Without realizing it, he was actually mouthing the words, as if addressing himself from nearby. *But nobody caught you yet. Nobody knows yet, asshole. Why not wait and see what happens?* He argued with himself for a while, then started the car and drove off.

He took the Route 23 four-lane north out of town. A few miles past the strip mall where the K Mart was, just down the road from Marlow Tackett's country-western bar, where he and Kathy had often stopped for a drink, he turned right onto Harmons Branch, a side road that briefly hugged the property line of a brick house whose lawn was bordered with a white wood fence. The car kicked up gravel; a man in shorts pulling weeds in the waning sunlight on his lawn paused to glower as he passed. Mark's heart raced; his jaw set, he drove slowly, painfully extending his throbbing right hand along the top of the passenger seat in an effort to look casual. It was a road he and Susan had taken before. If you drove all the way up past the strip-mine equipment shed, you came to some bungalows set back in the trees from the foot of a high hollow. But he wasn't going that far. He watched in the rearview mirror through the dust until he saw the man go back to his weeds. About a half mile up was the first mine road, now unused, which went up a few hundred yards into the ridge. Beside that was a ravine with a small creek at the bottom, thick with weeds. The car thumped, its bottom scraping the ruts gouged into the road by coal trucks. In this part of eastern Kentucky, once you got off a main road, the terrain was honeycombed with hollows and little creeks, mostly dry now. Through the trees, he could see some trailers at the strip-mine shed on a clearing a quarter-mile off; the area wasn't isolated, but he knew that not many cars used the road, especially at night.

When he turned in and stopped the car, he heard the brittle whine of dirt bikes, kids racing up and down on one of the mine roads. He couldn't see them, but they were not far away. Through the open window he felt the soft breeze of a late spring night. This was where he would put her, at the edge of a ravine overgrown with brush and saplings. This, he figured, was where they would find her.

Her body was heavy. His arms trembled; it was impossible to be gentle. He lugged her out, straining his ears for any approaching vehicle, but heard nothing other than the wind in the trees and the croak of the bullfrogs and the incessant whine of the dirt bikes. His braced his legs for leverage and dragged the body a little way down the ravine and just out of sight from the road. The slope was steep, and nettles scraped his arms as he struggled with his unwieldy cargo, limp in his arms. His feet got tangled in roots; he stumbled and fell with a shout. He began to cry. Then, getting a better hold under her arms, he pulled her down the hill as far as he could. They were about fifteen feet below the roadbed now, and this is where she would stay, barely concealed, like his guilt. Kneeling beside the body, his weight on his knees against stiff bushes like a prayer stool, tears streaking down his cheeks, he stroked her face and said, "I'm sorry." Carefully, he removed the clothes, tugging the T-shirt off. His shorts, thirty-two-inch waist, slid off easily. Susan never wore underwear in warm weather. He did not think about whether she looked pregnant now that he saw her nude body. She was barefoot; her sandals had come off in the trunk. He gathered the clothes under his arm, turned, and abandoned her in the leaves.

When he struggled up to the top of the ravine, he found himself looking into the eyes of a dark-haired young woman astride a chestnut quarter horse. There were riding stables a few miles down the mountain and the hour was late to be on a horse alone She stared implacably for a minute, with just a hint of a raised eyebrow, at the good-looking but disheveled young man climbing up from the bushes.

Mark was startled but he thought fast enough to tug at his fly, flash a grin, and say, "Nature."

The woman kicked her spurs and trotted off without a word.

It rained again that night. Great muddy sheets of water lashed at the hills. From his motel room Mark managed to call Kathy and the children, though he could not remember what he said to them. Afterward he was very hungry. He pulled himself together to drive out in the rain to the Log Cabin on Route 23 where he wolfed down a steak and drank a beer.

It was here that he had his next scare.

Myra Chico, the local radio reporter, had a part-time job tending bar there on weekend nights. Mark had known her for years and had tried to help her when she said she was interested in applying for the FBI. He and Poole had arranged an interview for her at the bureau office in Lexington, where the supervisors had liked her well enough to invite her to apply. But she decided she couldn't leave Pikeville.

She came by his table and said that she had to talk to him. "It's very important, Mark. Can you meet me after work? I've got to talk to you about Susan."

And so the next phase began. The beer and food had worked on him, and he was as tired as if he had swum five miles. He studied her pleasant expression and asked, "What time do you get off?"

"A half hour. Come on over to my place for some coffee."

He followed her home in his car, anxious and frightened, but strangely glad for the company.

He wanted a glass of 7-Up, not coffee, and when she had brought it, they sat cross-legged on either end of her couch and talked.

"What about Susan?" he asked tentatively.

"Do you know where she is?"

"No. Why?"

"Ron Poole told me she left the Landmark sometime yesterday and didn't go home."

"You know Susan."

"Listen, you got a problem, do you know that?"

He waited. *Tell me about it,* he thought.

"She's pregnant. Ron showed me the test. He says you know."

"She told me."

"She says you're the father."

"Ron tell you that, too?"

"She's telling everybody you're the father."

"You believe it?"

"No."

"I never touched her," he said, aware of just how grave a lie that was.

"Ron asked me to ask you—he wants to stay out of it—where Susan went to."

"I don't know where Susan is," he lied again. *Yes you do,* he thought. *She's up on that mountain where you abandoned her.*

Myra had no reason not to believe him, and none even to question him. They talked about other things. He seemed very tired, a little emotional, perhaps. She figured it was the strain. As a friend, she understood.

The motel was as quiet when he returned. At the front desk, a groggy clerk said there were no messages. Mark's room had been made up and smelled faintly of cheap soap and starch. He fell into bed exhausted. He switched off the lamp and tried to force everything bad out of his mind; after a while, with much effort, he succeeded. He remembered when they put Cat Eyes in jail. That had been their best time together, the time he wished he could freeze in place forever. God, it had seemed as clever as a spring caper. Who would have thought it would graft Susan onto his life? When they taught you about informants in the academy, they didn't explain that you bought not only a piece of their time, but a part of their history, too. He hadn't understood that in order to renounce her past, Susan had found it necessary to affirm a future with him.

You made me a hero, Susan.

But not without a price, of course. The urgent phone calls at home at night, as if her problems were now immutably his: "Mark, would you come and get me out of here please? Kenneth beat me up. Could you put me up someplace?"

The bad thoughts rushed back like a squad of cops breaking in the door of his consciousness. He turned the light on to wait out the rest of the night.

The next thing he knew it was after nine o'clock. He awoke in a nauseous sweat with the bedsheet knotted around his feet. He hurried down to get a Lexington newspaper out of the box by the service elevator. On his way he pushed the plastic bag containing Susan's clothes into a trash receptacle. He scanned the headlines as he walked back to the room. There was nothing—at least for today.

Numbly he pressed on with his work. A subpoena in the chop-shop case had to be delivered to a man out in Magoffin County, which took a good part of the day. When he got back into town, it was late afternoon and he had begun to think more clearly. The car was on his mind. He drove to a service station on Route 23 and in the car-wash area vacuumed the interior of the Ford. He found an earring on the floor and let it be sucked into the vacuum hose. Using a bottle of kitchen cleaner he had bought, he carefully washed bloodstains from the dashboard and console. He bent down to study the rubber floor mat on the passenger side and noticed what looked like dried mucus. He was afraid to throw out the mat in the gas station where he could be clearly seen.

Kathy had told him to make sure he stopped by the house on Honeysuckle Lane, which was still on the market, to check things over. As he'd told Self, the garage needed straightening to spruce it up for prospective buyers. On his way over, he stopped, looked around furtively, yanked the floor mat out of the car and crammed it into a trash-bin near a ditch beside the high school track where he ran after work.

At the house he ran into a neighbor, Cecilia Fish, who noticed the car in the drive and wandered over. She stared at his cut hand. He had lost the bandage and it had begun to bleed again. He explained that he had ripped it on a nail while stacking those paint cans in the garage, and she hurried into her house and came back with a new bandage.

The next day, having already run the Ford through a carwash in Pikeville and carefully cleaned the inside, he got rid of it. He drove back up to the tiny Huntington airport a hundred miles away and told the clerk at the counter in the terminal that the windshield had been cracked by a chunk of coal falling off a speeding coal truck. That was not an uncommon occurrence on those mountain roads, and they gave him another Ford Tempo without any problem. He made the long drive back to Pikeville.

He wondered why he hadn't heard from Poole. Usually, Poole was as alert as a burglar when it came to the comings and goings of Susan and Mark. Poole knew Susan wasn't in her room at the Landmark and he'd probably already called Shelby looking for her. But Poole did not call him, and Mark had no idea where he was. That night, Mark was so exhausted that he fell asleep while talking to Kathy on the phone.

On Monday, three days after he'd left Susan's body in the ravine, Mark took another step to cover up his crime. He made a phone call to Shelby Jean Ward in Freeburn and asked, calmly and deliberately, whether she had heard from Susan.

"No, I haven't heard, and I'm worried. It ain't like her," Shelby said tentatively, not wanting to show any courtesy to a man she believed had used her sister, gotten her pregnant, and abandoned her after she had served his purposes. Shelby thought that Mark Putnam had monumental nerve expressing concern for Susan at this point. Ron Poole had kept Shelby well posted on Mark's evasiveness about the pregnancy.

Mark said, "Listen, I'm worried, too. She told me she was going to meet—"

"Ain't nobody seen her for three days, after she was out to the Landmark," Shelby interrupted.

Mark told her, "I was thinking that if you don't hear from her, you should probably file a missing person's report."

"I know that. I already thought of that. Somebody already told me I should do that."

Mark didn't need to ask who that might be.

"You seen Ron Poole, Shelby?" Mark asked.

"Excuse me?"

"Never mind. Just tell him I was looking for him, please."

After talking to Shelby, Mark called the Pikeville state police and spoke with Paul Maynard. He told Maynard that he was worried about Susan. He said she had left the motel on Thursday or Friday and not returned to Shelby' house in Freeburn. He made sure to mention that Susan had told him she was planning to meet some of her drug contacts from up north on Saturday when they were to pass through West Virginia on their way south. He also told Maynard that he had called Shelby and advised her to make a missing person's report. "She thinks something might have happened to her sister," he said.

"Mark," said Maynard, "this girl has a habit of taking off: You know that."

Aware that Poole had already told people about his problem with Susan, Mark anticipated Maynard's next question. "Well, I've known her pretty well for two and a half years. If you need any help on this, send a couple of the boys over to talk to me."

Maynard thanked him for the offer.

Shelby had also phoned the state police that day. The initial report summarized her call succinctly:

> SHELBY WARD of Freeburn, Kentucky, telephoned Post to report that her sister SUSAN SMITH of Freeburn, Kentucky, was missing.
>
> Victim was brought to Pikeville by the FBI and left at the Landmark motel. She arrived on June 5, 1989, and stayed until June 8, 1989, when she left the motel for unknown reasons. She left a few articles of clothing and makeup in the room. Her sister talked to her last about noon on June 8, 1989. FBI agents state that they do not know where she went.

A report of this kind is routine, filed as an alert for possible reference in case an unidentified body is found in a highway wreck or some other mishap. It is not regarded as an indication of a crime.

The police assume that an adult is free to disappear if he or she wishes and does not break the law in the process. The standard police procedure is to wait seventy-two hours before initiating an investigation, by which time most missing people return home, call, or turn up dead.

Susan Smith had done none of those things by the time that period expired. When Det. Richard Ray came to work on Friday morning, he found her missing person's report on his desk. On it was a note from his boss, Lieutenant Maynard, instructing him to get in touch with the woman's sister Shelby Jean Ward and see if anything had turned up.

The detective called Shelby and took down the information quietly and politely, his big fingers thumping at a keyboard to enter into the state and national law enforcement data networks the facts of the missing woman's existence, as stated by her sister: Susan Daniels Smith; white female; twenty-seven years old; short brown hair; five feet five inches tall; 130 pounds; tanned complexion; no occupation. Address, Freeburn, Kentucky, lives with sister, Shelby Ward; missing as of June 8. Sister last saw her wearing white shorts, blue University of Kentucky "Wildcats" T-shirt, gold necklace with gold cross.

Ray looked this information over. He was the kind of detective who notices the wayward rustle of a curtain or the dent on a car even when he is not working, and he detected in Shelby's voice an angry undertone. He asked her a few questions, listening intently to the answers. Then he told her he would be out to see her.

At the age of fifty-four, Richard Ray was the most experienced detective in the Pikeville post, a distinction that gave him more leeway than most other detectives, who complained that they had to get permission for virtually every move they made away from their desks. Understaffed and chronically underfunded in a state where politicians were historically uneasy about having an independent-minded law enforcement network on hand, the Kentucky State Police tended to keep its detectives on a short leash and off balance. A detective with decades of experience could find himself starting a murder case in the morning unable to follow up in the afternoon because he was switched to highway patrol—and unable to find an empty desk or a free telephone when he got back to the office.

In Pike County, where the per capita felony statistics always came in near the top among the state's 120 counties, the workload was especially fierce. A detective might handle 130 or more cases a year and report to a boss who had spent most of his career in the driver's license department. As a result, case coverage tended to be, as one detective said, "forty miles wide and one inch deep." In fact, Ray had already decided that he'd had it with the state police. He was planning to put in his retirement papers the next year.

Freeburn was a forty-five-minute drive away, but Ray was glad that he took the time to indulge himself on a hunch. It seemed that the missing woman had enemies. She had worked as an informant and put one local boy in the penitentiary. Yes, she had run off before, but she always called to check on her two small children, who were with their father. He was also interested to hear that the missing woman had been over to the Health Center behind the courthouse a couple of weeks earlier for a pregnancy test—and had named as the father FBI special agent Mark Putnam. The sister evidently hated Putnam, from what Ray could tell, even though she had only spoken to him on the phone. Shelby explained that the other Pikeville FBI man, Ron Poole, had checked Susan into the Landmark motel so that she could confront Putnam with the bad news. And then she had disappeared.

Ray was a taciturn man, with eyes that betrayed no surprise, a man who saw no need to punctuate conversation with anything more than a nod. He took down Shelby's information, thanked her, and said he would be back in touch.

Ray knew Mark Putnam slightly. He thought of him mostly as a typical FBI man who had been taught never to trust the local cops. On the other hand, he had run into him on enough major investigations to regard him, if only grudgingly, as a hard worker who wasn't afraid to get his hands dirty. If he had to sum Putnam up in one word, from what little he knew at that point, the word would have been *overzealous*. But then that was how he would have described himself when he'd first started out as a state cop in Harlan County more than thirty years earlier.

On Monday, Mark was out of town serving a subpoena. The next day, Ray and another state police detective, Kenneth Sloan, found him at the federal building for a pretrial hearing on the case. During lunch break, they borrowed an empty office and spoke informally for about an hour.

Ray gave Mark a copy of the missing person's report. Mark read it quickly and saw that the document had only routine information—vital statistics, the fact that Shelby had last seen Susan in Freeburn on June 5 (that would have been the night before she first came to his room), that her dental and medical records were available, and where. In the space beside the words *Tattoos or Deformities*, he saw that Ray had printed *None* but added, between tactful parentheses, *5 months pregnant*.

Watching him, Ray thought that Mark was nervous but cooperative—a little too cooperative. He was all over the field, and the detective had to scribble fast to get everything down:

> *Agent Putnam told me . . . he knew Susan Smith and that she was a witness against Carl "Cat Eyes" Lockhart in the bank robbery trial. He said that Lockhart's girlfriend, Sherri*

Justice, had beaten up Susan while Susan's brother watched.
Putnam said that he had talked to Susan's husband, Kenneth
Smith, about being an informant against Lockhart. He said
that Kenneth demanded money and probation on a drug
charge and he would not deal with him. Susan had been paid
money for being a witness. Putnam said that Kenneth came
for Susan's $200 one day and he ran him off as Susan had
said not to give it to Kenneth. Susan was paid about $9,000
for being a witness and an informant.

According to Ray's report, Mark told him, "Kenneth would call me and complain about how we used Susan. Kenneth called my wife and told her I was fucking Susan. Susan talked to my wife and denied it. Susan was trying to help Agent Ron Poole with some drug buys."

Mark described to the two state detectives Susan's dependency on him and Kathy. He said that the last significant work Susan had done for him was in the fall, but that they had stayed in touch afterward and had spoken on the telephone a few times after he went to Florida.

Mark also told the detective that he had spoken with Susan at the Landmark several times during the week before she disappeared—once in his room—about "her problems." He said they discussed the possibility of her having an abortion, and that he had offered to help her find the money for it. She did not want to have an abortion, Mark said.

He said that the last time he spoke with Susan was about ten-thirty on Wednesday night when she phoned his room after he got back from his meeting in Lexington and asked him to join her in the lounge for a drink. He told her he was too tired and had to be up early. She then told him about a "strange phone call" she had received about a meeting in West Virginia in a few days with drug contacts, "some guys from Chicago, the amigos," she called them. She described one as a "Spanish cop" from Cicero. Mark said that she declined his offer to follow her to the meeting "in case of trouble."

Why was Susan at the motel in the first place? Mark told the detectives that Poole brought her there "to do some undercover work" for him.

Did Mark know she was pregnant? He knew she was saying so, he said, because she had told him herself just before he transferred to Florida. Had she told him that he was the father? No, he replied. Furthermore, he wondered if Susan really was pregnant, since she didn't appear to be showing. "I tried to feel her stomach at the motel, but she jumped away," he said. Did she ever tell him who the father was? "No," said Mark. "She wouldn't tell me."

So he hadn't seen her after the Wednesday-night phone call? No, Mark said. Charlie Trotter told him that Susan had checked out of the motel at the end of the week. He hadn't heard from her since, although he knew that Ron Poole was making inquiries, trying to find her. Mark offered to do whatever he could to help.

Mark sensed Ray's antagonism, but that was nothing especially remarkable. The detective had always been cool toward him, and Mark guessed that Shelby had amply filled Ray in on Susan's claims about their relationship.

Trying to be helpful, Mark described his whereabouts not only on the night Susan left the motel but also on the following night, Friday, when he said he had gone to the movies.

"What did you see?" Ray asked with casual interest.

With equal casualness, Mark replied, "Something called *Road House* or *Rock House*, something like that. Patrick Swayze was in it."

When Ray made a few more notes at the end of their conversation, Mark cast a quick glance and saw that the detective had jotted down the name of the movie.

The conversation with Putnam gave Detective Ray a lot to consider, not the least of which was the extent to which Susan had been dependent on the largess of the FBI. Everybody in Pike County knew that the FBI had money to pay for information, but Ray was surprised to hear Mark confirm that Susan had received at least $9,000. In fact, he was disgusted. Here was the FBI man—with a salary roughly equivalent to a state police captain's—peeling off big bills to coddle informants while he, a state police detective often working the same cases, had to go hat in hand to his boss for permission to put a couple of hundred extra miles a week on his police vehicle, even when he was working the extra hours on his own time.

For his part, Mark was puzzled by what he regarded as diffident questioning on the part of the detectives. He fretted over the encounter, unable to decide what he would have done if they had asked him directly, "Did you have anything to do with this girl's disappearance?"

He thought that his answer might have been, "Yes."

What if they had then asked, "Did you kill her?" He tried to be honest with himself, but his mind was swimming with thoughts of guilt and survival. Before he fell into a feverish sleep, he decided that his answer, then and there, might have been, "Yes; yes, I did." But perhaps he was deceiving himself. At any rate, they hadn't asked.

Mark flew back to Florida a few days later. Then a coal-mine strike in Pike County turned violent, with gunshots fired at trucks, and Ray was barely able to keep track of the Susan Smith case during the commotion. On June 23, Ray did manage to get a few hours free to sit down with Ron Poole at a sandwich shop on Main Street. Curiously, Poole claimed that he had been concerned about Susan's assertions that she felt threatened by both her ex-husband

and by outlaws in the Tug Valley who vowed retribution for her work as an informant. So Poole, who was by this time making his sexual intentions toward Susan clear, at least to her experienced eye, claimed that registering her at the Landmark would be a good way to keep her in sight and look after her. But he said that his main reason for putting her in the motel was to give her and his ex-partner Mark the opportunity to discuss this business about her being pregnant. Poole said he had hoped they could "work this out," because, frankly, he was "tired of hearing about it" in Pikeville from Susan while Mark enjoyed the good life in Florida.

Poole, too, seemed to be excessively helpful. He even suggested that Mark would come back to Pikeville to take a polygraph test "whenever we need him to." That struck the detective as a fine idea.

After his brief conversation with Poole, Ray studied his notes. It was possible that the two agents simply saw the situation differently, and of course there was the sensitive matter of the pregnancy and the bureau's well-known proclivity for protecting its ass, not to mention the ill-defined undercover operation that Susan was apparently talking about to everybody she knew. Local cops never expected to hear the full story from the FBI. Maybe they had stashed her in the witness protection program, although Ray couldn't imagine that this particular source had information momentous enough to earn that kind of treatment. What's more, Poole had denied it.

Another complication was Susan's reputation. Even Shelby, worried as she plainly was, conceded that Susan was a loose cannon, a woman who had run off in the past without telling anyone where she was going. Besides, hadn't Susan in her excitement about being an FBI criminal informant prattled on about the possibility that, if things got too hot for her in the mountain belt, Mark would recommend her as a candidate for the federal Witness Protection Program? In fact, Susan had not been lying about that. She and Mark had at least tentatively discussed that possibility, which was open to any person whose work as an informant for the bureau put them in a position where they were in grave danger from retribution.

Still, Ray couldn't put out of his mind how effusively helpful Putnam had been in providing details of his activities. *Too many details.* He wondered if he would have time to see which of them didn't check out.

Ray found the maid who had worked the second floor of the Landmark that week. She told him that the woman in Room 224 had kept mostly to her room, watching television all day with the door bolted. She had not seen her with anyone. Her checkout bill, which Poole had paid with his American Express card, showed that she ordered room service and ate in her room. Nothing extravagant—$9 one day, $10 another—certainly nothing to indicate that she was entertaining visitors. There were a couple of short local calls, and three long-distance calls to her sister in Freeburn, two of them on the morning of the day she disappeared, just as the sister had said. The maid had collected a few of Susan's clothes, including a pair of shorts, her purse, and some makeup that she had left behind and taken them down to the lobby. The fat FBI man took them with him when he paid the bill, which came to $251.46.

As a matter of standard procedure, Ray took the shorts and other items and labeled them as possible evidence.

Ray finally raised his concerns with his superiors in July nagged by the worry that he was missing something obvious, and frustrated by his inability to spend any time on the case. He was convinced it was time to formally question Putnam with regard to what he knew about Susan's disappearance. But he was told that there were probably better things he could be doing with his time as an investigator. Putnam had long since left town; there would be no state police junkets authorized to Miami, of all places, not without a good goddamned reason. Besides, wasn't the bureau itself looking into it? Wasn't Poole making his own investigation? Why waste time on a routine missing persons case?

The girl was wild, Ray was told again and again when he asked questions out on Peter Creek and in Freeburn. So what if an FBI agent or two had screwed her? Hadn't she run away before? Hadn't she always turned up? And if she were double-crossing a drug operation, she'd turn up for sure—in the morgue in Cincinnati or Chicago.

Yes, he thought. That much was probably true.

When August rolled around, there still was no sign of her. But Ray had only speculation, innuendo, and instinct to go on. If there had been any sort of unpleasant confrontation between the missing woman and either of the FBI men, he could find no one at the Landmark who knew about it. No one had seen Susan and Putnam together on either the day she disappeared or the day before; moreover, Charlie Trotter and another man staying at the motel who talked to Putnam that week said that Mark had made it clear he was doing everything he could to avoid her. Reasonable enough, Ray thought, since she was accusing him of getting her pregnant and running off. Furthermore, if they *did* have a confrontation—and from what Shelby had said, Susan was looking for one—Ray had found no one who saw or heard it.

The complications troubled him. He tried to separate what little he actually knew from the nagging suspicion that something was very wrong. A poor mountain girl who has been on the FBI payroll as an informant—something near $10,000, maybe more—turns up missing. From the way it looks, she and this FBI man were involved; she gets knocked up, he's gone to Florida with the wife and kids. He comes back to town on government business; the FBI sets her up in the same motel. *The FBI sets her up in the same motel with this guy who doesn't have any further government business with her?* And she turns up missing.

But the FBI man isn't the only one this girl has been involved with. To hear people tell it, she gets around pretty good. She is also a wildcat who fights at the drop of a hat, and just before her disappearance, she gets coldcocked by the girlfriend of the bank robber that she sent to the penitentiary. She turns up missing.

Furthermore, he thought, this is a girl messed up bad on drugs, whose ex-husband beats her up, not to mention the other enemies she has obviously made, being an informant out on Peter Creek where mountain people tend to frown on such things. Besides that, she has been known to run with a bad crowd out of Cincinnati and Chicago in the past and has supposedly been in contact with some of that crowd recently. And her sister Shelby Jean, who has had her own run-ins with Susan, and who is nervous about her working as an informant, takes a phone message for the girl while she's in the Pikeville motel at the FBI's expense. The message is that she is supposed to meet some drug dealers on Saturday at a rendezvous in West Virginia. On Friday, she turns up missing.

Assuming something bad happened to her, Ray thought, that made for a fair number of suspects. Even in normal circumstances, the first suspect was always the husband or ex-husband or boyfriend. And here was an ex-husband who abused her and whom she keeps going back to. That made one prime suspect. Then there were the drug dealers she was supposedly going to see. Add the bank robber's girlfriend, the bank robber's buddies, any other outlaws she'd informed on—not to mention Poole, the sister herself, and maybe even some still-unidentified pillar of the Pikeville community whom she'd tried to shake down in a motel. Hell, even without Putnam, that was already a regular damn Las Vegas chorus line of star suspects—assuming she hadn't just run away.

And Ray had to assume first that she had, in-fact, merely left town on her own. What Ray couldn't quite understand was why, given that, given all of the other likely suspects if foul play were actually the case, the earnest, well-chiseled face of Mark Putnam stayed in his mind as if it were painted there.

Aside from his bosses at the state police post, the only other person Ray confided his suspicions to was Myra Chico, who was friends with most of the cops in town. One night when Myra was tending bar at the Log Cabin, they were talking about Susan Smith's disappearance, and Ray surprised her by saying, "I think Mark Putnam had something to do with it."

Myra laughed and said, "Richard, you're nuts!"

Ray didn't often say things twice. He shrugged and changed the subject.

11

The change from Pikeville to Miami had been abrupt. Overnight they'd traded the black and gray of an Appalachian late winter for the sudden Technicolor blare of southern Florida in spring.

"Daddy, you can see the sky all over," Danielle had exclaimed with childish delight from beside the pool of the residence hotel where the bureau had installed them while they looked for a new house. At four, she was already learning to read and write. Mark Jr., at sixteen months beginning to exhibit his father's dark good looks showed his appreciation for the improvement in scenery in a way that reminded Kathy of her husband—he'd simply hurl himself onto the thick rich grass beside the pool and roll around in it like a pooch freed from its kennel.

Kathy felt like a woman awakening from a trance. She thought of the joke about pounding your head against the wall because it feels so good when you stop. At once, she was renewed; she felt young again, not haggard and ashen as she had been in the last months in Kentucky. The troubles in Pikeville swirled out of mind.

Only the phone calls intruded, and these she accepted with the mild annoyance of someone fending off telephone sales solicitations. Soon after they left, whenever Susan called for Mark, as she did several times a week, Kathy exchanged a few arm's-length pleasantries, handed the phone to Mark, and walked away to do other things.

There was plenty to do. It fell largely to her to settle her family into a new home, a task that she threw herself into with verve. Mark had a new job to acclimate himself to, and old business in Kentucky to finish. She figured that after the chop-shop trial, Pikeville and all that went with it, not the least of which was Susan, would be history, to be filed away with her old calendars.

For the first time, she felt like part of the "FBI family" that she had read about in orientation brochures from the academy. Mark finally had bosses, colleagues, and a support system at work. With help from the bureau's relocation office, she quickly found a house, a three-bedroom condominium in a new subdivision beside a canal. The town, Sunrise, lay at the western edge of the coastal sprawl, on the fringes of the Everglades, but still only a forty-five-minute commute from the FBI office in North Miami Beach.

And then, in June, the phone calls from Susan had stopped. With so much emotional and physical distance between them, Kathy accepted the news of her disappearance impassively. She had done her best with Susan, who never listened. If Susan had taken off for Chicago or Cincinnati, as Kathy assumed she had, the futility of what she had tried to do was another unpleasant memory to forget about and write off to experience.

So eager was she to embrace a new life that Kathy failed to calculate the emotional distance that still separated her from Mark. He was the more sensitive, introspective one, and the one who had shouldered most of the burden; she figured he required more time to rejuvenate than she did. In her elation, she discounted a number of signs that her husband was deeply troubled in the summer of 1989. He wasn't sleeping or eating normally. Sometimes she would wake in the night aware that he lay beside her motionless and alert. He was losing weight, and he had developed a nervous habit of scratching at his chest, to the point where a raw patch of skin appeared on his sternum.

These symptoms she attributed partly to Mark's anxiety about establishing himself in a new job in a competitive and hierarchical work environment. And the echoes from Pikeville hadn't totally ceased with the end of Susan's calls. Poole still checked in, usually with word that nothing had been heard of Susan. Myra Chico also called from time to time to pass on Pikeville gossip, but Kathy made it clear to Mark that she had little interest in it.

One night in the summer, after speaking with Poole, Mark abruptly mentioned to Kathy that Susan had been saying that she was pregnant right before she disappeared. "So who's the father?" Kathy said with a trace of sarcasm Mark shrugged his shoulders.

She found his diffidence irritating. "When are you going to put that behind you?" she demanded. "Forget about Susan. She isn't your problem anymore."

"How can I?" he said almost plaintively.

"Look, if she's still missing, the next thing you know, Mark, you could be pulled into this. She could be lying dead somewhere."

His face darkened and he replied quietly, without meeting her eyes, "Don't ever say that."

Kathy believed that, Mark's sluggish recovery aside, they had settled in happily. The cost of living in south Florida was higher than Kentucky; with Mark earning $33,000 a year, a little more with overtime, they had to make the money stretch, which Kathy always knew how to do. To put a little aside for their next summer vacation, she took a part-time job on Saturday and Sunday mornings, waiting tables at an International House of Pancakes near Fort Lauderdale. One of the waitresses she met there was a woman with two children and a husband in prison. When Kathy told Mark how sorry she felt for her, he looked away and changed the subject.

For Mark, there were many such moments as he contemplated the calamity that he knew lay ahead. In retrospect, he would wonder how he managed to fool anybody during that time as he waited for what he knew was the inevitable moment when he would either be caught or give up. "My insides were frazzled," he recalled.

Outwardly, he projected a sense of purpose. It helped that the work in the Miami Bureau was nearly as fast-paced as it had been in Pikeville, with the huge difference that he was not off on his own. The new environment offered both the collegiality of a large group of fellow cops and the reassurance, at least in those unguarded moments when he focused on the job and not on his secret, of being adequately supervised. For once, Mark felt he didn't have to make it up as he went along. He appreciated his circumstances with a sense of poignancy, aware that they would last only until he was exposed.

Nevertheless, he impressed his bosses. Without exception, his supervisors in Miami regarded him as likable, talented, and extraordinarily hardworking. In many ways, with his steady demeanor, polished manners, physical bravery, and good looks, Mark represented the FBI's image of itself, and in retrospect, it would help to explain why the bureau would be almost the last to believe the worst about him. In Miami, it was obvious to everyone except Mark himself that the young agent had a bright future in the FBI.

At several times during the year Mark believed his time was up.

Not long after he got back from Pikeville, on July 5, the day after his thirtieth birthday, he was summoned to the office of the top man in the Miami Bureau, the special agent in charge, William Gavin. But instead of arresting him, Gavin slid a memo across the desk from Louis DeFalaise, the US attorney for eastern Kentucky. It read in part:

I want to formally express to you our thanks and appreciation for the work and assistance of Special Agent Mark Putnam of your Miami office. Special Agent Putnam, prior to assignment to your office, was in the Federal Bureau of Investigation office in Pikeville, Kentucky. While that was his first office assignment, you would not know it.

While he was there only two years, his reputation for hard and diligent work left its mark in the area. Our office had the pleasure of working closely with him during his tenure and I can say confidently that he is a unique Special Agent whose career with the bureau will be long and fruitful.

I want to specifically call your attention to the excellent job he just completed leading up to the successful conviction of seven defendants in the case of U.S. v Vernon Andrew Mullins et al. . . . Special Agent Putnam was involved from its inception in the investigation of a multistate "chop-shop" operation centered in a remote section of eastern Kentucky. Following the execution of a state search warrant which uncovered the remains of millions of dollars of trucks and truck parts, Mark worked with one of our assistants in identifying the vehicles, tracking down the owners and ownership documents and preparing the case for trial. As stated, all seven defendants were convicted on a thirty-eight-count indictment. . . . Special Agent Putnam's in-depth knowledge of the case was primarily responsible for the government being successful in its case. He worked long hours and weekends assisting our office in preparing and presenting this case. Without his hard work and dedication, the result would not have been so satisfactory.

*Special Agent Putnam's departure has left a real void,
which will be hard to replace. You have gained a topflight
agent in Miami in Mark Putnam, one who exemplifies the
dedication and professionalism of a fine Special Agent. Please
convey to him our devout appreciation for his service to eastern Kentucky and to our office.*

Not long afterward, in August, Mark had another scare when he
answered his beeper on the street and got a message to contact his
supervisor immediately.

Feeling sick, he found a pay phone and called the office.

But his immediate boss, the supervisor of his squad, an agent
named Roy Tubergen, came on the line laughing. "Hey, you know
two good old boys named Hatfield and McCoy?"

"Yeah, I know them."

"That really their names?"

Mark sighed with great relief. "Yeah. Like the feud. Why? What
did they do?"

"Well, they stopped by here to see you. I'll tell them you're on
your way in."

Paul Hatfield and Fred McCoy, eyes wide with sleeplessness,
had driven all night to get to Florida. For months, they'd been
working together to expose corruption in the Pike County sheriff's office, which they knew was an issue Mark had planned to
press hard on before the transfer out of Pikeville. As part of their
investigation, they said they had had spent days at work wearing
hidden recorders, taping literally everything that was said. For
good measure, they had also videotaped each other reading long
statements about county funds being misused to buy campaign
hats and badges.

In Pikeville, with their evidence stacked up like the Watergate
transcripts, they had called a press conference to denounce the

sheriff's department as "a small Mafia" and the sheriff himself, a man named Fuzzee Kessee, as "the godfather." A few days later, Hatfield and McCoy were summarily fired. Announcing that they feared for their lives, the two then boxed up their tapes and drove straight through to Miami, where they had never been before.

"You're the only one we can trust with this material, Mark," said Hatfield, pulling at a long beard.

"Wait a minute," Mark said, not wanting even temporary custody of their cache of evidence. "I don't have responsibility for that stuff anymore!"

While they waited, their eyes darting anxiously around the bustling Miami FBI office, Mark called Tom Self in Lexington to ask for advice.

"Tom, you're not going to believe this. Paul Hatfield and Fred McCoy—"

"Tell me they're not down there," Self groaned.

"They're here. With a suitcase full of tapes that I don't want to listen to and I don't even want to touch."

Self told him to send the material to Lexington.

Hatfield and McCoy drove back home immediately to follow up.

Mark's fellow agents hooted and razzed him about the episode, and the following day, when he came in to work, one of them had on a big straw hat with a corncob pipe between his teeth. Mark chuckled in a good-natured way, but it bothered him. He had worked hard to fit in in eastern Kentucky, and he had succeeded. Hatfield and McCoy and the others were more than caricatures to him; even *hillbilly* had an ugly sting to it, like *dago* or *spic*.

In September, Mark and a colleague from Miami were sent to New York City for a few days to trade information on an undercover case with agents in the Manhattan office. After going to a Yankees game with a group of agents after work one night, Mark returned to his hotel and found an urgent message to call Lou DeFalaise at home "no matter what the time." Figuring that this was it, with a shaking finger Mark tapped out the phone number for the US Attorney in eastern Kentucky. As he heard the phone ringing, he steeled himself, *it's all over. He wants to tell me as a courtesy that I'm about to be arrested.*

DeFalaise was plainly agitated. "Mark, what the hell is going on? All hell is breaking loose here."

Mark felt tears well in his eyes, until he realized that the federal prosecutor wasn't talking about Susan Smith. He was talking about the antics of Hatfield and McCoy, who had called another press conference—this time to accuse the US attorney's office of seeking to cover up their investigation.

Still shaking, Mark gave DeFalaise his assessment of the situation, which was that as diligent as Hatfield and McCoy were in tape-recording everything spoken, they really didn't have a case. And authorities apparently concurred because no action was taken against the sheriff. DeFalaise thanked him cordially. Mark put the phone down and slumped in his chair.

While there was a new camaraderie in Mark's work life, there were no close friendships. He declined invitations to dinner, cookouts, and drinks after work. He was afraid to make friends. His time was running out, and he did not want to embarrass any other agent who might have the misfortune to be close to him when the end came. As a consequence, some of his new colleagues in Miami saw him as aloof. To others, he was quiet, diligent, careful, and dependable—a good team player, a man who could be trusted in all circumstances, but still, a hard man to get to know.

One of the agents who worked with him on a five-person undercover operation against a ring of property thieves tried to get close and failed. In fact, Mark liked this agent enormously—for his honesty, tenacity, and sense of humor. On several occasions, most notably on an all-night surveillance job when he relaxed enough to regale his companion with stories of Kentucky law and order, Mark had to restrain the impulse to confide in him about Susan. Bitterly, he withdrew from the incipient friendship, thinking, *Can I put him in that position, being a friend to the guy who's about to be a pariah? Do I even have the right to have a friend?*

The year was full of painful irony. Once, he and Kathy invited a young agent from the office who was having personal difficulties to dinner at their house. Warmed by the glow of affection and security he had felt in the Putnam household, unaware of just how fragile it was, the agent told everybody he saw in the office the next day what a wonderful time he'd had.

"This guy has everything—a beautiful wife, good looks, two beautiful kids, a great job," he told a group of colleagues, clapping a hand on Mark's shoulder when he came by. "What more could a man want?"

Mark's heart sank. "Everybody has their problems, John," he said, smiling wanly.

If only they knew, he thought. He had lost fifteen pounds since the summer. Nearly every day he had diarrhea. Nights were worse. He was afraid to go to sleep He did not know if or when he would confess. He always assumed they would find Susan and arrest him, and he was bewildered that so much time was passing without any indication that an end was in sight. Again and again, he replayed the scenario until he was convinced that he believed it. They would come to him and ask, "*Did you do this?*" In his mind, he always gave them the same reply, without hesitation: "Yes."

In the winter of 1990, Kathy's younger sister, Chris, who had been living near Miami, came to stay with the Putnams temporarily while she was going through a divorce. Chris, as easygoing and laconic as Kathy was intense and expressive, admired Mark very much. He had helped her to find a job as an officer with the Florida Marine Patrol. She regarded him as an ideal husband and father who had become almost a big brother to her. When she'd visited Mark and Kathy in Pikeville, she had known that their life was difficult and stressful. In Florida, she didn't notice anything alarming about the way Mark was behaving.

As she later recalled, "Mark was kind of hyper anyway, not in an odd sense, but just a real active guy. He ran every night without fail. If he was watching television, he was also reading a book at the same time. When he and my sister first got together, he always had two jobs. All the time I knew him, he was always working. The only thing unusual in Florida was he had developed this nervous habit, this scratching at his chest. I thought he was like anxious to get back to work."

One other thing she noticed was that he bought several newspapers a day and flipped through them methodically, as if looking for something small—always first checking the pages that had state-by-state news items in *USA Today*.

"Why's he read all those papers?" Chris asked Kathy once with a laugh. "Don't they all have the same news in them?"

Passing time burnished Mark's nerve. He wondered how long he could wait. He still heard from Poole often, but Poole had his own anxieties about Susan, who had told people that she slept with him, too. Baffled as to what had happened to Susan, perhaps suspecting that Mark knew more than he let on, Poole told Mark of Richard Ray's request, unsuccessful so far, that the two of them be given polygraph tests.

"Ron, I don't care," Mark said boldly. "I'll take their polygraph."

Poole replied, "I'll take one, too. I don't give a shit what these hillbillies do." And he added, "Well, buddy, you and I got to stick together on this thing."

What thing? Mark thought contemptuously. What did his ex-partner feel he had to hide? It was almost amusing to think that Poole was worried. For the first time, Mark felt that he had the advantage in these verbal jousts. If Susan turned up dead, whose problem was it going to be?

Still, Mark resisted the urge to probe for information on the investigation that he knew was going on in Pikeville. He did not know much about it and didn't ask, preferring to be seen not as disinterested but as disengaged. With Myra Chico he remained circumspect, afraid that if he gave any indication that he was worried, that anxiety would be conveyed to the state police.

Had they found the body? That was the main thing he didn't know. Stubbornly, he didn't ask. Still, how could it *not* have been found, lying there just out of sight in a place where people came by on horses and trucks, where kids ran their dirt bikes up and down the ridge? Maybe they had found the body and were keeping it quiet, building their case. Every time the phone rang, he jumped.

He did not expect any respite from the obsession. Susan was the first thing he thought of every day: she flashed into his mind as if a switch were thrown the moment he awoke, and she stayed there until he managed to fail asleep at night. To live with himself, he had settled on a term to describe what had happened, as if supplying the kicker to a headline: *tragic accident.*

There were frequent reminders of what he had already lost. The most painful came when Tubergen took him aside one afternoon to ask if he would consider a transfer to a smaller office elsewhere in Florida, where he would be promoted to a supervisory rank. It was an invitation onto the management track. But what would have been fabulous news to the man who had dreamed about a career in the FBI since high school now had a bitter sting. Mark mentioned the overture to Kathy, but told her that he had turned it down because they had just gotten settled and the kids were thriving in their new home. He said he didn't want to see his family uprooted again so soon. In his mind, he knew that he was protecting the bureau from the further public disgrace of having a supervisor led away in cuffs.

While he waited for time to pass, he thought often of the father he had revered. The man had exuded dignity, even during a tragic and prolonged death from cancer in middle age. In a way that he could not quite articulate, Mark had believed it was his responsibility to ratify his father's memory. But, instead, as he had always secretly feared he would, he had disgraced it forever.

There had been times during the year when he had edged toward confession and pulled back. As early as September, he had told Tubergen about the rumors in Kentucky that he had been sexually involved with an informant who was now listed as missing. Mark asked Tubergen if he would contact OPR, the Office of Professional Responsibility, the Justice Department's internal affairs unit with supervision over the FBI, and request them to investigate the disappearance of Susan Smith to "clear up" the ambiguities associated with his relationship to the missing woman.

Literally, he was told not to make a federal case out of it. A missing persons case was a state police matter. The rumors had already filtered down to Miami through the FBI grapevine, where discreet inquiries had been made to assure supervisors that Susan Smith was the sort of woman who ran with a dangerous crowd and had gone off before. Mark was seen as naïve and excessively punctilious, a young man who had been through a tough tour of duty in a rough place and had acquitted himself with honor and distinction, even if he had stupidly become involved with an informant. He was a man above suspicion.

Besides, Mark was told, he was due for a promotion in grade, which would mean a higher salary. An open OPR investigation, no matter how pro forma, would put that on hold.

Once, while leaving for work, Mark looked up to see his daughter gazing at him from her bedroom window. She met his eyes and held them in her gaze, and he thought then that she knew something was very wrong.

He thought, *How can I face her day after day, year after year, knowing what I know? What kind of a father can I be to her?*

Sometimes, he would pretend that it had not happened. He would place himself ten or fifteen years into the future. He would still be in Florida, a good, solid, low-profile agent who knew all the ropes. He would be at his desk reading a case file, the family portrait propped beside the phone. Danielle, a young woman now, as pretty and smart as her mother, would pop in unexpectedly to ask him to lunch as his colleagues watched with envy.

Or he'd spend the day with little Mark, an adolescent now allowing him to play hooky from high school on the opening day of spring training. In the bleachers, they would feel the hot sun on their necks as they argued about the new crop of pitchers.

Or he thought of himself with Kathy, middle-aged and still in love, strolling south Miami Beach. In a gentle ocean breeze they would hold hands and look at the lights strung along the low-roofed art deco hotels on the strand. He would guide her body toward his. They'd mold perfectly, as they always had. Their lips would meet, their tongues touch. He'd feel her breasts against his chest. She'd arch her long back slightly in his arms as they looked for a deserted place on the beach.

Relentlessly, he supervised these three daydreams like a movie director who is never satisfied with the take. Again and again he replayed the same scenes in his head, varying the nuance and inflection, as if he needed to get them perfect before fixing them in his mind.

Running was a way to pass through time without thinking. For a while, he hadn't been able to do even that. "When I got back to Florida after Susan's death, I stopped running for a while," Mark would later recall. "I was afraid to go out, to be alone. Especially at night. I was even afraid of a dark room."

In time, he forced himself to overcome his fear and go out to run every night. The wind blew away everything but the churning of the legs, the pumping of the arms and lungs. His regular nightly route took him along a remote stretch of road, beyond a canal at the edge of swampland. On that stretch one night, he tripped and fell. Scraped and bruised, he sat on the ground, arms clenching his knees, and cried.

"The day of reckoning is coming, Susan," he said aloud to the black sky. "It is. I promise."

By the winter, he reached the point where he realized his guilt was diminishing his effectiveness as an agent:

He had been investigating a major organized theft ring operating out of the Port of Miami, a bazaar of criminal activity. Laboriously working informants and poring over insurance records, he made inroads until finally he had a suspect in a major insurance-fraud case, a businessman named Tito who was as arrogant as he was crafty. If he broke, Tito would lead to bigger fish, Mark knew.

Mark stopped at Tito's computer-parts business in Miami one day and told him, "Listen, pal, I'm on to your sorry ass, and I'm going to see you again."

"No problem," Tito said in his singsong voice.

Finally Mark had enough evidence to nail the man, who was just arrogant enough to try to bluff his way through a polygraph and take questions afterward.

"Listen, I've got you by the short hairs on this thing, man," Mark said as they sat alone at a conference table in the office. "I've got documents here, with your fingerprints on the documents. You took a lie detector test and flunked it. That's not admissible, I'll give you that, but it's important because it confirms to me that you are lying. The people who receive my report will know that you did it, and continuing to lie to me will only make it worse."

Insulted, Tito insisted that he had not lied. The machine may have lied, but he never did.

Assuming the frown of a suspicious tax auditor, Mark opened his thick folder and turned pages slowly, occasionally grunting at something he pretended to read. Out of the corner of his eye, he noticed Tito was unconsciously telegraphing the classic signs of a worried man—clearing his throat, squirming, brushing imaginary dust from the table, swinging his feet slightly but hastily, as if they would propel him right out the door if they touched the rug.

Mark heard the telltale sound of a sniffle and looked up expectantly. Tito met his eyes and said, arrogance now gone, "I got a business, man. I got a wife and kid. You know how those guys down the Port are. They can lean on you pretty good."

"I know what you're going through," Mark said sympathetically, thinking how nice it was to actually have a textbook example of what they taught in the academy about how to usher a wavering suspect into a confession:

You aren't the typical criminal. You seem like a man under terrible pressure. Nobody is perfect—if the perfect person walks into this conference room, we will both get down on our knees. This is probably the first time you have done something like this. You can stop with this. Did you know that eighty-five percent of people who deal with merchandise steal something at some point? You seem to be basically an honest man, a man like you said, with a wife and kid that you obviously love. You've probably been dealt a pretty bad hand. I've always been curious about what motivates a person to do something they do not feel is right. What caused you to do something so dumb? You're an intelligent man, you got in a jam. But could you put your arm around your kid right now and feel right? You can make this right. Ever since the pencil was invented there have been erasers on it.

Tito started crying.

Mark looked at him with disgust that slowly curled inward as he thought, *I'm busting this guy's ass for some lousy computers. Who the hell am I? I killed somebody. There's a body out there with the bugs and snakes and whatever else is in those hills. There are two kids who don't know where their mother is because of me.*

"Tito, get the fuck out of here. I don't want to see you again," Mark said abruptly, standing up.

Tito was stunned. "What do you mean, man?"

"Tito, go home. I don't give a shit what you do. Just leave me the hell alone."

Tito's feet found the floor. He backed out of the office like a court attendant and practically ran to his car in the lot.

Later that day, an agent Mark passed in the hall said by way of greeting, "How you behaving, Mark?"

"Above reproach," he said quietly.

Each day he awoke more secure in his assumption that the body had not been found, and despising himself more for his cowardice. The diarrhea persisted. His urine had blood in it. He was haggard and sour. This could not go on, and yet it did.

One morning, Kathy heard him muttering in the bathroom. She called from the bedroom, "What did you say, honey?"

Standing at the mirror, he replied, "I said, 'Good morning, killer.'"

12

No one looking for Susan Smith could have anticipated how many tiny threads of her life she had left tangled.

One of the first calls Richard Ray made when he began his investigation was to the man who was the source of the mysterious phone message for Susan at the Landmark. This man was not in fact the drug contact from Cicero that she had been telling Mark and Poole about. It was another one, an old contact, a man from Milwaukee.

No, he told the detective, he had not met Susan the weekend after she disappeared. In fact, she never returned his phone call. The man said that Kenneth had called him the next week, looking for her. Then an FBI man also called.

Ray ventured a guess. "Poole? Ron Poole?"

"Yeah, something like that. FBI."

"Not Putnam?"

"No, the other one you said. Poole."

This should have been an indication that the FBI was investigating, but like everything else in this case, the answers were ambiguous. The FBI generally declines to confirm or deny whether it is investigating, but Ray had determined informally that there was no "active" investigation into the case.

What then was Poole doing? The way Shelby told it, Mark Putnam's ex-partner was persistent and involved. She told Ray that she had been talking to Poole almost every day. She said Poole told her that while Susan was at the motel, he took her with him one day to serve warrants. Shelby also said that Susan had mentioned that she might be spending a day with Mark in Virginia, also serving warrants.

And then there was Susan's brother, Bo, who appeared to be running his own independent investigation, questioning people who knew Susan, even trailing people he thought looked suspicious across the Tug into West Virginia. Bo wasn't sure what had happened. When pressed, he couldn't even say for sure that there had been a sexual relationship between his sister and Mark.

"They would keep it secret," he would later explain to authorities. "She was coming out here in front and calling him, and he was meeting her out back at the parking lot. And they would go and stay gone for two or three hours at a time."

What, Ray had to wonder, was *Bo* up to?

Ray worked quietly and moved easily among a great range of ordinary people: motel clerks, librarians, secretaries, truckers, drifters, outlaws behaving themselves between felonies—all felt comfortable with him because he didn't come on like a cop or a reporter: Gossiping with people outside a lunch counter, usually saying little himself, he kept track of the social undercurrents of the Peter Creek communities. Usually, he could get a fairly good line on current events.

Susan Smith was a tough one, though, because there were so many conflicting opinions about her. Everyone in Freeburn knew that she'd fight at the drop of a hat, that she was a heavy drug user, that she had a mouth on her, that she did outrageous things such as the time she went over to the car lot and mooned Bert and his friends. He also heard about the time she'd gone to the federal courthouse and lifted up her shirt to flash her boobs at the boys in the marshal's office.

But there was another side to this woman that took a little more patience and trouble to find. She seemed also to be someone who always picked up a phone and called when she was away. Up the hollow at Barrenshee, Susan's mother, Tracy, said that Susan never forgot to send a birthday card, Christmas card, Mother's Day card—"no matter where she was living." In Phelps, the high school principal, Beth Compton, had known Susan since she was in sixth grade at the old Freeburn school. She described her as "a young girl who fought her way through life. She had to struggle for everything she ever had in a world where a girl's greatest ambition was to get married and have children." But she also recalled a transformation in Susan when she came back home after those years living in the city. Then, she said, "Susie had suddenly developed into a strikingly attractive young woman who projected poise." And, at least when Compton saw her with her two children, Susan appeared to be "an interested and concerned mother."

Something was not adding up.

The rumor mill of Peter Creek, which had ground along chronically malfunctioning since the days of the Hatfield–McCoy feud, also made it difficult to sort out information. Every time it appeared as if Susan Smith was indeed missing, and possibly dead, another rumor seemed to pop up to throw the theory out of whack. Almost weekly, Ray drove out Peter Creek to check out the latest hearsay. Much of it was difficult to evaluate. Among the things he heard, from Shelby and others, was Susan's apocryphal tale of the Putnams' parrot. Ray also had to consider Shelby's wide-ranging speculations. Perhaps, Shelby had once mused, Susan had followed Mark down to Florida and was simply lying low waiting for him to leave his family and come to her. Or maybe she was temporarily and safely ensconced in the federal witness protection program, and could not reach out to anyone at home. Or maybe she had gone off to hide out with another sister, who lived in Texas.

A man in Turkey Creek named David Blankenship, whose deceased brother had been married to that sister, said that he, too, thought that might be where Susan was "because she was close to her sister and missed her." But he also reported that Kenneth had informed him that Susan "took off with a detective." Moreover, Blankenship said, he had heard that Susan recently went up to Cicero to get drugs and came home bragging that "she could sell all the drugs she wanted and not get busted" because the FBI was protecting her.

On August 8, Ray had called Shelby to get an update on the case, and she told him that a Phelps man named Johnny Stump had gotten a phone call from Susan. But when Ray drove out to see the man, that turned out not to have been the case. Stump explained Susan had once bought a 1979 Ford LTD from him and had not made the payments. He had filed a judgment against her, and she had failed to appear in court when the case came up two weeks, earlier. He complained about her, but he said he hadn't told anybody he'd heard from her.

Meanwhile, Shelby's husband, Ike, said that he had heard Susan say, on the night Ron Poole picked her up to take her to the Landmark, that she was actually going to stay for a few days at the house of a former sister-in-law, though he believed this to be another of Susan's stories.

Bewildered, Ray decided that Shelby ought to take a polygraph test, "to see if it was some kind of plot, if she knew where her sister was at." Shelby was insulted, but she complied. On August 22, she took the test and passed. The results showed that she didn't know where Susan was and that she was "very concerned, very worried about her." Moreover, she insisted that the people they ought to be strapping to the polygraph machine were Kenneth, Smith, and Mark Putnam.

This proved to be no easy chore. Ray and Paul Maynard went to Capt. Gary Rose, the commander of the Pikeville state police post, who in turn called Terry Hulse, Mark's former supervisor in Covington. But word came back that while the FBI would of course cooperate in any investigation to the extent it saw necessary, it saw no reason to involve an agent. "Polygraph the ex-husband," Captain Rose said he was told. "Maybe he had something to do with it."

The difficulties in tracking down Susan were compounded by the reports that she was involved with a drug gang. However, aside from Susan's own apparent exaggerations as she tried to get herself reactivated as an FBI informant after Mark was transferred, even if it meant she had to work with Poole, there was no indication that she was involved in anything much grander than petty local drug deals. "She was a known drug user and would on occasion sell drugs to support her own habit," Maynard said.

Meanwhile, Ray would later recall, "The FBI people just kept putting us off." Apparently they had talked to Mark about the investigation and had come to believe that "this is a plot by the people up there to discredit him, to cause him trouble." What Ray did not know was that in Miami, Mark Putnam had already approached his superiors and volunteered to take a lie detector test to clear up the matter, and they had told him he was being silly.

Kenneth Smith, who Susan had claimed had actually caused physical harm to her in the past, turned up in custody—his own. In October, Kenneth was sentenced to thirty days in jail for a series of motor vehicle violations. Because he was the sole guardian of the two children, seven-year-old Miranda and four-year-old Brady, the judge allowed him to serve an alternate ninety-day incarceration at his place in Freeburn. With an electronic device strapped to his leg to monitor his movements, Kenneth wasn't available to come to Pikeville to be polygraphed until January.

By then, Kenneth declared that he was making an effort to straighten himself out and provide a decent home for the children. He had a job as a night watchman at a strip-mining company. On January 12, Ray and Bert Hatfield called on Kenneth, who told them what they already knew, that he had been married to Susan for three and a half years until they were divorced six years ago, and that they had lived together off and on since then for the sake of the kids. According to Ray's notes, Kenneth said that Susan had been going to Pikeville frequently to see Mark and also, at times, to buy drugs.

Kenneth said that Susan "told me that she loved Mark and he loved her. I called Mark's wife and told her about it. Susan said she hoped Kathy would find out so she would leave Mark." In early June, he went on, "Susan spent a night with me and the kids. The next night she was at Shelby's, and around midnight, the FBI came and got her. I have not seen her since . . . Susan told me she was pregnant about three weeks before she left. She said she had discussed it with Mark and that he had agreed to help keep the baby up."

Asked if he had any idea where Susan was, Kenneth replied, "I think she is in Florida with Mark Putnam."

Ray suggested to Kenneth that he accompany them to Pikeville to take a lie detector test, and Kenneth readily agreed. Actually administering it successfully proved problematic, however. On January 16, Kenneth took the first polygraph test at the state police post in Pikeville. The operator, Charles Hines, believed that Kenneth was telling the truth when he said he knew nothing about what had happened to Susan, but it was difficult to get a good reading because of the chemicals in Kenneth's system.

"He's pretty bad hooked on drugs and we had a hard time," Ray reported afterward. After two inconclusive tests on successive days, Kenneth was kept overnight in a Pikeville motel under state police guard, "to try to straighten him up" for the next day's test. That test was not much more conclusive. Finally, Ray concluded what the machine could not. Kenneth apparently didn't have a clue.

And then it seemed again that Susan Smith had surfaced. In January, Shelby phoned Captain Rose at the state police barracks and said happily, "You can stop looking for Susan now.

"What do you mean?" said Rose.

"Josie Thorpe has gotten a call from her," Shelby declared. Thorpe was a fifty-two-year-old distant cousin whose rusted trailer sat on a wedge of land hacked into the low ridge on the road into Freeburn. Susan occasionally went to visit her and bring clothes.

Ray hurried out to Peter Creek, as Shelby was spreading the happy word that Susan had turned up after all. As usual, the detective stopped by Bert Hatfield's little car lot, and Bert went with him to talk to Josie. The door was open, though it was the dead of winter. When they rattled the screen door, which was missing one of its hinges, there was a muffled commotion just inside, followed by silence, and then the unmistakable click of a shotgun. Ray looked at Bert and thought, *Someone is going to shoot me.*

Hastily they called out, identifying themselves. A voice responded, inviting them in. As they edged inside the doorway, a younger woman in a housedress tore past them and ran down the hill toward the road shrieking, "The law! The law!"

Inside, an older woman put down a shotgun and eyed the intruders warily from the couch. "Well, what do you want?" she said evenly.

Bert introduced Ray to Josie and started to explain their business. As he did, Ray glanced curiously at the cast-iron stove that was radiating a wall of heat from the corner. He was wondering about the dark yellow smoke that seeped from under the lid when something inside the stove exploded with a great boom that caused both men to experience something akin to cardiac arrest.

"Damn girl!" their hostess yelped. While the smoke cleared, she apologized for the cherry bomb someone had popped into the stove.

The ice having been broken, they persuaded Josie to describe her telephone contact with Susan Smith. Shelby had said that Josie told her she had in fact received two or three calls from Susan, and that she was all right. Josie quickly confirmed the report.

But Ray's relief dissipated like the yellow smoke from the stove when Josie added, "At least, she *said* she was her. Now, I had never talked to her by phone before, but it sounded like her. She would only talk a couple of minutes and hang up. She said she had left a sweater and fingernail polish at Shelby's and that I could have them."

Josie looked at them sweetly and jabbered on, describing how Susan, or whoever it was on the phone, she wasn't at all sure now, told her to be sure to take her medicine. "It could have been a tape recording or a prank," Josie said with a frown. "I take a lot of medicine and am not well. I don't know why she would call me, and I don't remember her saying she was Susie Smith. Besides, my number is unlisted."

The two officers looked at each other and got up, thanking the woman for her time.

Poole, Ray discovered, had already supplied Josie Thorpe with a tape recorder to record future phone calls from Susan, but Josie did not report any further contact, real or imagined.

Not long afterward, Ray tracked down Charlie Trotter at his home in McRoberts, far up in the hills of Letcher County. Charlie confirmed that he had stayed at the Landmark, on the FBI tab, for nearly five months, including the week Susan and Mark were there in June. After testifying successfully in the chop-shop trial, the nervous star witness had checked out in August. Soon afterward, he got his final payment of $30,000 from the FBI.

Charlie said that he hadn't seen anything at the motel to indicate any problem between Mark and Susan Smith. He said that Mark was usually gone most of the day during that week, not getting back till late at night. He seemed perfectly normal, Charlie said, other than complaining that the US Attorney's office was "jerking him around" in Lexington all day when he really needed to spend more time preparing his witness to testify. Charlie didn't think Mark saw Susan for more than a few minutes during that week.

"Why do you think that?"

"Well, I saw her come out on the balcony a couple of times looking for Mark. He would park in the lot under the balcony. She gave me the impression that she was coming on to Mark, and he would hide in his car and try to dodge her, like she was after him or something. I don't think Mark was fooling with her."

How did he learn that Susan was missing?

"Ron Poole told me about the girl being gone," said Charlie. "I never saw anyone talk to her except Mark Putnam and Ron Poole."

Charlie also said, "She was rougher looking than the picture you showed me."

By January, Richard Ray figured he had chased every goose and run down every lead. The holidays were past, and Susan hadn't contacted a soul since the day she disappeared. He went to his boss Lieutenant Maynard and told him it was time to get tough with the FBI. Assuming something untoward had happened to Susan Smith—and that was precisely what he was assuming by now—there was at least one easy-to-find suspect who hadn't been eliminated yet. It was time, Ray said, to demand that the FBI have a talk with its agent Mark Putnam, preferably with a polygraph machine strapped to his arm.

Later, testifying to a grand jury in Pikeville, Maynard described the frustration he and Ray felt as they tried to find out where Susan Smith had gone, or what had happened to her. He testified, "We had investigated and pursued leads during the entire year to no avail; we could not get a line on where she might be or anything like that. We had information that she had been in different parts of the country and we had contacted different police agencies and requested assistance from those people and tried to locate her, but all the leads turned up to be dead-ends. We couldn't locate her."

Mark Putnam's name kept turning up in gossip and speculation, but Maynard and others felt that a highly regarded young FBI agent like him was initially above suspicion criminally, even if he was sleeping with the girl. "From the beginning of the investigation, of course, the information we were getting was that she may have been having an affair with FBI agent Mark Putnam. Initially we accepted this due primarily to the person's position of being an FBI agent, it was very hard for us to believe that he could be capable of being involved in her disappearance or death," Maynard said.

By January, though, the state police were more willing to accept the idea that an FBI agent could be involved in causing harm to Susan. Wasn't it time to at least sit Putnam down to answer some questions? The state police were unaware that in Miami, Mark Putnam, wracked with guilt, was already suggesting to his aghast superiors that perhaps an interior investigation might be launched to put the questions at rest. Meanwhile, supervisors in the FBI's main regional office in Louisville once again responded civilly but firmly to the entreaties from Pikeville. They were not prepared to produce a federal agent for questioning by Kentucky cops just because the state police were unable to find Susan Smith.

The reasoning behind their attitude was logical enough. First, there was no evidence that a crime had even been committed. Furthermore, there was plenty to suggest that the missing woman, a reputed small-time drug dealer with an abusive ex-husband and a passel of enemies, had simply gone off somewhere. Yes, there was speculation, but there was always speculation in places like the Tug Valley. The agent whose name was being bandied around, Mark Putnam, had compiled a distinguished record fighting crime in eastern Kentucky, gossip about his personal relationship with the missing girl aside.

Shelby also kept pressing for answers and was furious about the rebuff she got from Terry Hulse when she'd phoned to demand that the FBI question Mark. "He acted like she didn't need to be found," Shelby would later say. She claimed that Hulse told her that Susan would undoubtedly turn up alive, at which time "we'll do a pregnancy test to determine if it was Putnam's baby or not. But from what I've heard, your sister fooled around with everything in Pikeville." Shelby was bristling. "They just talked to me like I was dirt under their feet," she said. "It is impossible for me to understand why they would feel that this was a problem for the Kentucky State Police when we all knew Susan was a paid informant for the FBI and had testified and given information about several potentially dangerous people."

Of course, part of the difficulty was that although Shelby never wavered in her insistence that Mark Putnam had been personally involved with her sister, she herself had given investigators various theories about her sister's disappearance, with no evidence for any of them. All she really knew was what she said Susan had told her. She had never even laid eyes on Putnam.

But Ray had sorted through the various accounts and come back down the blind alleys increasingly certain that Mark Putnam knew more than he said about what had happened to Susan Smith. Convinced now that the woman was dead, stymied by bureaucratic lethargy within a state police hierarchy that was reluctant to incur the ire of the FBI, he decided to go through outside channels. He stopped by the downtown office of the county prosecutor, commonwealth's attorney John Paul Runyon, to ask for advice.

Ray told the prosecutor that he thought the FBI's refusal to take any role in the investigation was inexcusable. The woman had *worked* for them, after all. She had put herself in danger for them. "They don't seem to understand that they have a special responsibility to this girl," he said.

Once he had heard the detective's full description of the dilemma, Runyon readily agreed that the FBI needed to pay attention and step up. He himself had long been troubled by what he regarded as the cavalier way the FBI used its money to buy informants. He thought it was basically a cynical system that encouraged a kind of outlaw welfare state, with little genuine long-term law enforcement benefit.

This seemed to be a perfect example, he decided. A poor mountain girl disappears; the federal agent who has put her in danger pulls up stakes and goes off to Florida. Didn't the FBI owe her family at least the courtesy of an active investigation? Missing persons' cases were not under FBI jurisdiction, but tampering with a federal witness sure as hell was. Besides, as Ray brusquely pointed out, the FBI had always managed in the past to find a way to insert itself into a local investigation when it felt like it, especially if the case looked as if it might yield some glory. Where was the bureau now?

Runyon told the detective he was making it his business to find out.

Kentucky's county-based commonwealth attorneys perform the function of district attorneys, prosecuting felonies. But in the state's unusual political structure, where power is concentrated intensely within the county courthouses, a commonwealth attorney wields significant influence over a wide swath of civic life, especially in poor rural areas such as Pike County. Now in his sixties, approaching the end of his fifth term in office, John Paul Runyon was the dean of Kentucky commonwealth attorneys, a man both widely admired and feared in Pike County.

He also happened to be an occasional hunting buddy of Richard Ray's, and he respected the veteran detective's levelheaded comprehension of the societal currents in isolated regions such as Peter Creek. An athletic man, six feet four, with thick white hair and chiseled features, Runyon prided himself on his accessibility. His storefront office on a side street in downtown Pikeville was the kind of place where a man with a grievance could come in, stroll back to the prosecutor himself, sit down at his desk, and say, "John Paul, you sent my cousin to the penitentiary five years ago, and he always told me you was fair . . ."

Runyon was also acutely aware of his public image. His predecessor as commonwealth attorney, a blustery coal tycoon named Thomas B. Ratliff, had attracted the ridicule of the national news media in 1967 by leading a posse in a midnight raid on the farmhouse of a couple who were active with Vista, the federal antipoverty group then calling attention to the destitution of southern Appalachia. Ratliff announced the discovery of a cache of "communist propaganda" in the house—actually, he'd found a handful of newspaper clippings about civil rights marches in Alabama—and successfully prosecuted the bewildered couple for sedition. By 1972, when the case was overturned by the United States Supreme Court, Pikeville had more important things on its mind, such as the giant mountain Cut-Through, one of the largest earth moving projects in US history. It allowed Route 23 to be rerouted and the flood-prone Levisa Fork to be diverted, freeing Pikeville's downtown for new development.

Runyon, a county official previously credited with bringing new state roads through the mountains, personified the desire of Pikeville to present itself as a progressive and vibrant commercial center, not a backwater hillbilly hamlet. He was first elected commonwealth attorney in 1972 and had been reelected, with increasingly wide margins ever since, resisting blandishments to run for statewide office. He liked to tell the story of a man he knew who had once run hard in a Democratic primary for governor and had unexpectedly gone down to decisive defeat. "You got beat because you didn't want to *be* governor badly enough," Runyon had told him. "Unless you wake up in the middle of the night in a cold sweat screaming, 'If I don't get elected governor, I'll *die!* I'll *die!*' you are simply not going to be governor. I could see you didn't have that."

His own aspirations were clear. In 1990, he was planning to round out his career with election to one last term as commonwealth attorney the following year. He wanted to win it without opposition—hell, by *acclamation*, if possible. And his acute small-town political instincts told him that the Putnam case, with its undertones of exploitation, cover-up, and official betrayal, was a booby trap. He did not intend to stumble into it blindly.

While Ray sat in his office, Runyon picked up the phone and called Lou DeFalaise in Lexington. The US Attorney told the prosecutor that he happened to be on his way to the Justice Department in Washington.

"Well, kick somebody there and get them working on this, will you, Louie?" Runyon said.

Runyon also got together with Captain Rose, who recounted his own frustration in dealing with the FBI. He was especially unhappy since the state police had now heard, from Poole and other sources, that Mark Putnam had already said in Florida that he would agree to take a polygraph test. Yet every time the state police tried to take Putnam up on the supposed offer, the bureau stalled and finally, in early February, said flatly no.

Rose said that Putnam was now the "main suspect" in Susan Smith's disappearance and strongly suggested that Runyon meet with Shelby Jean Ward, who, he warned, was threatening to call a press conference to charge that law enforcement authorities were engaged in a cover-up of the murder of her sister, a federal informant.

On February 9, a very unhappy Shelby Ward met with Runyon and state police officials in the prosecutor's office.

Shelby was quite serious about her threat, and it had some weight. National tabloid television programs would quite probably be interested in the story, which had all the right ingredients: the poor coal miner's daughter; the dashing prep-school FBI man; treachery, cover-up, intrigue, and, of course, illicit sex.

While he figured only a federal investigation would get to the truth, Runyon knew that putting Mark Putnam on a polygraph machine, even if he could get Putnam to agree, was not building a criminal case. Polygraphs are inadmissible as evidence in court. Essentially, there was no case without evidence that a crime had been committed. And there was a conspicuous absence of evidence in the one at hand.

Shelby, as the state police had found, could offer the prosecutor little more than anger and speculation. "Is your sister the type of person who would just up and leave like that, maybe go off and stay in an apartment or something with Mark Putnam?" Runyon asked her.

"It's possible," she said

"Or leave with somebody else?"

"That's possible, too," Shelby allowed.

Explaining that he had no significant involvement in the investigation yet, and that no solid information had been developed, Runyon asked Shelby to consider that if the FBI man was in fact involved in her sister's disappearance, premature publicity could "run Putnam to ground" and let him escape. They knew where Putnam was, and he wasn't going anywhere. Runyon asked Shelby to stay quiet for "two or three weeks to see if I can build a fire and get this thing moving."

Reluctantly, Shelby agreed.

When she left, the prosecutor, now believing that a full scale federal investigation was the only way to "shake this thing loose," called Terry Hulse and suggested strongly that the FBI should get involved in the case, if only to clear their own man's name, which was being dragged through the mud in Pike County.

Hulse prudently made some calls. In Washington, the bureaucracy stirred. There was a request from the Justice Department for Richard Ray's case file.

A month passed. The case was reported "under review." In April, two federal officials visited Pikeville for a briefing on the case. They were Sarah Pickard, a supervisory special agent with the FBI, and David P. Bobzien, an assistant counsel with the Justice Department. Hulse drove down from Covington to participate in the meeting.

The federal agents confirmed to Runyon and the state police that there was no current investigation, either professional or criminal, into the allegations against Mark Putnam. If Poole had been investigating, he was working on his own, as usual.

"I can't believe that you people don't have *any* kind of investigation going on into Mark Putnam," Runyon snapped.

Ray would later recall, "After talking to them, I had a little hope. They read my report. They weren't really aware of what we had here; they seemed pretty concerned. They assured us that once they got back to Washington, this case would take a little higher priority than what it had been before, which was apparently none. I think some of the FBI people had heard about it, and they didn't think it was very serious or something. They figured that probably this woman would show up somewhere. Which I knew she wouldn't."

A few weeks later, Captain Rose called Runyon. He had heard back from the Justice Department. The message, he said, essentially was, "We're not interested. You handle it."

Runyon sighed impatiently and told Rose, "That's a serious mistake. To start with, you don't have the resources. You don't have the jurisdiction—the boy you need to talk to is in Florida. And you can't talk to him without permission from the Justice Department. Let me see what I can do."

This time he was less delicate in his approach to the FBI. "Listen," he warned Bobzien, "you people have got a problem. You people are in this up to your eyeballs. You threw this young girl to the wolves, and if you don't get off your ass, I'm going to have Geraldo Rivera breaking down your office door sticking a camera in your face, and saying, 'Where is your missing informant?'"

13

The FBI investigation began. With twenty-three years in the bureau, supervisory special agent Jim Huggins had seen his share of hotshot rookie agents roar out of the academy in a blaze of energy, thinking they were the greatest thing to happen to federal law enforcement since Eliot Ness, and then burn out before they qualified for their second week's vacation.

Not so, he thought, with this Putnam fellow. Huggins had run into him only a few times when Mark came up to Lexington for gun training, but he knew enough about his reputation down in Pikeville, where the kid was practically a one-man band, to regard him as one of the best young agents he had ever encountered. Huggins believed fervently that the future of his beloved FBI depended on a steady supply of sharp, hard-working young agents just like Mark Putnam.

On May 1, Huggins met with Terry O'Connor, the special agent in charge of the Lexington office. The discussion was about some talk of trouble in the Pikeville office. The commonwealth attorney down there was "bouncing off the wall" and threatening a media circus if the FBI didn't deal with questions that "needed to be resolved" about the relationship between a young agent and a female informant who had gone missing.

Resolving them would turn out to be the most emotionally wrenching experience of Huggins's career.

At the start, Huggins and the other agents who were sent down to Pikeville—there would ultimately be ten of them in all—believed that they would be looking into a simple missing person case that had been mishandled by the state cops. Not that the bureau was totally without fault; it was clear that Putnam had some explaining to do about the missing informant. And there was the delicate underlying problem, "the Pikeville horror story," as one agent put it, of an office out of control, with a rookie agent doing the work of four people in partnership with an agent as disreputable as Poole, who'd been moved out of the mainstream and sent down to Pikeville because supervisors didn't want to deal with him. Clearly, the Pikeville office had been trouble waiting to happen. The bureau's vaunted public image, which every agent was trained to protect at all costs, was in peril.

Huggins met first with Captain Rose, who, he said, "made available all of the resources of the post." These resources consisted primarily of Det. Richard Ray, a burly and taciturn cop who was somewhat resentful at being assigned to escort the newly arrived FBI agents as they essentially duplicated his own investigation, at least as he saw it. It was clear to him that the FBI's elite squad thought they had been sent down to straighten out the mess that the hillbilly cops had made. Their attitude, he thought, was, "Let's do a thorough job, clear our guy, and find the guy that really did it"—assuming "it" had been done at all. He felt he was supposed to play tour guide, driving the agents—most of whom, he said, knew nothing about mountain people and had never seen Pikeville before—on their rounds as they checked off likely suspects.

Years later, Huggins took strong issue with Ray's characterizations.

"I had no idea what was going on in Pikeville, which was under Covington," he said of the way the FBI offices in Kentucky were organized, with Covington and its agent in charge, Terry Hulse, having the supervision of the small Pikeville office.

He said the first he heard of the Mark Putnam problem was when Sam Smith, the agent who had been in the Pikeville office when Mark Putnam was first assigned there, came into Huggins's office in Lexington one morning at the end of April.

"Jim, can I talk to you for a minute?" Smith said.

Huggins shut the door and Smith explained, "I was just out in Pikeville talking to a couple of my buddies, and there's a missing informant down there, and they think Mark Putnam might know more about it than he is saying."

Huggins, aware of Mark's reputation as a first-rate young agent, was incredulous at first. So were the supervisors in the main regional office in Louisville when he called to ask if they had heard the rumors. They had not, and asked him to find out what he could.

He immediately phoned Capt. Gary Rose, the commander of the Kentucky State Police post in Pikeville, to find out what was going on. Why hadn't the FBI been informed that there were questions involving an agent and his missing informant?

Huggins recalled, "Gary said, between you and me, Jim, I'm not about to accuse an FBI agent of any wrongdoing or even contact you guys without any evidence—but I'll tell you, from what I'm hearing about this thing, I think you better come down and take a look. He might be involved. And I said, 'Holy cow, we need to resolve this, Gary.'"

After speaking with O'Connor on May 1, Huggins contacted superiors in Louisville and was given the go-ahead to commence a preliminary kidnapping inquiry, a procedural matter that allowed the FBI entrée to a missing person case by invoking a presumption of possible kidnapping, which is a federal crime.

"The order was, let's get to the bottom of this," said Huggins, who was told to pick a few of his best agents and go to Pikeville to launch a joint investigation with the state police there.

"So I picked four guys—Sam Smith and, who of course had been down there for years; Bill Welch, another guy from the mountains; Tommy Gayheart, who was born and raised in Harlan; and Tim Adams. All of them knew the territory. Richard Ray didn't know any of them except Sam."

Captain Rose instructed Ray, who bristled at having to put up with an elite squad of FBI agents barging into his case, to cooperate fully when they arrived in Pikeville and began reviewing his files.

"Our guys said, 'Hey, what's with Richard Ray? What's he so pissed about?' I said he probably thinks that we're trying to make him look bad, which was not true," Huggins recalled.

All of the agents stayed at the Landmark, Pikeville's only major motel at the time, and thoroughly read through Ray's comprehensive missing person's file on Susan Smith.

"I said, OK, guys, you've all read the report. Let's just go around preliminarily here. Let's say this girl did meet with foul play, somebody killed her. Based on what you've read, who is the likely suspect?"

"I think it was probably her husband. He had the motive; he beat her before; he's unstable," Agent Welch said.

"Yeah, I think it probably was Kenneth," Gayheart concurred.

"I'm guessing it's old Cat Eyes. She testified against him, so he had a motive," Smith said.

Adams shook his head. "I think it was Mark," he said, stunning everyone in the room.

Huggins recalled, "We all went '*What*?'"

Adams replied, "Well, look at the guy. If everything we read is true, that he's alleged to be having an affair with her, that she threatened to expose him, he definitely had a motive. We can't rule him out."

Huggins had to agree. "So I said, let's eliminate him or make him, one of the two. Let's zero in on him, from the minute he arrived in Pikeville to the minute he left."

The FBI agents quickly went to work, sorting through the rumors, half-baked speculation, and false leads that had confounded Ray for months. They, too, soon gathered plenty of indications that Susan was unreliable and disreputable, a drug user with criminal friends—and enemies. Informants often—almost inevitably—became disgruntled. Agents were routinely falsely accused by unhappy former informants cut loose from the gravy train. If this woman had been harmed, it would appear, at least on the surface, Mark Putnam barely made first cut on the list of likely suspects.

For example, David Blankenship told them that Susan's brother Bo had told him that he believed Kenneth had killed Susan. According to the FBI's investigative file, Blankenship said that Susan claimed she had been paid $12,000 for her work on the Cat Eyes case and described to him the way she had subsequently set up Cat's uncle in another bank robbery. Susan "feared for her life because people had threatened her," he told them.

A few days later, Ray drove agents Adams and Welch across the Tug to Vulcan, to talk to Ronnie Mounts, one of the old friends who used to sit around the kitchen table for hours on end with Kenneth and Susan, drinking beer and playing cards.

Mounts said Susan was mainly a "pill popper." He told the investigators that, while he had no idea where Susan was, he had heard reports that she had gone off to Chicago. But he had also heard she might be staying with a sister of hers in Texas. On the other hand, he said, Kenneth had told him that he thought Susan was somewhere in Florida—though Mounts hadn't seen Kenneth in weeks and thought he was "on the run," too. He said that he knew Kenneth had accused his ex-wife of "going with Mark Putnam." Mounts said he hoped they found her soon.

"Why?" he was asked.

"Because she owes me sixty-five dollars."

In early May, the agents fanned through the area re-interviewing many people who had already talked to Ray for his own report. Just as Ray had found, the FBI discovered the people who knew Susan had a multitude of theories to explain her disappearance. Most mentioned her drug use and drug connections. Mark Putnam's name often came up, but always in the context of second-hand information.

Pam Daniels, a thirty-year-old former neighbor on Barrenshee Hollow, was among those who told agents that Susan had a "bad drug habit." She claimed Susan had come to her house in the spring after being "run off" by Shelby and her husband during an argument over her relationship with Mark Putnam. She also said that Susan told her that if Mark did not give her enough money to support the baby, she was going to "set him up," which Pam Daniels interpreted as a threat to tell his wife about the affair. Daniels said she did not allow Susan to stay at her house after Shelby kicked her out because of Susan's drug habit. Instead, Daniels said she gave Susan a pillow and a blanket and she "believed that Susan probably slept in her car."

According to another bureau investigative report by Smith and Gayheart, Troy Ward, Shelby's husband, described Susan as "the type of person who would make stories up and make statements that she knew who was involved in a criminal act when, in fact, she would have no idea who committed the crime." He also told agents that Susan was a heavy cocaine user who would take any kind of drugs except marijuana and would do "anything" to obtain them, although that had become more difficult for her because of her reputation as an FBI informant. Personally, he said, he thought that Susan was dead, "possibly killed by drug dealers or someone she testified against."

Ward told the agents that Susan, who "had lived with him and Shelby off and on since they had been married," had told everyone who would listen that she worked for the FBI and was "bonded." It was Ward's impression that "Susan felt superior to other people by running around with FBI agents." He said he had never observed Mark with Susan, although he had once seen Poole pick her up at the car lot. Still, Susan was "in love" with Mark and would have done anything for him. He added that while he seldom believed anything Susan said, he did believe she had an affair with Mark and was pregnant by him.

Ward also told them about the beating Susan had received from Sherri Justice, who, he said, "threatened to kill her." Further clouding the picture, he said that Shelby had told him a man Susan knew as a drug dealer had, in the past, said he and his family "would keep her" if she ever needed a place to live.

Ward certainly underlined a number of motives that implicated many possible suspects that could have done Susan harm. According to the agents' report, "Ward stated that Susan had made many people mad at her and since it was widely known she was informing to the FBI, she was having difficulty buying drugs from people for her own use. He stated that Sherri Justice had threatened to kill her."

The agents' report on their interview with Troy Ward concluded: "Ward advised that he was not trying to get anyone in trouble and would not swear against Mark Putnam or Ron Poole because all the information he has is hearsay and that Susan was a cheat and a liar."

Shelby herself was more specific on the relationship between her sister and Putnam, but her account, too, mostly lent support to the notion that Susan had a lot of enemies. According to the agents' report: "*Shelby stated that Susan, Kenneth Smith, and Tennis Daniels went to the Pikeville FBI office to pick up the money for testifying, and supposedly later in the day, Kenneth stole the money from Susan, who later got the money back. Shelby does not know what Susan did with the money, because Susan and Kenneth were both heavily on drugs at the time. The money was supposed to be for Susan to get out of the area, because Susan was getting a lot of threats from Sherri Justice and Cat Eyes, who said if he ever got out of prison, he would have her killed.*

"*About the first part of May 1989, Sherri Justice beat up Susan, causing cuts and bruises, and also smashed out a window in Susan's car. Justice swore she would kill Susan. . . . Shelby stated that she and Susan would often talk about the threats made against Susan, inasmuch as Susan was very afraid of Sherri Justice and Cat Eyes and wanted to get away. . . . Shelby advised that during the two-year period Susan worked for Putnam, Susan and Kenneth fought continuously, with Kenneth getting physical with Susan. Kenneth was very jealous over anyone. . . . Shelby advised that Susan was on cocaine bad enough that she had to have it, and that was Susan's reason not to completely stay away from Kenneth. . . . Shelby further added that Susan lied a lot. However, she told the truth a lot also.*

"*. . . On Thursday morning June 8, 1989, Shelby received a phone call from Susan. Susan seemed real happy, being with Putnam and talking about the baby, and laughed about Putnam not giving her money, and that Putnam would send her money when he got back to Florida and got straightened out. Susan was going to get Poole or*

Putnam to bring her back to Shelby's. Susan was not upset and was
laughing.

"About two hours later on Thursday morning, Susan called
again, and her attitude changed. She was not happy. Susan wished
there was some place she could go with the kids and be away from
Kenneth. Shelby wanted Susan to come home, and Susan told her
that she loved her, but could not stand to be around Kenneth and
could not take it anymore.

"Shelby advised it was very unusual for Susan to say she loved
her. Shelby stated if someone would have given Susan money, she
would have left. Shelby advised this phone call on Thursday was the
last time she had heard from Susan . . ."

Meanwhile, there seemed to be a new wrinkle in the FBI investigation. The agents had come across a witness who had actually
heard from Susan Smith, five months after she had supposedly
disappeared.

They had found the loquacious Josie Thorpe.

The official report of the FBI interview with Thorpe, who had
already been ruled out as categorically unreliable by Ray, read as
a model of just-the-facts investigative objectivity. Any one reviewing it at a desk far away in Lexington or Washington would have
had cause to wonder just what the fuss over Susan was about, since
she appeared to be still alive.

"Josie Thorpe, date of birth December 19, 1937, Freeburn, Kentucky,
advised that she knew Susan Smith and Susan would visit with her
on occasion. Thorpe stated that sometime after Susan's disappear-
ance she got several telephone calls from her. . . . During one call,
Susan inquired as to how Thorpe was getting along and if she was
still taking her medicine. Susan also inquired about her own chil-
dren and told Thorpe that she (Susan) had a dark blue sweater and

orange fingernail polish that she had left at her sister Shelby's house and that Thorpe could have them.

During the last telephone call, Susan inquired about her children, Miranda and Brady. Thorpe stated that the telephone call had to be after Thanksgiving, since she told Susan that her ex-husband, Kenneth Smith, and the children ate Thanksgiving dinner with her and that she served spaghetti. Thorpe stated that she told Susan that people were worried about her and looking for her and that she should call her sister Shelby. Thorpe also told Susan that Ron Poole, Federal Bureau of Investigation, had also interviewed her regarding Susan's telephone calls Susan told Thorpe not to tell anyone that she had called or she would not call anymore.

Thorpe stated she believes the person she was talking to was Susan and that Susan was alive. Thorpe stated that she has had her telephone number changed and that Susan had called her on the old number, which she could not recall . . ."

The Huggins task force had come up with the same snarl of conflicting information that Richard Ray had uncovered in his investigation. The case was thoroughly perplexing. Like Ray, they concluded that Putnam's role required further investigation, and they had an advantage that the state police lacked. They could ask Mark Putnam himself about it. To Ray's great relief, Huggins returned to Lexington with his squad determined to do just that.

Mark was aware of what was going on in Pikeville because both Poole and Myra had called to say that Huggins and his men were in the area retracing the state police investigation. Mark received the information with an odd mixture of dread and relief. In a month, Susan would be dead for a year. Mark was intensely aware—the thought, he later said, never left him—that she had been out there in the woods all that time. When he looked at his own two children, he often thought of hers, a little girl and a little boy who had no idea where their mother was.

In early May, feeling close to the abyss as Huggins's team was starting its work in Pikeville, Mark had gone in to see Roy Tubergen once again, repeating his request for an internal Office of Professional Responsibility investigation "into the allegations against me."

"No way," the supervisor said, aware of the bureaucratic complications posed by an official OPR investigation and the potential damage it could do to an innocent young agent's career. But, he did bring up the polygraph. "If the Kentucky state cops want you to go on the box, would you do it?"

"Yes," Mark said, not certain in his own mind whether this reply was motivated by a desire to confess or to appear eager to deal decisively with the situation and get it behind him. Later, he would understand that it had been both.

A week went by without further mention of the situation. Then, at the end of a workday, Tubergen took Mark aside and mentioned that Jim Huggins and a couple of state police detectives wanted to come to Miami to talk to him.

"It's strictly your call," Tubergen said.

Mark felt his toes and fingertips go cold. He forced himself to be steady. "I have no problem whatsoever with that," he said.

He needed a little time, he thought, to brace himself. He had been overwhelmed with work lately on a major undercover theft investigation. His unit had rented an apartment in Fort Lauderdale to set up a sting. It had been a heady experience, almost like the thrill of the chop-shop case, except that this time he was part of a well-oiled unit, not a lone wolf who had to watch his back even against local cops. Now he was a professional among professionals, all prepared to go the extra mile for one another. He could see himself now, however transiently, as the agent he had always wanted to be—but never would.

He savored the thought briefly, but was quickly overcome with another wave of fear, shame, remorse, resignation, submission, and mental exhaustion. His life had become a severe headache that never eased.

Okay, he thought, *I'm ready.* But he wasn't about to simply surrender. The outcome was inevitable—he would lose it all, and soon—but he wouldn't just give it up, not after all of the decent things he had done. *They're going to have to work a little bit to take it away from me. And then that's it.*

He struggled to stop from reflecting on what was about to happen to Kathy and the children. It was as if he were watching his family from afar as they were about to drive off a cliff—he could see the deadly hidden turn in the road, the car accelerating, the coal truck bearing down—but there was nothing he could do. It would be futile to shout.

On the afternoon of May 15, he left the office, telling the receptionist that he had an interview to do. Knowing he would be alone, he drove to the apartment the FBI had rented for the sting. He sat on the couch, in the orange slats of late-afternoon sunlight. In his hand was his bureau-issue Smith & Wesson .357, which he studied as if he had never seen it before. He could smell the oil. The gunmetal was cool in his hand. He raised the barrel and pressed it hard against the perfectly squared sideburn at his right temple. How would it look? Who would find the mess? Would there be pictures? He lowered the gun and tapped the barrel thoughtfully on the palm of his left hand, probing his feelings as if poking at a broken filling with his tongue. He tried to cut through the bullshit: *If I do this, who benefits?*

He lowered the gun. Had he just spared his own wretched life? Or was this an exercise, another step he had to take to face his fate like a man? Again, the fragment of a headline came to mind: *tragic accident.*

He was cop enough to know they didn't have much of a case against him. He had the case all in his head. Had the flurry of FBI activity in Pikeville meant that they had found her body? If so, why hadn't they simply arrested him? Why talk now? If they had the body, they still obviously didn't have any other evidence. Did this mean that he could make his inner peace with himself and with Susan, whatever the cost for the rest of his life, and brazen his way through the rest for the sake of his family? All trouble got easier over time. Why not this?

He left the apartment utterly unable to decide. He stopped back at the office to check out and before heading home. Roy Tubergen spotted him at his desk.

"They're coming down tomorrow," Roy said.

All Mark remembered driving home was looking down to see the speedometer needle edge past ninety on I-95 out of North Miami Beach. He let up fast and checked the rearview mirror for a sign of a police car's flashing lights in the line of cars strung out behind. Queasy with guilt, he imagined that a Florida highway cop who pulled him over for speeding would easily guess what everyone else failed to see—a murderer. He could see the cop's impassive face at the window, his nostrils sniffing the panic sweat, his hand poised with his gun.

Mark found himself turning into the driveway, his temples throbbing. It was almost six o'clock, the usual time. The kids tackled him at the door. Little Mark tottered off into the playroom while Danielle wrapped her arms around his legs and held on, chattering about her day. But when he only stood there silently for a minute, she stopped talking and looked into her father's eyes, and he thought that he read there a deep and sudden sorrow. He knew then that he was going to prison for a long time, and that when he was a part of her life again, she would be grown.

At dinner, Kathy hung back, sensing that something was very wrong. She guessed it was Pikeville again. After the kids were in bed, they talked for a while in the screened-in porch outside the kitchen. Was everything okay? No problem, he said. Just work. He got up and went out for his run.

The night was muggy and warm, the dark sky streaked with milky clouds. He started out easily, feeling the energy build as he picked it up. He was at about the halfway point, two miles, on a stretch of county farm road, when a car full of teenagers roared by. *Fucking asshole!* he heard. An empty beer can sailed by his head and clattered onto the asphalt. He stopped, panting, and watched the taillights on the road. Joy-riding was just the kind of thing he had avoided assiduously as a teenager, so worried about his "record" as a youth that he ran like a rabbit even from a girl with a can of beer. Snorting, he circled back behind the beer can lying on the road. Picking up his pace, he kicked it in stride, watching it rise through the air and bounce ahead. Breathing evenly now, he quickened his stride, adjusting his step as he approached to boot the can again. It sailed away in a perfect arc and clattered down twenty feet ahead. The wind gathering force through trees on either side of the road sounded like the roar of a stadium. Again he approached the can, shifted stride, and met it with a powerful stroke of his right foot. The roar was deafening now. He could see the American flag on its staff high above the stadium, a postage stamp stuck on the corner of a bright blue sky. Again, he came up fast on the can and booted it in a fury. It sailed out of sight. He heard it clank to rest somewhere ahead in the dark.

Winded, he tripped and fell, sprawling nearly spread-eagle on the asphalt. He crawled to the side of the road and sat in the wet grass beside an irrigation ditch, scraped and bruised. He looked into the sky, lighter in the east with Miami's cold glow, falling off to darkness to the west, where the Everglades swamped the land eighty miles wide.

He dreamed of Susan again that night. She was closer to him now. He knew that he had called out her name because the sound of his voice woke him. Kathy slept on gently. He looked at her beside him and groped for the right emotion. Was love even possible, with what he had done to her and what more was to come? Would remorse ever be enough? He kissed her arm lightly, careful not to awaken her, and slipped out of bed.

At work, he busied himself with papers on his desk, avoiding the phone, until he saw them come in. It was May 15. As he had expected, Richard Ray was there. Paul Maynard came in with him. Jim Huggins, whom he recognized from the Lexington office, led the way. Mark kept his head down and found a reason to leave the office on an assignment.

Mark's immediate supervisor Roy Tubergen was astonished by the investigation.

"Did you know this guy in Kentucky?" Tubergen had asked Huggins.

"Not really. He wasn't under my supervision, but I heard nothing but good things about him," Huggins had replied.

"He's one of the best agents I got down here, he works his butt off. You mean to tell me that you all suspect him of killing an informant? You're crazy!"

"Well, Roy. We are not accusing him. We're down here to talk to him because he is a suspect because of his relationship with this girl who has not been found. So all we need is for him to clear it up."

The special agent in charge of the Miami office, Bill Gavin, called all the supervisors into a big conference room and introduced the visitors.

"Jim Huggins is here to conduct an investigation to determine if Mark Putnam had anything to do with a missing informant in Pikeville," Gavin said.

There was vocal consternation. "Holy shit, are you kidding me?" one supervisor said.

Gavin quieted them down. "Look, I don't want to hear any more discussion about this, all right? He's got a job to do, it's not a pleasant job and we're going to get to the bottom of it one way or another. I don't want any interference from anybody here; I don't want to hear any rumors going around the office, and don't discuss it with your squad until we get this resolved. Is that understood?" Gavin gave Huggins an office to work out of and a bureau car to use.

The next morning, at 11 o'clock, Mark was summoned into a conference room for the first interview with Huggins and the two state police officers. They each had file folders and a legal pad on the table in front of them.

Huggins cleared his throat and advised Mark of his rights as an employee of the Justice Department to answer questions voluntarily. Huggins nodded to Maynard, who looked directly at Mark and recited words that startled him with their familiarity from a far different place.

"You have the right to remain silent. Anything you say can and will be used against you in court. You have the right to talk to a lawyer for advice . . ."

Mark closed his eyes.

"You sure you don't want a lawyer, Mark?" Huggins's voice intruded into a serenity that had settled briefly over him.

Mark looked up. "Positive. I don't want a lawyer. I'm ready."

He was asked to provide a detailed day-by-day account of what he remembered about the week during which Susan Smith had disappeared. But Mark was not going to make it that easy for them. He would confess, but he had decided he would make them sweat for it. They wanted details? They'd get them, but let them show what kind of cops they really were. *Gentlemen*, he thought, *make yourselves comfortable, because we're going to be here for a while.*

Speaking slowly in response to Huggins's questions, Mark went over his career in Pikeville, incident by incident as it reflected his association with the missing woman. He described how Bert Hatfield introduced him to Kenneth Smith and Susan. From their first meeting, he explained, the relationship between agent and informer was dogged with "ridiculous" rumors that he was having a sexual relationship with Susan. Susan herself was one of those who spread the rumors, he said.

"How old is Susan?" Huggins asked at one point early in the questioning.

"She was twenty-eight," Mark replied. Huggins felt a shock at Mark's use of the past tense.

Mark kept responding in detail to Huggins's questions about himself and Susan. The payments to Susan for informing on Cat Eyes and others. Susan's clamoring for more money, for protection from threats. His and Kathy's attempts to help her find a new life away from Kenneth. The gifts Susan pressed on him. The intimations about a drug operation she had resumed contact with involving the policeman in Cicero, Illinois, and Poole's interest in that.

He recounted the 4:30 a.m. phone call in early February, in which Kenneth had told Kathy that Susan and Mark had had an affair. "He was extremely jealous of me because of the informant relationship with Susan," Mark said, effectively highlighting the potential motive of another suspect.

"Just before Christmas, 1988," he explained, "I got her a motel room at the Goldenrod Motel in Pikeville. I registered it in my name and told her she could stay there to get away from Kenneth . . . I paid in cash."

Similar arrangements were made on two other occasions in January or February of 1989, he said. He didn't need to add that haphazard utilization of informants, motels, and government money had become standard practice, actively encouraged by the bureau in its zeal to keep undercover investigations active and statistically fruitful, not to mention private.

As for Susan, "she had a reputation around Pikeville for telling people that she was having sex with various individuals in the Pikeville area."

When had he first heard that Susan was pregnant? "Sometime around the middle of April 1989," Mark said. He had received his transfer orders to Miami; Susan called to discuss her wretched personal problems; she was broke, strung out, battered, afraid, and forlorn. In that context, he said, she mentioned that she was pregnant. "I asked her who the father was, and she said it was none of my business."

Later, in Miami, there were odd telephone calls from Poole, reporting on Susan's despair and imploring him to call her and try to help. When he did, Mark said, "she started crying and told me that I was leaving her out in the cold. She told me she was feeling bad, and that she had been beat up by Sherri Justice. I asked her what I could do to help, and she said, 'Fuck you. You don't give a shit about me.'"

Two hours had passed since Mark started talking. Ray could sense the agent's mind racing as the chronology moved inexorably toward that final week in June of 1989. He thought, *This guy is going to slip up. He's just too cocky.*

Huggins pressed on with questions. Mark described his return to Pikeville, in June, and recalled his surprise at finding Susan at the motel when he checked in. How had she known he was coming? "I assume Poole told her," he said. He said Susan came to his room to talk about her troubles. That was news to both Ray and Huggins. It was a detail that no one had turned up, relevant only, Ray knew, in that Mark had seen a need to mention it.

What did they talk about in his room? "Again, she never accused me of being the father of her child," Mark said.

Ray watched him with hooded eyes, wondering if he had caught a whiff of panic.

"I got upset with her." He stopped short. *Upset?* Mark couldn't believe he had used such a stupid word! His heart beating fast, he went on evenly, and made another mistake. "During this conversation, I raised my voice and grabbed her by the arm, but did not in any way hurt her."

The cops at the table, Mark included, registered this tactical blunder immediately. No glances were exchanged. Mark's mind flashed urgent warnings about the "indicators of deceit" that every good cop knew to watch for in a suspect who was about to cave in. He took instant stock of how he was projecting his mental state. Body language: Do not shift position. Do not move. He glanced at his hands resting casually on the table and resisted the overpowering impulse to touch them together, form a blockade with his arms. Keep your voice at the same pitch. Do not lick your dry lips. Do not sigh or yawn. *Do not swallow!*

He imagined that he was on a small rubber raft, in fast water now, listening for the low thunder of the waterfall ahead.

He knew that if any one of them had stood up and pointed a finger at him at that moment he would have spilled his guts. He was ready to take his punishment and be done with the lies and the shame. The impulse to confess was crushing, yet the need to go on was overpowering. No one looked at him. No one rose to denounce him for murdering Susan Smith. With grim resignation he drifted on.

He explained that he flew into the airport in Huntington, West Virginia, "because it was closer than Lexington, which was the next-closest major airport, and I believed at that time that most of my work would be in Pikeville." Eyes downcast, he took a breath, not wanting to meet a gaze at the table. "At Huntington, I rented a car—"

Huggins interrupted him: "Hold it, hold it. You rented a car? What kind of a car?" In fact, Huggins was well aware of the rental car already.

Mark shot an incredulous look at his fellow agent. Was this a bluff to knock him off-balance? How could they not have known about something as basic and obvious as the rental car? How the hell did they think he got around town that week, drove back and forth to Lexington? The question surprised and even exasperated him, but he tried to sort out the ramifications before answering. There were rental records, expense vouchers—easy-to check, routine stuff. Mark considered Ray a first-rate detective: methodical, perceptive, tenacious, smart. Had the FBI thrown that many roadblocks in Ray's way? Was the state police brass that terrified of going against the FBI and being wrong? How hard had the cops *really pushed* here?

To a man who had thought he was cornered and was merely playing for time—Mark was calculating days, not even weeks, by this point—the implications were breathtaking. He paused for an instant, sifting possibilities, wondering almost playfully if the hole was big enough to kick a ball through. *What else didn't they know?*

He had always believed that Susan would eventually be found, that he would be confronted, and that he would confess and put her soul and his to rest. It was only a matter of time. In the past few weeks, as they closed in on him, he had assumed that they had new evidence and that they had finally had the body. Now, looking around at his questioners' faces, blank with the indication deliberately planted by Huggins, he knew for certain that they had not found her.

"Yes, I rented a car, a blue Ford Tempo," he said calmly.

"Go on."

He was thinking, *Can I bullshit my way out of this?* The prospect unsettled him deeply because it required more introspection
and there was no time for that. In a weary voice, he went on, lying
with confidence now about his activities on the day Susan disappeared and the days that followed. He felt like a man lifting a bar-
bell, muscles trembling with tension and pain, desperate to put it
down, determined to press just a few more.

Huggins and Ray detected the change in Mark's tone and watched
him carefully. Was that a glint of sweat on the man's upper lip?

But Mark forced himself to keep going, methodically touch-
ing on each of the points of the chronology that he assumed they
had already established. His talks with Charlie Trotter. His trips to
Lexington, with arrival and departure times. His several encounters with Susan (he was careful to mention the phone message
she said she received from Shelby about supposedly meeting her
drug-dealer friend). The perplexing calls from Ron Poole checking on Susan. His routine on the night she was last seen. He went
on, describing his trip to Lexington the next morning for another
meeting with the assistant US attorney. Back in Pikeville, dinner
at the Log Cabin, followed by the friendly talk long into the night
with Myra Chico.

So far, it checked out as well as the evidence could support.
But Mark was going too fast, layering in too much detail. He had
passed over the critical time, the hours during which Ray believed
he had killed Susan Smith, but there was something he seemed
impatient to explain.

Mark said that on Saturday, June 10, two days after Susan disappeared, he left the motel at about 8:30 a.m. and drove out of
town to serve a trial subpoena on a witness. "I returned to Pikeville around noon," he said. "I then went to my old house, which
still had not been sold and still had some personal belongings in
the garage. I pulled my car in the garage, checked out the house,

and went back to the garage to discard some old paint cans that were stored under a workbench. Reaching under a shelf, I cut my right hand on a nail that was protruding from the shelf. The wound began bleeding very heavily; I got in the passenger side of the rental car and started slinging my hand up and down, causing blood to splatter on the passenger seat and on the dash. I wrapped my hand in a towel to stop the bleeding."

Mark paused. If they didn't even know about the car, why was he blurting out something else that they never knew about? Besides, the blood was his, not hers! He thought about the cracked windshield and struggled mindlessly to explain it: "While sitting in the front passenger seat of the car, I was extremely angry over cutting my hand; in an act of frustration, I kicked the front windshield with my right foot. It caused the windshield to slightly shatter in the area of the middle of the right side between the mirror and the right post."

If Richard Ray, for one, had had any doubts, he now knew for certain that Mark Putnam had killed her. Only a guilty man in his last shrieking ride down the chute would babble on, providing new information without prompting. Ray felt a strong urge to stand up and arrest the suspect immediately, not only for murder but also for insulting the intelligence of a police officer. But he remained silent as Mark went on and on: How he took the car with the cracked windshield back to the rental agency in West Virginia, blamed the damage on a chunk of coal flying off a truck, and got a replacement car. "I lied about the damage because I didn't want to have to pay for the windshield." How he had lent Susan his gym shorts and shirt. How Susan had told him about rebuffing Poole. How she "may have met up with the group from Illinois on a drug deal" and come to harm. Or how "her ex-husband, Kenneth Smith, could have harmed her, since he had beat her up on numerous occasions in the past."

He was exhausted, morally and physically. "I have no idea where Susan Smith is at the present time," he said. "Both Ron Poole and I cared about her very much and are concerned as to what happened to her. I certainly did not kill her intentionally or accidentally, because I could never do anything like that."

The signs of guilt were clear to the cops at the table. Mark had bowed his head. He was perspiring and seemed to be fighting back tears.

Huggins kept returning in his mind to the shock he had felt early in the interview when he had casually asked Mark, "How old is Susan?" *She was twenty-eight*, Mark had said.

It was a low-key interview for the most part, though it went on for more than six hours. Huggins was worried that Richard Ray in particular might intervene with strong-arm questions that would intimidate Mark into halting the interview to get a lawyer, but that did not happen. Hour by hour, Huggins's sadness deepened as he realized Mark was steadily dissembling, and that his statement would begin the process of damning him.

"I treated him respectfully and we kind of just talked," Huggins recalled. "I didn't hear something I suspected to be untrue and scream at him, 'That's a damn lie, you lying piece of shit,' the way, you now, you might treat a bank robber. So I just went on with one question followed by another, like a general interview, like, 'Hey, Mark, how'd you find that house down there you and Kathy had?' and he'd go on about that. But I could see that he realized I was leading him down the garden path."

Before the interview started, Huggins had told Maynard and Ray that he knew that this was basically a state investigation. "I said look, guys, this is your case. If it turns out that Mark's involved in this, then it's going to be either a murder or a manslaughter and that's a state case. So you guys feel free to jump in here at any time during the interview if you see something I missed or you want to expand on something.

"But they never said a word till the very end of the interview, when Richard Ray reached into his briefcase and pulled out a pair of gym shorts. 'These look familiar?' and I'm sitting there thinking, where in hell did that come from?"

"Nope," Mark said truthfully.

The shorts were among the possessions of Susan's that Poole had collected from her room at the Landmark after she went missing. They had no bearing on the case.

"So Ray just put them back into his briefcase. That was his whole contribution to a seven-hour interview," Huggins recalled with a laugh. "I called it a day. I said, hey guys, anything you'd like to ask Mark? And they agreed, no, you pretty much covered it.

"And then I told Mark, you know, buddy, there are some problems. There's some stuff we have to go over. It's been a long day. Let's continue in the morning."

Mark replied eagerly, "Yes, sir, Jim. I want to get this over with."

Huggins, Maynard, and Ray went back to their hotel nearby in Fort Lauderdale, had dinner, and made arrangements to meet in the restaurant early the next morning before going back to the FBI office to question Mark again. That night, Huggins stayed up until dawn, rereading the missing person's report and jotting down questions to ask Mark the next day. But Huggins now knew that Mark was guilty.

14

Kathy was in the kitchen making dinner, monitoring the noises of the kids playing out back near the screened-in porch. From the canal two blocks away, a breeze drifted over neat lawns deep green from spring rains.

Absently, she glanced up and saw her husband standing mutely on the other side of the breakfast counter, his shoulders slumped and his tie undone. As he peeled off his suit coat and dropped it on a chair, he sagged with weariness. He tugged at his holster and took out the .357, and, to her annoyance, laid it on the breakfast counter. They had an inviolate policy about that gun. It belonged high up, usually on the upper shelf of the bedroom closet, in the back. She scowled at him and placed the gun pointedly atop the refrigerator. When she turned, he was standing right beside her. He took her in his arms and kissed her clumsily.

"You know I love you."

She did, but she hadn't been hearing it much lately and was curious about why she was hearing it now, with a pot lid rattling on the stove. Laughing uneasily, she moved away and studied his face. His eyes looked sunken; he was pale, as if he hadn't seen the sun in a year.

"What's the matter with you? You look awful."

He looked drunk, in fact, but Mark seldom drank, and never more than two beers, and never before coming home from work.

He sat her down and tried to guide her into a channel he knew was soon going to become deep and fast. "They came down to interview me today. It went on for a long time, all day after lunch. I'm a little worried."

Susan, again. So they'd finally come down from Pikeville. She and Mark had discussed the possibility that he would be questioned, especially with the first anniversary of Susan's disappearance approaching. Cops got nervous when anniversaries passed without results. Poole had been calling with the play-by-play every week or so. Kathy wouldn't talk to him, but she could tell by Mark's clouded expression when Poole was discussing Susan. Kathy knew that Shelby was making noise. So *fine,* she thought. She was sick of the innuendo and gossip. She was sick of Poole's constant probing. She had warned Mark that Susan was trouble, yet there was no satisfaction in being right. All she wanted was for Susan to be out of her life.

"The thing with Susan?" she ventured warily.

"Yeah."

"Has she turned up?"

"No. That's what they wanted to interview me about."

"Mark, who came to interview you?"

They had gone in to sit on the couch in the living room. "The FBI's been getting into the investigation," he said. "A guy named Jim Huggins from the Lexington office. He came down, and so did Richard Ray and Paul Maynard." She could see he was holding back.

She had met Richard Ray. He was always on the big cases. She also knew that Ray would lock up his granny if he had evidence, and she did not like the idea that the Kentucky State Police, who were so cheap that a man on a stakeout couldn't even put in for a cheap motel room and was expected to catch a nap in his car, had sent detectives all the way to Florida for what should have been a mere formality of a phone interview.

Kathy felt her anger rise. In fact, if it hadn't been after office hours, she would have got into the car and gone right to Miami to let Mark's boss have a piece of her mind over what she regarded as an example of stupid harassment of an officer who had done his job well under difficult circumstances and deserved to be left alone to continue doing that job. The bureau questioning Mark was one thing. She welcomed that as a way to finally clear the air and put Pikeville behind them. But the Kentucky State Police? What business was this of theirs?

She said, exasperated, "Richard Ray is handling this investigation?"

"Yeah." Mark got up unsteadily and trudged up the stairs to change.

Later, after watching Mark talk to the kids with forced animation and pick listlessly at a late dinner, she put Danielle and little Mark to bed and came down feeling it was time for her to step in and put an end to the nonsense. She had, in fact, already spoken with Terry Hulse about what she regarded as the whining in Pikeville over Mark's deeply misunderstood relationship with Susan. The more she thought about it, the more infuriated she was at the idea that her husband should be put in the humiliating position of being questioned by a pair of hillbillies from the Kentucky State Police who couldn't even find a missing person.

She and Mark had finally gotten things back on track. Their marriage, she felt, had begun to renew itself in Florida, despite the lingering distractions from Pikeville. Mark had been asked to become a supervisor. Things should be going beautifully. Too much was at stake for her to let them continue pushing him around.

"Mark, you are just too trusting," she said in the sternly reproachful tone she used when she thought his good nature overwhelmed his good sense. "Tomorrow morning, I want you to call in and tell them you'll be a few hours late. You stay with the kids. I'm going down to the office first thing in the morning. They're going to hear me out before this goes on any further."

He didn't object, and he didn't ask her what she was going to say. She figured he was so beaten down from it that he didn't care.

He went out to run. When he returned, he found her out back smoking in the darkness of the porch. He pulled up a lawn chair and sat facing her.

She pressed her palms against his hot cheeks. "Is there anything you haven't told me about, Mark? No matter what, we'll work it out."

He felt tears again. He broke eye contact. He tried to force himself to tell her everything.

"No," he said. "There's nothing else." Across the stockade fence, the neighbors' electronic bug-zapper crackled and went quiet.

"Do you remember when the windshield broke in the rental car?" he asked after a minute.

"Mark, what does that have to do with it?"

"Well, if they ask you any questions about that, I just wanted you to know that it wasn't a piece of coal that fell off a truck and broke that window. Remember that's what I told you?"

She only vaguely remembered. It was nearly a year ago, after all. He had phoned from Pikeville, worried that the car rental company was going to make him pay for the goddamned windshield, cracked by a chunk of coal bouncing off a truck, a common enough occurrence on the mountain highways. The kind of Boy Scout earnestness Mark conveyed in that phone call was one of the few things that truly irritated Kathy about her husband. Here he was, a G-man, worried that a rental agency would yell at him for an accident. She had suggested to him that he simply return the car and tell them how the windshield got cracked. It was the last she'd thought of the matter until now.

"I just wanted you to know that that's not how that happened," Mark said, pressing on. "The windshield didn't break the way I told you it did."

"What does that have to do with anything?" she said, gesturing impatiently, as if to dismiss the topic.

"Do you remember when I smashed my hand?"

That was the same trip. Cleaning the garage, a nail. Two weeks later, when he got back to Florida, his hand was badly swollen, gashed across the knuckles. He thought he'd broken a finger, but it was healing. Hard-charging Mark was always banging something up, on the job or at home doing chores. Of course she remembered.

"Well, I said it was a piece of coal off a truck because I was worried about what you would say," Mark continued deliberately. "The truth is, I was working in the garage, and after I snagged my hand, I got mad and kicked the windshield of the car. That's how it really got cut. I didn't want to tell you that because you would think, how could he be so stupid? What if the insurance company makes us pay for the damage? I didn't want you to worry. If you go down there tomorrow, they'll probably ask you some questions about the windshield, and I want you to know what really happened."

A warning bell went off in Kathy's head. She realized that she was not the first person today to hear this incidental piece of information, this *adjustment*, from Mark. "Did you tell them that when they interviewed you today?" she asked sharply.

Uneasily, he replied, "Yeah, I did."

"Jesus, Mark! What are you telling them about something like that for? Why did you even *mention* the goddamn windshield? Don't you realize how that makes you look? How could you be so stupid? What does that have to do with *anything?*" She folded her arms, simmering.

"Because Kathy, they think I had Susan in the car and I took her head and smashed it into the windshield."

The bluntness of the statement stunned her. Not even Shelby was saying anything quite like that. Kathy tried to analyze the situation. If, God forbid, Susan was dead, if she had actually turned up dead, it would be reasonable for the authorities to question Mark, since he had been so close to her. *Fine*, she thought. *He should tell them what he knows and that will be the end of it.* Why was he compounding the equation? Why in the world was he babbling about the goddamn windshield?

He got up to pace, and she knew he was looking not at her but somewhere out into the darkness. "They wanted to know about my activities that week," he explained wanly. "I have to tell them everything that happened as it happened." He explained that after the meeting with Ray and Maynard, he dug the car rental agreement out of his travel voucher file and gave it to Huggins.

"This is totally out of hand!" Kathy shouted, her almond eyes flashing. "You're fueling this yourself now!" She stormed into the house, letting the screen door slam behind her, and went to bed.

As she lay there, many bad thoughts barged into her mind. The night he returned to Florida from Pikeville, it was clear that his hand had been very badly cut. Now she thought: A nail? A *nail?* Closing her eyes tight, she fought to expel her misgivings. But the misgivings intruded. The morning after he had got back from Pikeville, almost a year earlier, she had walked into the bathroom as he was stepping out of the shower. There were purple scratch marks on his neck. "They're from crawling under a truck when we were wrapping up the chop-shop audit out there in the hills," he explained. But she wondered, those scratches must have been pretty deep to be still showing.

An hour later, she was awake and fuming when he climbed into bed next to her. There were things she did not understand, and Kathy was a person who demanded clarity. She lay pointedly on the far side of her half of the mattress so their bodies did not touch. For a long time, neither of them spoke.

Grinding her teeth, Kathy decided to take charge, though she was uncertain about what she was taking charge of. She thought, *I am goddamned if this nonsense is going to continue. We worked hard to get where we wanted to be—that Pikeville nightmare was supposed to be behind us.* Finally, still without acknowledging her husband's presence, she drifted off to a fitful sleep.

The next morning when he went down to breakfast at the hotel Huggins was surprised to find Maynard sitting alone in a booth.

"Where's Richard? He's running late?" Huggins asked.

"No, he's on a plane. He left early to rush back to Pikeville," Maynard said.

"What? Why?"

"He said he was having stuff done around his house and there was a message that they were delivering concrete today, so he had to get be back."

Huggins shrugged and thought, *Why in hell would a guy leave when this has to be the biggest case of his life, to make sure some guy delivers concrete?* But he didn't press the matter as he and Maynard drove to the office, where Tubergen met them with a worried look.

"Kathy Putnam is in my office," he said.

Brimming with indignation early that morning, Kathy had gulped down a cup of coffee and drove to the FBI offices, which were housed in a nondescript modern office building just off the interstate in North Miami Beach. Even agents' wives are required to show identification, so she brusquely dropped her driver's license on the reception desk and stated her business with a cool succinctness that struck the receptionist as arrogance. "I'm Kathy Putnam, Special Agent Mark Putnam's wife. And I'm here to see Mr. Huggins." The receptionist picked up a phone, murmured a few words into it, and asked Kathy to take a seat.

As she waited, she had studied the agency's seal on the wall between the two mahogany doors leading into the inner offices and snorted quietly at the slogan depicted on a banner beneath the scales of justice: FIDELITY—BRAVERY—INTEGRITY. We'll see about that, she thought. Above the seal, a video surveillance camera peered obtrusively into the reception area, recording on a tape that no one would ever watch.

After a few minutes, the door to the left opened and a man who looked to be in his fifties appeared with a hand extended and one foot planted on the reception-area rug. He introduced himself as Roy Tubergen and asked her in with a cordial flourish. It was the first time they had met. Kathy shook his hand briskly and got right to the point. She saw no need under the circumstances to play the role of the prim careerist wife or waste time with a man who probably didn't have a clue about what had gone on in Kentucky.

"I don't mean to be rude, Mr. Tubergen, but I came here to see Jim Huggins. I want to see Huggins, and I want to see that state trooper from Kentucky."

Tubergen was behind his desk, an immense glass-topped expanse on which he displayed a spray of miniature flags in a planter. Tubergen's hands were folded casually beneath parchment-stiff cuffs and squarely fastened with shiny silver links. Teeth gleaming, he smiled at his visitor, who sat erect in a chair placed carefully just to the side of the desk. A plush dark carpet and billowing tropical plants required only the accompaniment of a lazy wood blade ceiling fan to complete the impression of a concierge station at a first-class Moroccan hotel.

"I know you're upset, and I know Mark's upset," he said with studied sympathy. "Why don't you tell me what's going on?"

By this point, Kathy had no use for pleasantries. "Listen. I want to talk to them, not to you. As far as I'm concerned, the bureau owes me right now. I went through hell in Kentucky. I slept with a gun for this agency. And I'll be damned if I'm going to be jerked around or let you do what you're trying to do to my husband. I'm sorry!"

"I'm really sorry that you're upset like this," Tubergen said, assuming that her tears were about to arrive. His hand brushed at the handkerchief peeping out from his breast pocket.

But her brown eyes flashed anger instead. "No, you don't seem to understand. This is not a matter of my being upset. When an agent's name—*Mark's* name—is thrown out in the way it obviously has been in Kentucky, the FBI should have been all over it before it escalated to the point where my husband's integrity was on the line. I have never seen my husband like this. And now they are *questioning* him? I am here with information that should have been included in this investigation a long time ago, and I want it straightened out. I demand to be interviewed. The FBI is going to hear me." Her chin was set.

Tubergen had had only a short time to prepare himself for the prospect of an agent under his supervision being the possible target of a criminal investigation. He had taken no time at all to anticipate an assault from that agent's wife. However, a career in the federal bureaucracy had prepared him with the requisite etiquette. "Let me get Mr. Huggins for you."

Tubergen vacated his office with relief and found Huggins with his office door closed. He was well aware that Kathy had arrived.

"Kathy Putnam wants to talk, and I am glad she is talking to you and not me because she is pissed," Tubergen told Huggins, who stood, buttoned his coat, smoothed his tie, and waited for Tubergen to bring her in.

Huggins later recalled, "I'm thinking, what a great way to start off what is going to be an awful day. So Roy brings her in and she's friendly at first: 'Mr. Huggins, I am Kathy Putnam and there's some things I want to talk to it talk to you about.' For about two minutes she was cordial while she built up a head of steam."

"Where is Richard Ray?" she said.

"He had to go back to Pikeville this morning," Huggins told her.

She let loose on Ray, accusing him of many things that were new to Huggins. "That no good son of a bitch Richard Ray doesn't have the balls to face me?"

Huggins listened politely but he was thinking, *what kind of an unholy mess is this going to turn out to be?*

Not having Ray on hand was a major disappointment. Kathy had wanted the Kentucky cops there when she said her piece. Yearning to comfort her, Huggins heard himself giving assurance to Kathy's obvious belief that the investigation was routine, a technicality perhaps muddled by police ham-handedness. He did not let her see his own misgivings about the previous day's questioning of her husband.

"I understand why you're angry," Huggins said. "Look, all I can do is explain to you what the FBI is doing. We are officially involved now in the investigation, and we're going to see to it that this thing is taken care of once and for all. There are questions that need to be answered—you know as well as I do the kinds of allegations that are flying around in Pikeville. Well, now the big guys are involved." He smiled. "The bureau is on the case, and we're going to get to the bottom of it, no fooling around now. Everything's going to be fine once the air is cleared."

Kathy relaxed a bit, satisfied that she had at least staked out a defense of Mark's honor. She figured the investigation would get the questions answered—Mark would take a few lumps, of course. He had been sloppy with informants such as Susan, who should have been closed out long before she disappeared. But it wasn't Mark's fault the FBI had let that office get out of control, and besides, Mark had plenty of credit in the bank. Wasn't he one of the bureau's fair-haired boys? Police work was never neat. You got kicked in the teeth at times; he'd recover. And besides, Kathy wasn't about to let her husband take the heat alone—she remained determined to make the bureau confront and concede its own culpability in sending a rookie agent to a hellhole like Pikeville with all of sixteen weeks' training, including a *two-hour* class in working with informants. With no supervision. And then compounding the error by stashing a manipulative fuck-knuckle like Poole there? Dick Tracy would have had a hard time under such circumstances.

"Mr. Huggins," she said calmly, "it's no secret that we went through a terrible ordeal. I don't know how far you've looked into what was going on in Pikeville, but they've used me and Mark. My family was almost destroyed because of what happened down there. As I said, I don't understand when Mark's name was thrown out initially why the FBI wasn't all over this thing." This time there actually were tears in her eyes as she pressed on. "Where were you? Nearly a year has gone by since Susan supposedly disappeared and all of this talk started. Mark is *distraught* over this thing. When he came home last night, I've never seen him like that. And it's his own people doing this now. We left Pikeville behind, but it keeps coming back to haunt us. And Mark's own former partner Poole is up there taking part in the whispering campaign. That has to stop!"

"Kathy, I hear what you're saying. Mark is one of the finest young agents in the bureau. That's why we're involved now. Why don't you tell me what's on your mind?" Huggins took out a yellow legal pad.

She obliged, launching into an indictment that she had mentally prepared for months, honed the night before, and rehearsed on the drive down from Fort Lauderdale. Right off, she threw in the person she held almost as responsible for Mark's difficulties as Susan was.

"As far as Mr. Poole is concerned, I have absolutely no respect for that man. He's got no business carrying a badge. If you want to talk to somebody who's had a relationship with Susan, don't forget Poole. From what Susan told me, Poole spent an awful lot of time trying to get her to go to bed with him."

"Poole," Huggins grunted, scribbling some notes, realizing that this could get complicated. One by one, Kathy spelled out her grievances about the Pikeville office, impressing him with her command of details about FBI business in an operation that had clearly gone badly out of control. Informants tripping over each other and making secret, often conflicting deals. Crossed signals. Huggins's pencil worked furiously to keep up. He hadn't known about the abortive drug sting; he'd never heard of an agent's wife being encouraged to risk her neck like that. That alone was very, very irregular. And then, Kathy's allegation that Mark's partner leaked it to an *informant*? For a man like Huggins, who took great pride in the professionalism of the FBI, what Kathy told him was gravely disturbing.

Clearly, Mark Putnam was not the only one who needed to come up with some answers. And whatever happened with him, there would still be the fury of Kathy Putnam to contend with. This was not a woman who stayed in the background. And while he realized that Kathy was projecting some of her anger and frustration onto Mark's former partner, she was also prepared to hold forth in detail on matters that would add complications that this investigation, highly touchy to begin with, that he did not need right now. Especially if she went public.

When she wound down, Huggins sat back and exhaled loudly. "I can't believe what went on down there," he said, then asked, "You don't think Poole killed her, do you?"

"No," Kathy replied, sitting back and smoothing her skirt over her knees. The fact was she didn't even believe Susan was dead. Had Huggins invited her to make a guess, she would have guessed the same thing the authorities in Pikeville had assumed, that Susan was hiding out somewhere, lying low because she had shot off her big mouth once too often and someone was threatening to shut it up permanently. That was Susan.

Huggins cleared his throat and thanked her for coming. "We're going to see to it that we check all these things out, and that this is resolved as quickly as possible."

That sounded vague but promising to Kathy, who drove home with a degree of satisfaction that she had at least laid out the outlines of the Pikeville problem, had given them enough information to investigate properly, make their report, and let Mark get on with his career and them with their lives. So confident was she that things were moving along in the proper direction that she welcomed Huggins's seemingly offhand suggestion, delivered as she was leaving, that Mark might want to take a polygraph test, just for the record. Mark had been ridiculously eager to cooperate anyway. "Oh," she had said with an airy goodbye wave, "he'll have no problem with that."

She was glad to find Mark at home out back watching Danielle and little Mark splashing in the inflated wading pool. She could tell he was nervous by the tentative way he asked her how it went at the FBI office.

"Everything's going to be fine," she assured him. "You've got to relax. I gave them enough information to clear this thing up. If anybody has anything to worry about now, it's Poole."

"Well, I don't know about that," he ventured uneasily.

She wished he would just let her handle it. "Mark, you don't realize the kinds of thing an investigation like this can uncover." Hardly incidental to her concern was a desire that Mark not realize the extent to which she had confided in Poole during the winter about getting them transferred out of Pikeville.

Yet Mark remained as apprehensive as he had been the night before. "Well, I'm going to get dressed and go to the office." He kissed the kids and turned to go in the house. "I just want you to know how much I appreciate your going to bat for me."

"We're in this together."

He didn't say so, but Mark knew that was absolutely no longer true.

After Kathy left and while they waited for Mark to arrive for more questioning, Huggins called Capt. Gary Rose back at the state police barracks in Pikeville. "We interviewed Mark for about seven hours yesterday and I think we've got some problems that we're going to have to run through." He also mentioned Kathy's anger at Richard Ray.

At noon, Mark entered the office where Huggins and Gavin were waiting. His feet felt as if iron blocks were attached to them. He was acutely aware that his lengthy twenty-five-page signed statement from the previous day, which had already been typed up, was full of holes.

Gavin told him as he stood there, "We've been reading your statement and in talking to Jim here, there's a few things we'd like to ask you." Gavin asked Mark to sit in a chair and demonstrate how he could have managed to kick a car windshield to crack it. Mark tried half-heartedly, and dropped his head.

"Just checking, man," Gavin said sadly.

Huggins said, "Well, Mark, you know you're the only one here who knows the truth. You said you would be willing to take a polygraph."

"Absolutely, Jim. Let's get this over with."

Very quickly, it was set up with headquarters for Mark and Huggins to fly to Washington that night, and for Mark to be polygraphed the next morning.

Mark went home early to pack. After much wavering in his mind, he was now certain that they didn't have a body. No one had found Susan. No one could prove that she was dead. But again, he had to think, *She has been out there for a year.* Wasn't it time to bring her in?

Now he was measuring his time in hours. Would there be one more night with the kids? He did not know. He did know that very soon, it would be out of his hands.

Kathy had hoped to see a glint of optimism in her husband's eyes, but he looked worse than ever. With more resignation than she thought appropriate, Mark told her that he had decided he had to take the polygraph, though Huggins and Tubergen had assured him it was strictly voluntary. To get it over with, he was planning to fly to Washington that night. The test was the next morning. She watched him stuffing underwear in an overnight bag.

"Do you want to do this?" she asked, frowning at his mechanical motions.

"It's to clear my name," he said without much conviction, turning to her with a look of helplessness. "Do you think I should or not?"

Kathy took a deep breath and exhaled slowly. To her, the important thing was to get this behind them. After thinking for a moment, she accepted his decision. "I guess it makes sense for you to take the polygraph and straighten this out. Calm down. You're making this into a bigger problem than it has to be. This is going to work itself out. How could it not work itself out? I don't understand why you're so upset."

"You're right." He seemed to brighten.

★   ★   ★

Kathy made an early dinner. Mark didn't eat much, and he barely noticed the kids at the table. Before he left for his flight, he went through his usual ritual of reading the kids their bedtime story. Kathy lingered in the hall and looked at the three of them on the bed, a tableau of familial trust, fatherly love, childlike devotion, framed in the doorway of Danielle's room. Kathy unconsciously hung it like a photograph in her mind. Then she went out back to smoke and think.

Her afternoon courage faded with the daylight; with a sick feeling, she considered what she should have realized a long time ago, the likelihood that her husband had had an affair with Susan. Nothing else that she knew of could explain his prolonged agitation, and what she now recognized as his abiding guilt. She despised the thought, threw it against the wall of reason, but it bounced back. He had. The son of a bitch had.

If that was true, agreeing to the polygraph was a mistake. When he came out to say good-bye, she said, "Look, Mark, something's obviously wrong." She was thinking fast, trying to review the options realistically through her growing pain. "Whatever it is, you've got to know by now, with everything we've been through together, that we'll work it out. If there's something you have to tell me about, about you and Susan, or whatever, tell me now before you go and do this thing tomorrow. If there's something that you're hiding when you take this polygraph, it's just going to make you look guilty. Whatever it is, you can tell me. Tell me what it is now and we can get through this, Mark. If we got through Pikeville together, we can get through this." Desperately, she wanted an admission before he left her alone in the night with her thoughts.

He didn't comply. "Well, what would you think if I had?"

She didn't want to say, "Had what?" Instead, she tried to hurtle forward in time, forgive him, and start the healing. "Mark, we'll work it out. If something happened between you and her, we'll deal with it. There isn't anything you can't tell me—"

"What if I had—"

"—*nothing*, Mark," she repeated, fighting tears as the truth displayed itself.

"I want you to understand something. I have to take the polygraph tomorrow. I have to do it. And then I'll tell you everything. You'll understand."

And then he left for the airport.

Huggins met him at the Fort Lauderdale airport and they sat together on the plane for the two-hour flight to Washington. Huggins kept the conversation off the obvious matter at hand. Instead they talked about the weather and the University of Kentucky basketball team. Huggins wanted to ask about Kathy and the kids, how they liked South Florida, but he thought the better of that. Instead, he reached into the seatback pocket for the inflight magazine. Mark pretended to read a copy of *Sports Illustrated*, trying to shut everything else out, including Huggins's obvious discomfort.

It was late when they got in to Washington National Airport. Mark remembered arriving there in 1986, a new agent in training, on top of the world. On their way to Quantico, the thirty-five rookies in the FBI class checked each other out for what they could spot: attitudes, guts, brains, physique. Looking for the edge. Hoping they'd make it. Wondering who among them would not.

At the same airport on a Thanksgiving weekend, on a three-day leave from the academy, he was met by Kathy and two-year-old Danielle, all dressed up. They stayed at the Crystal City Marriott and visited the monuments with the happy tenacity of Japanese tourists. Would the baby remember the sense of proprietorship her old man felt when he showed her the Capitol, the Lincoln Memorial, the White House? Would she ever think of her father as a federal agent, in this city, that wonderful time, the three of them in love?

He and Huggins took a cab to their hotel. Huggins went his own way. Mark put his things in his room and went back out to wander the empty streets of the capital. The walking gave him the boost of energy he needed. He was still an agent of the government he swore to protect. A damned fine agent, one of the goddamned best. Hardworking, focused, a self-starter, a guy you only had to ask once. He wasn't the smartest or the best educated or the craftiest. He was naïve. But he was ethical and honest, and he would match his dedication against anybody's. Briefly, he savored that.

He thought of getting rip-roaring drunk, but quickly ruled that out. He walked for hours. God, he had wanted to belong. This is where he belonged, in this meticulously dignified capital with its monuments like alabaster tablets forced on the sky by floodlight.

He turned back to the hotel. As he walked, he spoke to her. "*Well, Susan, my time is up. I don't know how you're feeling about this, but it's time to get this thing squared away. It's time to bring you home.*"

He went to bed feeling at peace.

In Florida, his wife found no peace that night, nor any other night that followed. Kathy went to bed crippled with doubt. *Okay,* she thought. *He did it. Yes, the bastard slept with Susan!* She cringed to recall how pathetic she had found Susan at the time. She closed her eyes and thought hard, as if to summon the unknowable: *When and how did they do it? Where did they do it? How did they keep it from her? They. They.*

Susan blabbed about everything—how could she have kept her mouth shut about such a coup as sleeping with Mark? For that alone, Kathy hated her, for mocking her so effortlessly.

But her imagination recoiled. No, she decided abruptly, it was not true. Mark never lied to her. It had never happened. Oh, it *almost* happened, probably, but it never got that far. He had better sense than that. Her heart flooded with love and gratitude for the loyalty her husband had shown, at a time when their marriage was strained; she cherished him for the guilt he must have felt, at what he almost did to her—and to Danielle, his sweetheart, to dapper little Mark . . .

She kicked off the covers and lay there, wide-awake, her thoughts spinning. Nothing stayed in place long enough to make sense. She steadied her impressions, fixed on them one at a time, ran down a mental checklist. The hazard lights were flashing. Come *on*, she told herself brutally. There was something seriously wrong with Mark's demeanor and behavior, and there had been all year. She could see it now. A man who was never sick suddenly always complaining about diarrhea. That scratching at his chest to the point where he had to go to the doctor to get medicine for the rash. Mr. Easygoing, now so distracted he couldn't brush his teeth without moaning. What the hell was wrong with him?

And that rental car! The cracked windshield, his bandaged hand. Why had he lied about it? Why had he gone to so much trouble to bring it up when she had pretty much forgotten about it, would never have given it another thought? She could see his boyish face, lying as brazenly and haplessly as a child. And Susan throwing her head back with that shrill laugh. How foolish she must have sounded to her: *Susan, you are an intelligent, attractive, and worthwhile woman. Mark is not the only man in the world. You can have what I have, Susan. Don't sell yourself short.* Susan! Susan always looked for the easy way. Susan was a thief. She took what she wanted when she knew she could get away with it. Of course she took Mark. Of course she did! Only an idiot wouldn't see that!

She burrowed into the covers feeling desperately alone. *You can have what I have, Susan. You have to set goals and work toward them.* How delicious that must have seemed to her lying in Mark's arms, against his body. And she had; Kathy now knew it as surely as she knew her children's names. Susan had slept with her husband.

Dammit, she was closer to Susan than Mark was! Susan was her friend! She'd been the one to teach that trailer-trash hillbilly how to behave like a lady! She knew all of Susan's tricks, all of her brittle fears, her inadequacies, and futile, ridiculous ambitions. Susan was pretty, if you liked the Daisy Mae type, but she was dumb as a doorknob. Kathy and Mark used to make cruel jokes about her. For a fleeting, righteous instant, Kathy resented her husband deeply for the contempt he had shown *Susan,* her friend and admirer. Hadn't Susan even started dressing like her, *talking* like her, for God's sake? Hadn't she begun to say *you,* not *y'all?* Susan had told her she loved Mark, that Mark was "gorgeous." Kathy merely shrugged that off.

Kathy began to probe the wound again, fixing on the moment of betrayal, when he unzipped his pants. She tortured herself with the image. She looked at Mark's pillow, demanding an accounting. Details, goddammit! Chapter and verse, buddy boy! When? How many times? What were you wearing? What did she do that I don't do? How many times, Mark? Did she come? Did she squeal like a little hillbilly pig? Did you kiss her precious little face, hold her precious little hand, walk her in the precious goddamn woods? Did you! What did you say to her? Did you laugh about me? What did you tell her about me! What did you say! *Why didn't I know about this!*

How stupid she felt. Of course she should have seen it. But a worse fear was overwhelming her merciless insistence: the ramifications of the affair, not the least of which was the possibility that the rumor she'd dismissed as ridiculous—that Susan had been pregnant with Mark's child—might also be true. That there could be a baby—her husband's baby—Danielle and little Mark's half brother or half sister! Kathy struck her clenched fist on the mattress with each word: *"That's why this had such an impact on him."*

The only sensible thing to do was to divorce him. She groped through doubts: Can I live with this? Do I throw away eight years, especially knowing what I know about Pikeville, who Susan was, where she came from? She meant *nothing!* They would never see her again! Then it struck her anew: if he had had an affair with her and lied to cover it up, it was going to make him look guilty if Susan really was dead. She thought of the damaged hand, the disjointed comments, the phone calls and brooding looks of the past year. *What if he did know something about her being missing?* What *about* the lies about that windshield? There were too many lies leering like hobgoblins in the shadows.

At last her mind began working like a cop's. Okay, they are in the car. They make love in the car. (How tacky, Mark! The car?) He has a short affair with her, and one night they are in the car and they get in an accident. She's hurt, hurt bad—he panics and leaves her. That could explain the cracked windshield.

No, Mark would never leave Susan lying somewhere, injured and helpless. But was there any other way Mark could have been involved in Susan's death—assuming Susan was dead? Say they skid off the road, hit a tree. Susan dies. Mark panics and then leaves her in the mountains somewhere. No, that would mean there would have been more damage to the car than just a broken windshield.

Or they're having an affair; they have a fight when they're in the car. There's a big argument, Mark gets pissed off, punches the windshield, Susan storms out of the car and wanders away . . . and later, one of these *other* things happens to her, like that scummy ex-husband catches her and beats her once too often, or one of those other lowlifes she knows kills her, one of the drug dealers or bank robbers who always seem to be in the wings of her life. So Susan is dead, and Mark is indirectly involved. This is possible.

Hellish images rage through her mind. His bandaged hand, their faces gazing at each other, Susan's inane giggle, countless casual comments now swollen with cruel irony. The way Mark brooded when they discussed Susan's disappearance, his reaction that time when Kathy mused, "She could be lying dead somewhere," now startling in hindsight: *"Don't ever say that!"*

Kathy weighed her own role. She was an adult, a child of the 1970s, an honors graduate of the sexual revolution. So he had a tumble with some mountain girl, big deal. He came home to his wife, didn't he? She thought of a defiant country-western song, *"You ain't woman enough to take my man."* It wasn't the end of the world; affairs happened to the best of people in the worst of times. But why did it hurt like this? She'd found the false base on her life, on their relationship. Her husband, once a part of her very being, suddenly seemed as alien as the man in the next car at a red light. She felt foolish and exposed. She had never measured up. She heard ghostly laughter rise in chorus, from a grade school in Connecticut over fog-chilled hollows of a Kentucky night. *"Ponticelli, your ears! Your ears are sticking out! Look at her!"*

She opened her eyes to a dull headache. The sun warmed the bed, flooded the room. Downstairs, she could hear Danielle lecturing her brother on the proper way to pour cereal into a bowl.

In the kitchen, as she banged the kettle down on the stove, the phone rang. It was Mark. His voice was shaky. She pressed her eyes shut against the sunlight, knowing that the nightmare hadn't ended.

"I just wanted you to know that this is not going to go well today. I'm really scared about this. I don't know if you're going to understand," he said.

An artery in her neck throbbed. "I'm glad you called. Don't do this! I want to talk to you first." She wanted to hear the truth in his own words, even if it meant a situation she could no longer control.

"I told you I have to do this. But be prepared." His voice broke.

"Whatever happens, whatever the results of the polygraph, don't talk to them until you talk to me. Don't give them a statement or any information. You don't have to do that, Mark."

He was noncommittal. "I'll talk to you afterward."

The FBI Polygraph Unit was located on the second floor of a nondescript office building a few blocks from FBI headquarters. Huggins was glad to see that Mark had arrived by 10 o'clock and was quietly reading the *Washington Post* in the waiting room. Huggins greeted him cordially and went into a separate room where a bureau polygraph examiner, a supervisory special agent who specialized in lie-detector testing, was just finishing up reading the missing person's case file. Huggins and the examiner spoke for almost an hour about the case.

Then Mark was summoned. He nodded to Huggins and followed the examiner into the polygraph room while Huggins waited down the hall in a vacant office, reading the newspaper Mark had left behind.

After wiring Mark up and asking the usual preliminary questions about name and birthplace, the polygraph examiner asked, "Did your rental car in June 1989 play any role in the disappearance of Susan Smith?"

"No," Mark said.

"Did you have anything to do with the disappearance of Susan Smith?"

"No."

"Have you ever been convicted of a crime?"

"No."

"Have you ever violated the FBI's guidelines regarding illegal substances?"

"No."

"Did you have sex with Susan Smith?"

"No, I did not."

"Did you cause the disappearance of Susan Smith?"

"No."

Only a few minutes had gone by. The examiner frowned over his graph, asked Mark, "Would you step outside for a minute?" and went to the office where Huggins was waiting. "You have problems with your guy. He's off the charts. Do you want to continue?" the examiner said.

"Let me talk to him," Huggins replied, heartsick. In a minute, Mark was standing beside the desk where Huggins sat. A bureau stenographer sidled in and sat in the corner, her pen poised above her pad.

Huggins avoided looking directly at him. "Mark, you've got some problems, buddy. I think you know that," he said.

"I know. It was the question about sex. I did kiss her."

Huggins shook his head sadly and murmured, "No, no, no, no."

Mark took a deep shaky breath and looked pleadingly at him. "Jim, I want to get this over with."

Huggins sighed and asked him to sit. Mark's lips were tight, then he said, "Before we do anything, can I call Kathy?"

Huggins was playing this by ear, and a part of him still insisted that maybe there was an explanation other than the obvious one. Huggins stepped out of the office so Mark could speak privately to his wife.

Kathy answered on the first ring.

"How did it go?" she asked.

"Not very well. Things are bad."

She was trembling. "Are they holding you there?" Her words sounded muffled and disconnected, like a television playing through an apartment wall.

"No, they're not keeping me. But they have a stenographer who is taking down everything I say now."

"No! Mark! Mark? Don't say anything! If they'll let you come home, come home and we'll talk about it here. Don't say anything else. Do you hear me? Come home."

"Okay," he said.

He sensed a flurry of activity outside the office after Huggins retuned. Someone on another phone, papers being shuffled. A different process being set into motion. He remained outwardly calm, but his mind raced. It was clear that the atmosphere had changed. Other agents were standing watchfully by.

Mark was exceedingly apologetic in speaking to Huggins. "Jim, I'm so sorry, but Kathy wants me to come home, and she doesn't want me to say anymore. Am I under arrest?"

"No, Mark. You're not under arrest. You're free to go."

"Jim, I really don't want to be uncooperative, but Kathy wants me to tell her first. I'm really sorry."

Sadly, and at last extinguishing in his mind the tiny ember of hope that Mark was innocent and an explanation would be forthcoming, Huggins told him, "That's okay, Mark, you go ahead and tell Kathy what you need to tell her, and when you get home, in the morning you get hold of Bill Gavin first thing. He'll help you get through this, Mark."

It was well after one o'clock. Huggins had a flight home later in the afternoon for Lexington; Mark to Florida. The two men grabbed their bags and walked without speaking to the closest Metro station, where they rode together to the airport.

In midafternoon on a Saturday, the subway car was nearly empty. Sitting beside Mark, Huggins finally broke the silence, speaking as softly but clearly as he could. "Listen to me, Mark. You don't have to say a thing, just listen. I think something happened when you went back to Pikeville. You didn't expect to see Susan there at the hotel. She probably started firing on you the minute she saw you. There was a hell of an argument, and then I don't know what happened, but I think maybe you did something accidentally. Something happened that you probably didn't intend to happen, and then you panicked. And here you are."

Mark did not reply. Eyes cast downward, he nodded. Huggins felt his lips tremble. He held back tears.

His flight was the last one into Fort Lauderdale airport, arriving around midnight. An after-hours glare harshly lit the faces of the stragglers shuffling past the darkened shops, shut cafés, and unattended ticket counters. Kathy found Mark waiting alone at the far end of a wide, empty corridor.

He started to speak, but she held up her hand and said, "Just don't talk yet."

In the car, she suggested that they stop at a Holiday Inn near the airport for a drink. It was a conversation neither of them wanted to have at home, where Kathy's sister, Chris, was still living with them. Kathy looked straight ahead and lit a cigarette in the car, something she hadn't had the nerve to do in many years.

It was nearly one o'clock when they walked into the Holiday Inn lounge. At the bar, Kathy ordered a double Black Russian for herself and a beer for Mark. Carrying the drinks, she led him silently to a table in the darkness. Across the room, a four-piece band was playing heavy metal; couples in their twenties, the last gasp of the fading Fort Lauderdale beach scene, danced under lights that flashed like those on a patrol car.

Defiantly, Kathy lit another cigarette and blew the smoke at a point just over Mark's shoulder. She moved her glass to the side and looked directly at him for the first time that night. She waited.

"This is really serious," he sputtered.

You're goddamn right about that, she thought. In a cold fury, she smoked and waited.

"I'm sorry—"

Get on with it, she thought angrily.

"It's—"

"Look," she said in the sarcastic tone of a prosecutor trying to dismiss the ridiculous before homing in on the self-evident. "Did you kill her?" She spat out the words with a street swagger she hadn't used since she was a teenager.

"Yes."

This was not an answer she had anticipated. She had been expecting a nervous chuckle, a "Come on, Kathy!" before she probed the painful details and watched him squirm. She blinked slowly, her mind two beats behind the words.

"So you slept with her!"

"Yeah, I did."

"And this could have been your baby." She flung the sentence across the table.

"Kat—"

"Just answer the questions! How did this happen?" He kept crying. "Was there a car accident?"

"No."

She let out a furious, thin stream of smoke. "It wasn't a car accident. Did you *shoot* her?" Her voice was rising. Out of the corner of her eye, she noticed a middle-aged man in a business suit drinking alone at a table a few feet away. He had been casually watching them, with his eye on her. Now he stiffened at what he overheard.

"No. I choked her." Mark made a feeble little choking motion.

"You choked her," she said in a sarcastic flat tone. Then her voice rose, her face contorted with sarcasm, and she made an exaggerated choking motion, as if to show him how it was done. "You *strangled* her?" With that, the eavesdropper at the next table abandoned any pretext of indifference. He got up, slapped a twenty-dollar bill on his table, and scuttled away.

She waited until the man was gone. "How do you know she was dead? If you left her, are you sure she was dead? Are you sure, Mark! They haven't found the body. She was unconscious. Maybe she just got up and walked away."

"I thought that a million times. She was dead. I know she was."

Mark had regained some control. His eyes were smarting from the smoke, which she was making no effort whatsoever to direct away from him.

"I want to explain—"

"All right," she said abruptly. "Tell me how it happened."

He said that he hadn't lied to her when she first asked him about Susan, back when Susan was shooting her mouth off about Mark. He had laughed it off as absurd. And it was—he hadn't slept with her then. That happened later, but except for the night Kenneth called, the subject hadn't come up again until now.

All of the pieces fell together with a deafening thud. There was another round of drinks that was brought by a waitress wearing a thong bikini bottom and a lacy push-up bra under a little red jacket. Kathy was dimly aware of her trying to make eye contact with Mark. Her mind careened through uncertain frames of time: Mark and Susan drive into the mountains; they park, argue some more, suddenly she's screaming, hitting—and he loses it. It's over in sixty seconds. He pulls her out onto the ground, desperate, but she won't breathe. Like that, she's dead. She's wearing his shorts and T-shirt, for some reason that Kathy forgets. He puts her in the trunk of the car and goes back to the motel. And then drives to a meeting in Lexington the next day and parks the car out front with Susan's body in the trunk. *He drives around with a dead woman locked in the trunk of his car, like a gym bag?*

"You have to remember, she was screaming at me, Kat. I was afraid that everyone else in the hotel would hear about it."

He succumbed to wrenching tears just as the reality of what Kathy was hearing slammed finally into consciousness. In a flash of contempt, she walloped him, smacked him so hard her arm resonated with pain. He tried to duck the blow, which caught him forcefully on the right side of his face. As he dodged, he lost his balance and fell to the floor, one hand grasping the little table on which the drinks had spilled. He was crying like a three-year-old when he came back up. She had never seen Mark shed more than a few sentimental tears and watched the spectacle with the detached interest of a motorist passing an accident scene.

"I want to get out of here. Kathy, please let's get out of here and go home and talk. I don't want the neighbors knowing our business."

She wasn't budging. "No, I'm not moving and you're not moving. I'm simply not ready to get up yet." She had mustered a degree of haughtiness now and caught the eye of the waitress, who had wandered over expectantly when she saw Mark fall. Kathy regarded the waitress contemptuously in her skimpy costume, ready to wallop her, too.

"Another beer?" the waitress asked Mark, and added with a look at Kathy, "Another double Black Russian?"

"Yeah, another double. And he'll have a beer."

Kathy turned back to Mark, but the conversation had begun to blur. Several surreal rounds of drinks later, she and the man she had long loved and respected, the father of her children, had explored every facet of the fact that he had killed Susan Smith.

In the car, Kathy lay back and blamed herself: "I could have stopped this if I had been paying attention."

"Hey, I did what I did. Nothing you did could have prevented this."

"Yes, I could have! I could have! You don't know what I know!" She was nearly hysterical.

She recalled making a few clumsy thrusts: "You bastard, how could you do this to us?" and "Why did you *tell* me! Now that I know, I can't lie for you!" She remembered him wordlessly and gently undressing her in their bedroom and taking his place in bed beside her. She sat up and shouted, "What am I going to do with the kids while their father is in *prison*, Mark! Did you think of *that* when you killed her?"

15

She slept for less than an hour. With her mind instantly reeling again, she bolted up in bed, sensing Mark lying beside her with his eyes open. She squinted at the glowing red numerals on the alarm clock. It was five-thirty. She was due at her part-time waitressing job at the International House of Pancakes at seven, to get ready for the first wave of the Sunday-morning church crowd. Her first cogent thought was that she needed to phone her manager to say that she wasn't coming in, in time for him to bring in a substitute. But it was still too early to call. She remembered that Mark had told her he had to be in the office at ten, to talk to the special agent in charge. She wanted to go with him.

Not knowing exactly what to do, she dressed quickly and walked down the hallway to Danielle's bedroom, where the sight of Chris, asleep in the spare bed, vaguely irritated her. *How could you be sleeping at a time like this?* she thought, shaking her sister until her eyes were open. "Wake up! I need you!"

"What in the world is wrong?" Chris asked sleepily. Kathy was put out, as if Chris should somehow know that a calamity had occurred. "I can't believe he did that!"

"Did *what*, for God's sake?"

"Mark killed that woman!" Kathy hissed like a madwoman.

Chris, fully awake now, gasped, "What woman?"

Kathy began to cry with frustration, sensing that this was only the start of the pestilence of explaining that lay ahead of her. "The one in Kentucky!"

Chris's own police instincts snapped into place. Full explanations could come later. "Should I get you and the kids out of here?"

"What for? No! He's fine!" Kathy sobbed, afraid of awakening Danielle, who slept on with her face turned to the wall.

"What do you want me to do?"

Kathy threw her hands up. "Leave me alone!" she said in a shrill whisper, and stormed into the bathroom, where she mechanically brushed her teeth. Absently, she fumbled in the medicine chest for her makeup and dabbed it at her face.

There was no protocol for starting such a day. The closest parallel was a sudden death in the family, but Kathy had not even had any adult experience with that—she was only thirty years old; her own parents were relatively young; even three of their parents were still alive. She found herself in the kitchen, staring in bafflement at the wall phone in her hand. She put it to her ear and heard it ringing at the other end.

Her father answered huskily. Why *him?* she thought furiously; why couldn't *she* have picked it up? Her voice quavering, she managed to say, "It's Kathy. It's serious. I need you guys to come down here right away," but that was, all she could get out. Sensing Mark's presence behind her, she slammed the receiver down on the breakfast counter.

"I'll handle it," Mark said, rushing back upstairs. Wordlessly, she put the phone to her ear, listening to her father's labored breathing. When Mark picked up the extension in the bedroom, she heard her husband say, "Ray, it's Mark. There's something I have to talk to you about . . ." With a trembling index finger, she pressed the button down and placed the phone into the cradle.

By now it was after six; little Mark had wandered into the bedroom, waking Danielle. Chris took charge of the kids and didn't ask questions. Once she had decided that no one was in any danger, she figured the best she could do was to keep the kids occupied and not worry about clarifications until Kathy and Mark sorted out whatever had occurred. She made a deliberate decision not even to speculate, beyond supposing that an accident of some kind had happened involving Mark and someone else when he was in Kentucky. She was vaguely aware of the problems they had experienced in Pikeville, especially of Kathy's misery there just before they left. She had heard something, during the time she had been living with them in Florida, about an informant being missing. But she figured these were just normal headaches of FBI life.

When she brought the kids down for breakfast, Chris spotted Mark on the couch watching her with a stricken and questioning look. She ventured a cheerful but shaky, "Good morning."

"Hey," he said very softly, forcing a smile. "How's it going, Chris?"

During the six years she had known him, Chris had come to respect her brother-in-law for his equanimity and his steady good sense. She thought, without any question, that Mark was the best thing that had ever happened to Kathy. The months she had spent living with them had only reinforced that assessment. If Mark was in control, how bad could it be? She had never even heard the man raise his voice. Kathy, the volatile one, was out in the kitchen making coffee, which was reassuring in itself, although Chris did observe that her sister had spilled the grounds in a small heap on the counter and had not poured any water into the machine. Furthermore, Kathy's makeup, usually light, appeared to have been jabbed on with a paintbrush, and her outfit looked as if it had been assembled in the dark. Chris took over the coffee making and said nothing.

Kathy broke down again when she called her boss at the restaurant. As gently as he could, Mark took the phone and explained that a family emergency had come up and she wouldn't be in. The manager was considerate and concerned. To Mark's relief, he didn't pry for details.

They had to leave around nine for the drive to the office to talk with Gavin, the special agent in charge of the Miami FBI Bureau, who had kept in touch with Huggins in Washington the previous day. It was a meeting both men dreaded.

At some point before they left the house, Mark telephoned his mother. Kathy could not imagine what he said to her.

A janitor let them in a side door at the FBI offices. Gavin was already waiting. A large, affable man who supervised more than three hundred agents in one of the FBI's most important regional offices, he had been fully apprised of a situation that was, as far as anyone could tell, unprecedented in the eighty-three-year history of the FBI: an agent, one of his boys, appeared to be facing a charge of criminal homicide. While Putnam had not confessed, he had badly failed the polygraph, and he wasn't exactly protesting his innocence. Making the situation even worse, for veteran FBI men such as Gavin and Huggins, men who had seen it all and remained true to the faith, was that the offender wasn't some rogue cowboy on some drug-addled flame-out. Of all of the eight thousand agents in the bureau, it had to be *this* guy—this walking personification of the goddamn Boy Scout code, this earnest, likable, gifted, indefatigable young man who seemed not only to avow, but to actually manifest and *project* every virtue that the bureau still imagined itself as representing.

The guy they would have put on a recruiting poster now qualified for a wanted poster.

Gavin greeted them in jeans and a short-sleeved shirt, which made
him look like an interloper behind his big mahogany desk. He was
accompanied in the office by his second-in-command, the assistant special agent in charge, Larry Torrence, who had on a suit
and tie. Gavin apologized gamely for the stifling atmosphere in the
building and sent Torrence out to see if he could find someone to
turn on the air-conditioning. He asked if they were comfortable,
if they wanted coffee. All Kathy wanted was to smoke; seeing her
desperation, Gavin went out himself to find an ashtray.

The social preliminaries were excruciating for Kathy. She was
mortified to find herself shaking with fright, which she knew was
not over the confrontation at hand, but over what would follow.
The fact was she and Mark had not yet been able to have a rational
discussion about their future. Sitting there trying to get her body
movements under control, she was suddenly afraid that her husband might not even make it home with her. She tried mightily to
order her thoughts.

Grateful for both the ashtray and the consideration Gavin
showed in holding a match to her cigarette, she drew in great
gulps of smoke, exhaling furiously between racking sobs, while
Torrence returned and the two supervisors persisted in discussing
the air-conditioning. "No dice on the AC," she heard Torrence say.
"It takes four hours for the building to cool down on a weekend."
Kathy was afraid she would scream, but she only cried quietly,
painfully aware that if either Gavin or Torrence had any question
at all about whether Mark was guilty, one look at the state of his
wife would give them their answer.

Trying to pull herself together, she asked where the ladies'
room was. Gavin invited her to use his private bathroom. She

splashed water on her face and stood at the sink trying to steady herself. Overcome by dizziness, she sat down. This was what Mark could have had one day: an office with a private bathroom. There was a vanity in there, with shaving things arranged neatly on it, and an extra tie folded carefully over a hanger. She put her head between her legs to stop it from spinning and saw a cockroach scurry across the floor.

When she rejoined the men, she heard Mark apologizing for the disgrace he had brought on the bureau. She followed the uneasy conversation between Mark and the two supervisors only in phrases that pierced her staggered consciousness. "I can't believe this has happened," someone said. "The FBI family" was invoked several times. She heard "worst-case scenario" mentioned. She struggled to focus.

On the sofa beside her, Mark was bowed, repentant, and, she saw with a mounting sense of alarm, *compliant*.

She fought to resist the allure of the empathy that wafted over the desk of the supervisor, aware that while so far they had talked *around* any specific mention of the awful event itself, the parameters of the discussion were slowly constricting. She heard phrases that sounded familiar from somewhere: *Stress of a cop's job . . . We've all been there. Things can happen in a flash . . .* She looked anew at the three men—the chief, brimming with concern and sympathy; his affable sidekick murmuring affirmations; the contrite, mortified suspect, abjectly grateful for small kindnesses—as if peering from an apartment window at a scene far below on the street, aware only that the participants were going through certain predetermined motions. Then she heard Mark utter the words, "I would like to take care of this and clear the air," and she saw the trapdoor at his feet, triggered to spring open. Her husband was about to confess to a capital crime.

"No!" she said, the force of her protest causing the three men to stop, shift their positions, and fix her with surprised stares. "Mark," she said with a glaring look, "we have to talk."

The interruption broke the momentum. Kathy now saw that Gavin was less assured about the process than she had supposed. There was a small bend in his tone; an opportunity for reflection crept in. Of course, if Mark wished to take care of this thing, he could make a statement now. A stenographer would be called in, he could lay it out, get it over with. He would be treated with respect and consideration: Kathy was now evaluating each word. Of course, on the *other* hand, she heard, perhaps Mark and Kathy wanted to discuss it privately. Maybe they wanted to think about getting a lawyer. Gavin said that it was not his role to recommend a course of action. Seeking legal counsel was a decision only Mark could make. Nevertheless, names of good defense attorneys could be provided, if Mark wished.

"Could we talk privately?" Kathy asked.

Mark had the look of a man who has no choice but to acquiesce to his wife's wishes. "No disrespect, sir," he stammered.

Gavin told them to go into an adjacent office and talk it over.

Jumping up, Kathy marched her husband next door. Just as she thought, Mark wanted to spill his guts. "I have to take care of this thing," he protested. "It's time."

Time? He could talk about time? She thought about time: How much did they really have? A day ago, to her, it was a lifetime; now what was it—days, *hours*, before they hustled him off to prison? Mark tried weakly to protest. "This is the FBI. They'll treat me right," he insisted. But she shook her head violently. "Those men are *cops!* They will *do their jobs!*" she told him, not caring that she had begun to shout.

The unspoken arrangement in their marriage was that on certain occasions, one partner could invoke an ex cathedra privilege and demand that the other shut up and comply. It worked both ways, which was why it worked. Now Mark listened, although sulkily. "They can arrest you and put you in jail *today!*" she said. "We haven't even told the kids!"

For the first time, they talked soberly about what would happen after he confessed. He had not given it any real thought. Thirty years? Life in prison? *Execution?* Neither of them really knew. In all the time that he had been obsessed with his guilt, over the entire year since he had killed Susan, Mark had never thought through his options. It had simply never occurred to him that he had any, except to confess, to "put things right" and accept disgrace and whatever punishment the authorities saw fit to impose. It was as if the problem were strictly an intensely personal crisis of conscience, with consequences so overwhelming that no single person could affect the outcome in any way. Kathy suddenly understood that she had been omitted from that estimation. Her eyes flashed with resentment.

While the Putnams were talking, Gavin called Lou DeFalaise, the federal prosecutor in Kentucky, for advice. DeFalaise told him that since there was no outstanding state or federal arrest warrant, Putnam would be free to leave the office, even if he gave a statement, pending the filing of charges once any statement he gave was corroborated.

Gavin also called Huggins at home in Kentucky. "He's talking to his wife now and they thought it was probably in his best interest to get an attorney," Gavin said.

"Of course," said Huggins, who had slept soundly at home for the first time in weeks.

"One more thing. Can you get back here? If something happens this week I need you here."

"Of course," Huggins said, "I'll be there tomorrow morning."

When he and Kathy came back in, Mark apologized for not being able to give his statement immediately. He asked for the names of some lawyers. Torrence made a phone call to a Fort Lauderdale defense attorney who had previously been an assistant US attorney in Miami. In the upside-down world into which the Putnams had tumbled, this was good, because former prosecutors were "cops' lawyers." Mark and Kathy retreated again to the privacy of the spare office, where he picked up the phone. "Don't say another word until you see me," said the lawyer, a former assistant US attorney named Bruce Zimet.

Long after that day, Kathy would refer to the calendar she kept for 1990 to try to sort out the chronology. She had made notes in big blocks of space on each page, next to the "Sesame Street" characters. It surprised her to see how compressed the events had been, how quickly things had happened, one after the other. At the time, it had seemed that they had neither beginning nor end.

At home, the household did not turn to shambles, though Kathy thought it had. Chris soon pieced the story together, although she didn't yet grasp the consequences. "Kathy was looking at me for a reaction, and I was like, is he going to be *demoted* at work?" she would later say. The house was immaculate; when she wasn't crying Kathy was cleaning.

Yet she moved through a mental fog. Late Sunday afternoon, she found herself at the airport, unable to understand why she was waiting at a gate, in what she noticed for the first time were mismatched clothes, her eyes swollen, holding her husband's hand tightly. She saw her mother and father hurrying up the corridor toward them.

"I don't know how he's going to react," she heard herself say. "Don't be surprised if he hits you."

"I hope he does."

Instead her father shook his hand. She collapsed on top of her mother, Carol. She felt safer yet more vulnerable than ever.

Back home, practical matters had to be dealt with. Mark was on vacation time, but that would end; the $600-a-week paycheck would stop. Kathy's pay at the Pancake House wouldn't keep the household afloat, not with child-care expenses. Lives were shattered, but the mortgage was due, with no grace period for calamity. Mark was going to prison, perhaps for the rest of his life. She had two young children. Flaming wreckage lay everywhere. The idea of simply soldiering on was terrifying.

There were moments of respite. She remembered having a drink and smoking a cigarette Sunday night with her parents on the back porch, the cool air coming in through the screens, lulling her into consideration of a future without Mark.

She was focused well enough to discuss plans: She knew she could go home but the idea of asking for her father's sanctuary again caused her deep anguish. Father and daughter faced each other from well-marked emotional positions.

She broached the subject of moving back to Connecticut. She could work, finish college, get her life together. Her mother listened stoically as her father's mind leaped forward to control the damage. He was anxious to have his daughter and grandchildren close by but he couldn't stop himself from glancing with disapproval at the drink she had in her hand.

"I am going to help you," he said, and Kathy stiffened. "If you want to go wherever Mark is going, I understand that—"

She exploded. "Sure, anything to get me and the kids out of sight!" Her father's mouth was agape. She rushed out, thrusting the screen door behind her. Even more infuriated that it would not slam, she stormed into the garage and rummaged frantically for something expendable. She picked up little Mark's lightweight stroller and smashed it again and again on the concrete floor until it was twisted and bent like an umbrella in a windstorm.

The appointment with the lawyer was scheduled for Tuesday. On Monday, they decided to see a child psychologist. Huddled together in their bedroom, with Kathy's parents and sister in the house and Mark's mother on her way down to Florida, having no idea what anyone would say, or even where everyone would sleep, they had struggled with the need to tell Danielle that her father had killed someone and was going to prison for a time that would outlast her childhood. Danielle, alerted by the activity in the house, the houseguests, the urgent verbal reassurances and muffled cries through bedroom walls, knew that something terrible had happened. They knew that she was waiting to see what it was.

"What do we tell her? 'You've always been Daddy's little girl, but now Daddy's leaving?'" Kathy said. "How do we not destroy her?"

Mark didn't have an answer. Kathy went down a list of psychologists in the yellow pages and made an appointment with the first one who was available that day. As soon as they saw her, they realized how impossible it was to explain their situation coherently to a total stranger. But the psychologist surprised them by restating the problem succinctly: "Your husband is going to jail for killing someone, and it is a total shock. You are both loving parents. How do you explain this to your daughter, who is five years old and loves her daddy?" She suggested practical ways to begin sorting out the situation for both Danielle and little Mark. Find a previous example of how the child had handled adversity well, explain it, and hold it up as a way to approach the current situation. Offer love and as much stability as possible. Above all, hear the child out.

That night, Kathy told Mark to wait upstairs until she brought Danielle. Sitting on the bed, he said, "I don't know if I can handle this."

"Just get yourself together I'm going to bring her in and we'll do it together, just the way we discussed this afternoon."

Kathy brought Danielle in. She scampered onto the center of their bed between her parents and asked her father why he was crying. He got up and went into the bathroom, where they could hear him sobbing loudly.

Kathy told her to wait. She returned with Mark leaning on her. Danielle watched quietly.

"Danielle, Daddy is so very sorry," he said, unable to go on. They both looked at Kathy.

She held her daughter. "Listen, do you remember when a couple of weeks ago, you were in the kitchen and Mommy was by the sink making supper, and dinner was cooking on the stove, and little Mark went over to the stove and he was going to reach up and maybe get burned? And you pushed him away and he fell and bumped his head, and he cried? And Mommy only saw you push him, she didn't see him reaching up for the stove?"

"Yeah, I remember it."

"And do you remember how you felt when I yelled at you?"

"I felt bad."

"But you really shouldn't have pushed him so hard?"

"I know."

Drawing a deep breath, Kathy explained that another bad thing had happened. Her father had done something impulsively. It was wrong; he had not meant to do it. A lady in Kentucky had been hurt very badly, there had been a fight, and Daddy had to be punished. The psychologist had stressed the need to explain that Mark was not bad, that the situation was. Moral nuances could be explored in years to come. "It wasn't as though Daddy had time to think about anything," Kathy said. "He reacted quickly, just like you did. Daddy had to tell the truth about what happened, but because of what happened, it was wrong. It was a terrible mistake. He's going to have to go away for a long time."

Danielle started to cry. She looked at her father and said, "Is that why you're crying, Daddy?"

Then she jumped into his arms and said, "If you're telling the truth, why do you have to go away?"

"Because what Daddy did was very wrong."

He told her that he would always love her, that he was proud of her, that she was a big girl, and he wanted her to be brave. "Can you do that for me?"

She said she could.

Kathy asked Danielle if she had any questions.

She didn't. She said, "Me and Mommy can take care of things." She told her father not to cry. "You're making your nose all red." And Danielle left the room.

Mark was shaking violently. Kathy put her arms around him and rested her head on his chest.

"I can't believe I did this to you and the kids," he said.

She left him there and went downstairs to the sounds of life. Danielle was outside playing. Kathy's mother was in the kitchen, making dinner. A storm had come up fast over the Everglades. Mark stood at the upstairs window and watched the Florida downpour, which would continue steadily for two days.

16

Bruce Zimet called Gavin at the start of the week and laid out the initial defense position. "You guys know you don't have a case without a body," Zimet told Gavin, an old friend.

"Well, with or without a body, we will not stop investigating. We're going to run every lead out, and I'll tell you, Bruce, I think I can get enough circumstantial evidence to make a case. And you also might want to tell Mark that John Paul Runyon, the prosecutor out in Pike County, can indict anybody for anything and be considered a hero."

"I'll be in touch," Zimet said.

In Pikeville, the commonwealth attorney's office had started moving on the prosecution of Mark Putnam the day after the state police detectives got back to Pikeville. Capt. Gary Rose had called Runyon at home on Saturday to tell him that Mark had just taken the FBI polygraph and failed it, and that he was going to be questioned the next day by supervisors in Miami. Runyon figured that Putnam either already had a lawyer or would soon be getting one.

On Monday, Runyon held a meeting with the state police; the FBI's representative from Lexington; Terry O'Connor; and the US attorney out of Lexington, Lou DeFalaise. The men gathered in the prosecutor's office knew that all they had on Mark at this point was that he had made false statements in an interview and during a polygraph test. Failing a lie detector test was not a crime, nor a legal indication of one. There had been no admission of guilt. They believed that he had killed Susan, but he hadn't yet admitted it, and there was still no way yet of proving it in a courtroom. There wasn't even enough to file a charge.

Runyon insisted that they evaluate the potential criminal case: In the absence of a confession, what did they have independently? Well, they could establish that Mark had a motive to cause Susan Smith harm. Several witnesses, Shelby most notable among them, would testify that Susan had said she was pregnant by Mark and had threatened to hound him until he met her terms, whatever they were. However, no one had actually heard her say these things to him. The motive was weak but at least presentable.

Furthermore, Mark had had the opportunity to commit the crime. His presence in Pikeville at the time Susan disappeared could easily be established; the two had been registered at the same motel. However, no one had been found who actually saw them together.

That, stripped down to its bare essentials, was their "case," Runyon acknowledged morosely. The major problem, obviously, was the absence of any proof that a crime had been committed. The investigation had run its course, they knew that. After a year, they still had no physical evidence, no witness to a threat—and no body. All they could do was wait for the killer's next move.

Runyon, who had prosecuted hundreds of homicides during his career, was a formidable opponent for any defense lawyer. Not only was he smart, he was convincing, which is often more useful in dealing with a jury. He had the unusual ability to cry real tears when summing up a case that particularly moved him. A performance of this distinguished white-haired servant of the people in front of a jury, literally crying for justice, was one that lawyers took time off to witness. After one trial, a judge had questioned the prosecutor about his remarkable theatrics. "Judge," Runyon replied apologetically in a slow drawl, "it is a strategy I never use unless I feel that it is absolutely necessary." To which the judge had snorted, "Hell, John Paul, in my opinion any lawyer has that ability and *doesn't* use it is guilty of malpractice."

Runyon knew that if he could get Mark Putnam indicted and in the dock in a Pike County courtroom, obtaining a conviction would be no great problem. He was already lying awake at night, rehearsing his summation to a jury of mountain people: "This slick prep-school boy from *Connecticut*, a college graduate"—here a knowing glance at the jury—"this highly trained *criminologist* for the Federal Bureau of Investigation who murdered, *in cold blood*, a poor, ignorant, pregnant mountain girl, a mother of two little children . . ."

But it was an exercise in fantasy. No matter how he shuffled the cards, he knew he did not have enough evidence to indict Putnam. And he worried that Putnam and his lawyer knew the same thing.

Runyon waited impatiently to hear from that lawyer, whoever it was. Monday passed without a word. Runyon was bewildered.

Finally, late on Tuesday afternoon, he received a phone call from a Fort Lauderdale attorney who introduced himself as Bruce Zimet, a former assistant US attorney, now in private practice, representing Mark Putnam.

Runyon said he knew the name.

Zimet wanted to talk hypothetically. But first he needed to invoke Rule 11 of the federal rules of criminal procedure. The prosecutor had been expecting that Rule 11 is a standard procedure that basically enables a guilty party to discuss a plea to a lesser charge, without being subject to criminal liability for anything that is divulged during those discussions. Under Rule 11, true statements "made in the course of any proceedings under this rule" are inadmissible if the plea is ultimately rejected or withdrawn. Prosecutors with a solid case do not agree to hold discussions under Rule 11.

Carefully, Runyon told Mark's lawyer to go on.

Speaking hypothetically, Zimet explained that while a client might be willing to confess, he was not willing to take the maximum penalty for a charge on which the state apparently had no evidence.

Two weeks of negotiations had commenced.

Runyon and his assistants researched their dilemma as the talks got under way. Their central problem was that, even in the unlikely event that evidence that Mark Putnam killed Susan Smith could be produced independent of a confession, an indictment for murder would be almost impossible to support in Kentucky, where state criminal law divides "criminal homicide" into four possible charges: murder, first-degree manslaughter, second-degree manslaughter, and reckless homicide. The requirements for a charge of murder clearly reflected the historical realities of justice in a frontier state. Only cold-blooded homicides really fit the definition:

A person is guilty of murder when, with intent to cause the death of another person, he causes the death of such person or of a third person, except that in any prosecution a person shall not be guilty under this subsection if he acted under the influence of extreme emotional disturbance for which there was a reasonable explanation or excuse, the reasonableness of which is to be determined from the viewpoint of a person in the defendant's situation under the circumstances as the defendant believed them to be.

Even with a body and independent evidence linking Mark to the killing, the requirement for intent would have been difficult to meet. Moreover, even with a riled-up jury a prosecutor would have a difficult time countering the defense that Mark's state of mind, reflected in facts that no one disputed, was consistent with "extreme emotional disturbance," which was defined under Kentucky law as "a temporary state of mind so enraged, inflamed or disturbed as to overcome judgment and to cause one to act uncontrollably from its impelling force, rather than from evil or malicious purposes." It would not have taken Clarence Darrow for the defense to establish that Putnam met those criteria.

If this was a homicide case, it appeared to meet the definition of first-degree manslaughter:

A person is guilty of manslaughter in the first degree when: (a) With intent to cause serious physical injury to another person, he causes the death of such person or of a third person; or (b) With intent to cause the death of another person, he causes the death of such person or of a third person under circumstances which do not constitute murder because he acts under extreme emotional disturbance.

Still, manslaughter was a major crime, carrying a maximum penalty of twenty years in the penitentiary. But even in a cut-and-dried case—with the perpetrator found standing over the body holding a smoking gun—twenty years was an ambitious goal for a prosecutor. Runyon had his staff research the court statistics on homicides in Pike County during the 1980s. The average sentence for all homicides (murder and manslaughter) was 7.6 years. For manslaughter alone, the average sentence was about half that. Nationally, the average time actually served for these crimes was nowhere near twenty years. A national study of homicide cases from 1976 to 1987 in eight states—California, Georgia, Montana, New Jersey, New York, Ohio, Washington, and Wisconsin—found that the median length of confinement for defendants found guilty of murder was five years. Aware that he would have to vigorously defend whatever verdict he obtained on the Putnam case, Runyon was determined to hold out for the stiffest sentence he could manage. But he had to be careful how he did it. As both a sportsman and a politician, Runyon knew well that hooking a fish took a lot less skill than bringing it in. He spent restless nights deconstructing his problem, not knowing—not even able to eyeball—his quarry circling at the far end of a telephone line. Yet Runyon knew instinctively that in the churn of mountain politics, a prosecutor who lost a case like this—the case of an outsider, *a federal agent* who killed a poor coal miner's daughter, dumped her body, and left her there for a year—would be vulnerable not only to defeat, but equally bad, to derision and scorn. And he knew very well that this case *could* be lost. The killer could manage to wriggle off the hook, even if he conceded doing, it, on the *technicalities*—he could practically hear the word curling from the lip of an as-yet-unknown political opponent, some Pikeville populist grabbing the opportunity to bring down the invincible John Paul Runyon.

If Mark Putnam walked, it would not matter politically that the state police and the FBI between them had not managed to produce a shred of evidence that a crime had even been committed, even though the brass from both agencies were now busy clapping themselves on the back for cracking the case. All that would matter would be that the prosecutor had let a murderer slip off the hook.

The prosecutor had no way of knowing that Mark Putnam was grimly determined to throw himself into the boat.

Back in Florida, Mark insisted that he was going to prison for thirty or forty years. "I killed somebody, Kathy. I've got to go to prison for a long, long time. You and the kids need to cut your ties to me," he told her in conversations that started at dawn and continued until they fell asleep exhausted at night.

His fortitude confounded his lawyer. Zimet had been stunned by the story that Mark and Kathy told him when they came to his office in Fort Lauderdale on Tuesday morning, but he immediately saw the advantages his client had in negotiating a deal. It did not make sense that Mark wasn't interested in negotiating. In fact, when Kathy stepped out for a minute to have a cigarette, Zimet asked Mark whether he was actually protecting someone else, such as his wife.

A suspicion of misguided gallantry was perhaps reasonable for someone who did not know the Putnams. Not many criminal suspects begin their case stipulating that they are guilty, even to their lawyers. Fewer still insist that they intend to admit to their crime. It took a while for Zimet to understand that Mark Putnam meant everything he said. Mark had been anticipating this reckoning for a year, focused entirely on the guilt that crushed him and the confession he needed to make.

It also took Zimet some time to see that, stricken as she appeared to be, struggling to keep her hand steady enough to sip coffee from the china cup in which it was served by a secretary, Kathy Putnam could be a strong force on her husband's will. For Kathy, the disaster had just happened. She was like an earthquake victim crawling out of flaming rubble. But as she got her bearings and began to look ahead, she tried to impress on Mark the idea that assuaging his conscience was not the only consideration. There was also the fate of his family, and any hope they had of putting a life together at some point, no matter how far in the future. She worked hard to persuade him that he did not have the luxury of acting unilaterally. He owed it to his family, if not to himself, to begin thinking like a defendant. She realized that without Mark's confession, the authorities did not have a good case—if they had one, they would obviously have made it by now.

On Wednesday, when she and Mark returned to Zimet's office to hear his assessment after his initial conversation with Runyon, Kathy had already identified a number of options, the most sensible of which, she had decided, was to deny everything. Let them make their case and prove it in court.

Though he was uneasy dealing with a spouse who had positioned herself squarely between him and his client, Zimet had come to the same conclusion.

"You don't want to plead out on this," Zimet told Mark. "You won't have to do a day. They just don't have enough of a case. They don't even have enough to indict you."

But Mark wanted to put an end to the ordeal. He refused to elaborate on his reasoning, but he knew that it had much to do with guilt and pride and little with legal strategy. If he could avoid it, Mark had no intention of letting a Pike County prosecutor put him on trial. He would rather prosecute himself by pleading guilty. Furthermore, he had been tormented for a year knowing that he had abandoned Susan in a mountain ravine. Even while he had delayed it as long as he could, he had always known that there could be only one resolution. Susan would have to be found, and he would have to confess to killing her. There was no other way he could live with himself.

"It wouldn't be right to try to beat it," Mark explained darkly. "I tried it for a year. Look at me." The lawyer had no way to compare, but Mark had by now lost over thirty pounds, and his face had the drawn, sallow look of a deeply troubled man. Besides, he argued, a trial could badly damage the all-important image of the bureau. A single agent pleading out on a homicide was one thing. In a trial, the whole sorry mess—systemic abuses of informants, shoddy procedures, indifferent supervision of agents—was likely to come out. He was not willing, he said, to cause further damage.

Invariably he returned to the bottom line: "I killed somebody. I did it. There is no excuse for what I did."

Zimet suggested that Mark and Kathy go out to lunch to talk it over.

At a restaurant across the street, Kathy tried to breach the wall he had erected around his guilt. "What do they really have, Mark? You're going to give them everything. I understand that. I accept it. But you can get some concessions in return. You don't have to spend the rest of your life in prison. Think about what you're doing to us, Mark."

He repeated his mantra. "Kathy, I killed that girl."

"Mark, if you go to jail in Kentucky, they'll kill you."

Overhearing this, a busboy who had been clearing the booth behind them dropped a plate. The crash brought a look of recognition to Mark's face.

Kathy went on. "Mark, you have to think clearly. Think of Danielle and Mark and me. You have some power in this." She was imploring him as she never had before. Finally, his mind managed to move past the word *deal*. By the time they went back, he had agreed to let his lawyer negotiate one.

In Pikeville, the prosecutor had guessed at Putnam's rationale. A more cynical man might have scoffed at the notion, but Runyon finally sensed that Mark was being impelled, step by step, not by his lawyer but by his conscience. Runyon didn't know how long that situation would last—consciences can fade when things get tough. He had no idea how far he could push.

In what quickly evolved into a high-stakes poker game, the phone calls flew back and forth between Kentucky and Florida every day for two weeks. Runyon told his associates at the onset of the plea negotiations, "I can never be sure when I hang up the phone today whether he's going to be talking to me tomorrow."

The prosecutor presided over a small group of people who had an interest in the case and whose judgment he trusted. They gathered daily around the conference table in the windowless second-floor library of Runyon's office, where the speakerphone provided a disembodied link to the suspect in Florida. Always on hand were Richard Ray and Rick Bartley, the assistant commonwealth attorney. At various times they were joined by Lou DeFalaise, Terry O'Connor, Jim Huggins, Gary Rose, and Paul Maynard.

DeFalaise had more than a passing interest in the homicide investigation against Mark Putnam, which was a state matter. As the US Attorney's office in Lexington entered the initial phase of its long-planned investigation into political corruption throughout eastern Kentucky, it was evident that several of the cases that had been developed in the Pikeville office, both by Putnam and by Poole, could be part of the interlocked framework on which that federal initiative would have to rest. There was concern about what might come out in a trial of Mark Putnam. No one knew what to expect.

At the initial gathering, Runyon laid out the dilemma: "We know the boy did it—but gentlemen, we can't prove that in a court of law. We can't even prove that a crime has been committed."

What if Putnam backed out?

Runyon didn't like to consider that possibility: "We've got to turn up the heat as high as we can."

Richard Ray huffed and puffed at the notion that Putnam might be able to cop a plea, but he was a good enough detective to know that there was probably no other choice. "We have no way of locating her body," Ray conceded.

Runyon went around the table, polling each participant individually. None of them disagreed with the plan to negotiate the best plea agreement possible under the circumstances.

"You going to hold his feet to the fire?" Ray asked morosely.

"You bet I am," Runyon replied, though he was not at all certain that he would be able to deliver on the boast. "I'm not going to take anything less than a twelve-year sentence."

There was a low whistle. Someone said, "Good luck, John Paul."

Under instructions from the Putnams to proceed on plea negotiations, Zimet had laid out the broad outlines of what he anticipated. A prison term was inevitable. The only question was how long. And with a defendant determined to plead guilty, that seemed to be a matter largely in the hands of the prosecutor.

"I wanted ten years," Zimet told them at the end of the first week of negotiations while Mark listened in stony silence. "If this had happened in Florida, there is no way you'd serve more than four. But Runyon says he won't sleep with less than sixteen."

Mark surprised them by engaging in speculation for the first time. "What do they really have? I told them about the car, so I guess they can find the car, but I checked it over pretty carefully. The floor mat is long gone. Of course, if they want your ass in Pike County, they can find anybody to testify to anything. But really, only that girl on the horse can put me on the scene."

Startled, Kathy asked, "What girl?"

Mark looked, at her blankly. *The one on the horse!* The young woman who had ridden off without giving a second thought to the dark-haired young man she had encountered climbing up out of the ravine—the woman whose knowing face, fleetingly as he had seen it, had not left his mind for a single day in the past year. The one who could put him at the scene! He couldn't believe they didn't know whom he was talking about.

The men gathered around Runyon's conference table were making grim bets on whether the talks would collapse.

"You think they're going to back out today?" someone invariably asked.

"Not today," said the prosecutor. He never knew about tomorrow.

Early the following week, Zimet made a formal offer: Mark would plead guilty to first-degree manslaughter in exchange for a guarantee of an eight-year sentence.

"I couldn't live with myself at that," Runyon said, digging in hard with a bluff. "It's got to be eighteen."

As he talked, Runyon doodled abstractly on a yellow legal pad. Later, he would see that he had put down the number *18* but crossed it out. Beside it, he had written 16 and underlined it in hard black strokes, with an arrow drawn right at it. But the fact was, he was prepared to take twelve.

The next day, Zimet had a new gambit. If Mark pleaded guilty to whatever sentence they agreed on, he wanted to serve his time in a federal prison, not a Kentucky penitentiary.

Richard Ray felt he had to object strenuously to this as a matter of principle. "What if I did this?" he asked. "What would happen to me? Could I serve my time in a federal prison?" He would never actually say it, but he felt the responsibility of speaking for Susan Smith, and maybe for generations of other poor, ignorant mountain people. But he knew that if this was the major concession they needed to make to get a stiff sentence, and if Runyon was ready to take the inevitable heat for making it, it should be made.

In fact, the cops, Ray included, were the most worried among the group that gathered in Runyon's office. Collectively, they had seen too many defense lawyers wreck too many criminal prosecutions, and they understood that this one could collapse in a minute if Putnam bolted out the door of Zimet's office. As Runyon himself had pointed out in amazement when he realized Putnam was willing to talk, "any defense lawyer in Pike County would tape that boy's mouth shut and tell him to take a long vacation until his conscience stopped bothering him."

Runyon replied that he was willing to go along with the federal prison. On June 1, the Kentucky Department of Corrections tentatively agreed not to object to Putnam's serving his sentence in a federal facility. This handed Runyon his last card to play.

"Runyon won't go for twelve," Zimet told the Putnams when they came in that day. "It's got to be sixteen." He broke it down. "Sixteen years. You won't do more than twelve; you're eligible for parole after eight, and it's in a federal facility."

Mark looked uneasily at his wife, who nodded shakily. "Let's go," he said.

Runyon's letter spelling out the plea agreement was drafted and faxed back and forth until both sides signed off on the final language. It was dated June 1. The key portions of it read as follows, with italics representing the additions Zimet insisted on:

This will confirm our conversations with regard to your client, Mark Putnam. As a result of these conversations it is agreed by and between the Commonwealth of Kentucky and Mr. Putnam as follows:

An investigation into the disappearance and possible killing of Susan Smith is being conducted by the Kentucky State Police and the Federal Bureau of Investigation.

Mr. Putnam will be completely forthright and truthful with this office and federal and state law enforcement agents with regard to all inquiries made of him regarding Susan Smith. Mr. Putnam will give signed and sworn statements if same are deemed necessary. In any interviews conducted pursuant to this agreement, Mr. Putnam may have counsel present if he desires. *These statements will be exclusively made pursuant to this agreement. If this agreement is not fully consummated for any reason, these statements cannot be used against Mr. Putnam.*

It is anticipated that evidence obtained from Mr. Putnam as well as evidence obtained by law enforcement investigators will be presented to the Pike County Grand Jury and that an indictment will be sought against Mr. Putnam *on or before June 11, 1990* charging him with *manslaughter in the first degree relating to Susan Smith.*

In the event that Mr. Putnam is indicted for murder for his role in the killing of Susan Smith, the Commonwealth of Kentucky, by and through John Paul Runyon, 35th Judicial Circuit Commonwealth Attorney, agrees to amend the charge to manslaughter in the first degree. If the grand jury returns an indictment charging Mr. Putnam with first-degree manslaughter, no amendment to said charge will be recommended by the Commonwealth.

Mr. Putnam will plead guilty to the charge of first-degree manslaughter on June 12, 1990, or within ten days thereafter Mr. Putnam may voluntarily appear for his guilty plea.

The maximum penalty to which Mr. Putnam will be exposed by virtue of his guilty plea is imprisonment for a term of 20 years and the minimum penalty will be imprisonment for a term of 10 years. Kentucky law does not provide for the imposition of a fine for this charge. Court costs of $57.50 and a $10.00 payment to the Crime Victims Compensation Fund will be paid in full on the date Mr. Putnam is sentenced.

The Commonwealth will recommend that Mr. Putnam will be sentenced to a 16-year term of imprisonment following his guilty plea.

Acknowledging that sentencing is "within the sole discretion of the court," the agreement letter nevertheless stipulated:

> In the event the Court rejects this plea agreement *or refuses to follow the 16-year recommendation of the Commonwealth* and Mr. Putnam refuses to plead guilty or withdraws his guilty plea, pursuant to Kentucky Criminal Rule 8.10, nothing contained in any statement or testimony given by Mr. Putnam pursuant to this agreement or any evidence developed there-from will be used against him in any further criminal prosecutions.

Only a few loose ends remained. Zimet wanted assurance that Mark would not face a related charge over the death of a fetus if it was indeed true that Susan had been pregnant, and in the unlikely possibility that an autopsy on a body that had lain exposed for over eleven months would still show evidence of it. Kentucky law was clear on that point. The state Supreme Court in 1983 had held in the case of a man who killed his wife while attempting also to kill her unborn baby that a "fetus was not a 'person,' as that word is used in context of criminal homicide statutes, and could not have status as victim of criminal homicide."

Negotiations concluded with that. On Monday morning, June 4, Paul Maynard and Jim Huggins got on a plane and flew to Florida. A state police unit was ordered to stand by to recover the body of Susan Smith.

Accompanied by Maynard, Jim Huggins arrived at Zimet's well-appointed office in Fort Lauderdale just after five o'clock. Mark had asked Kathy to stay home. He was ready this time when Maynard read him his Miranda rights.

Speaking softly, Mark confessed that he had killed Susan Smith and told where to find her body.

The directions he gave were so simple that the officers standing by in Pikeville didn't believe him. He said the body was in a ravine on the left side of a gravel road on Harmons Branch, five miles from the center of Pikeville, not even a mile off Route 23, on a surface mine site a few hundred yards from a cleared area with a shed where the mine company stored earth-moving equipment and parked coal trucks. Just before the ravine, also on the left, was a slope back through the trees where kids rode dirt bikes.

It sounded preposterous. "There's no way she could be laying there," Ray scoffed to Maynard over the phone. "Somebody would have found her."

When this was repeated to him, Mark muttered that that was the point. He thought they would have, long before now.

With a scrawled map and the directions, Ray drove a small and gravely dubious group of searchers up the road on the low ridge above Harmons Branch. Accompanying him, in two vehicles, were state police lieutenant Ed Shemelya; two FBI agents, Sam Smith and Tim Adams; and Fred Davidson, a state police officer who had brought along his excitable German shepherd, which he called a "body dog."

Driving slowly over deep ruts, Ray spotted the clearing where it was obvious that dirt bikes had clawed into the loose soil on a hill. Above, a high black ridge went on for miles, blocking out most of the thin sunlight. Ray found the turnoff and stopped the car on a mud-caked siding beside a narrow and bumpy coal-truck road that climbed sharply up to the strip-mine cut. With the light fading, they wouldn't have much time.

Mounds of fresh dirt and debris were pushed up at the side of the road, on the lip of the ravine. It appeared to be rubble from the strip mine, pushed down from above by bulldozers. They climbed over it and peered into the ravine, which was thick with undergrowth. After the first ten yards, the ground fell off sharply. They used ropes tied to the truck to ease down, one by one, lurching for the nearest bush or an occasional sapling for support. The dog thrashed ahead. The trickle of a small creek could be heard coming from the bottom of the ravine, but it was difficult to see through the brush. About halfway down, the way was blocked by a weed-covered pile of dirt and trash, remnants of tangled wire-mesh fencing, rotted mine timbers, and moldering trash bags. The rubble appeared to have been pushed down from the roadbed some time ago.

The dog was making a commotion somewhere below, but it scrambled back toward them, whimpering. Ray had no faith in the dog anyway. He had never known it to find anything before. It climbed on up toward the road, peed on a bush, and barked at the searchers stumbling downward.

Ray heard a shout from the brush about ten feet below. "Hey, it looks like there's some bones here!"

Ray stumbled and slid down to where Tim Adams had braced himself between two bushes and was staring down at the bones, which appeared to be from a skeleton that had come apart. At first, Ray thought they looked like the bones of a child. A flashlight glinted off metal; prodded with a stick through the dried mud and matted leaves, it proved to be a thin gold chain with a tiny cross.

Shaking his head, Ray squinted back toward the top of the ravine. The remains of Susan Smith lay not fifty feet from the road.

A radio transmission was made back from the scene to the state police post in Pikeville, where the message was relayed to the small group in the lawyer's office in Fort Lauderdale. Maynard put down the phone and said, acknowledging Mark's distressed look, "They found her just where you said."

Mark took a few minutes to collect himself. Then he continued talking as a stenographer took down the rest of his confession.

★   ★   ★

It was dark by now. The cops who had found the body waited until another state police vehicle arrived with two officers who would remain to guard the scene through the night.

Just before eight o'clock the next morning, a police car and a pickup truck lumbered up to the site. A man from the state medical examiner's office, a forensic anthropologist named David J. Wolf, got out, to supervise the removal of the remains.

Complaining about the difficult climb, Wolf worked slowly, taking copious notes. Some of the bones were entangled in the wire mesh, as if tugged at by animals. "Evidence of scavenger activity was visible," Wolf wrote.

To Ray, who had returned to the scene with Wolf and some other officers, Mark Putnam's claim that he had placed the body near the top of the ravine seemed plausible in the bright daylight. The hill was too steep for a man to have carried a body down that far, where anyone standing at the side of the road would have had to look hard to see it. Wolf's report described the scenario:

> *Though heavily vegetated with briars, weeds and grasses, the embankment had very few trees closely spaced that could impede a body rolling down the steep incline. . . . Based upon the topography, it became obvious that the body rolled down the embankment from the crest of the brim alongside the road until it became entangled in the wire mesh fencing which stopped its further progress downhill. Due to the steepness of the slope, the unevenness of the slope, the vegetative cover, as well as the quantity of wire mesh fencing, it would have required a truly herculean effort for one person to have carried the body to the site where it was found and deposited it among the flattened coils of the wire mesh.*

As a police photographer took pictures, Wolf supervised the collection of the bones and the loose soil on which they were scattered. He reported: "During the troweling activity, small bones (wrist, ankle, finger, etc.) were observed but were not individually collected at that time."

Annoyed by Wolf's officious direction, the state cops removed the material and placed it in ten-gallon coal buckets. They used wire cutters to cut away the pieces of fencing. According to Wolf's inventory, "several dark human hairs, a gold-colored chain with crucifix attached, and several fingernails as well as toenails that had been painted with red polish" were found in the debris along with the bones. "Flecks of nail polish that had exfoliated from the nails were observed. No other physical evidence (e.g., clothing, jewelry or personal effects) were observed on the surface at the scene."

Holding on to ropes tied around trees near the road, they passed up the buckets containing the loose soil and bones. When they were finished, a worker from the mining company drove up in a truck and asked when they would be finished.

Wolf said they were finished now.

When Ray asked the man why he wanted to know, the driver explained that the mining company was planning to abandon the mine and bulldoze the mounds of backfill into the ravine and landscape the area. Within days, Susan Smith's remains would have been buried under sixty feet of debris.

The detective felt a little better about the plea agreement with Putnam. That eliminated the nagging thought that perhaps the body would have been found by chance. It meant that the only other potential physical evidence was the car in which the crime had taken place—the rental car that Putnam had told them about when they questioned him.

The FBI, in fact, had already located the car. The rental agency had long since sold it to a man in Virginia who lived, coincidentally, not far from the bureau's renowned forensic laboratory in Quantico, Virginia. There, bureau technicians tore the car apart piece by piece and finally discovered a tiny speck of human blood between two layers of foam inside a front-seat cushion. Jim Huggins would later say that this discovery showed the bureau at "its truly most impressive combination of dogged searching and use of technology." But Ray didn't see much ground for boasting since the blood sample didn't match either Susan's or Mark's. The FBI technicians concluded that it must have come from an assembler in the factory where the car was built. There had been no physical evidence at all linking the killer to the crime.

On Friday, June 8, Mark Putnam's brief career with the FBI officially came to an end. He had typed out a short letter of resignation, just a few sentences, which he planned to take to the office personally. But he was no longer welcome at the office. Instead, Gavin and Torrence said they would come by his house in Sunrise. Huggins, unable to face that wrenching emotional ordeal, had gone home to Kentucky.

When Gavin and Torrence arrived at the front door, the two supervisors asked Mark if he had any bureau property in the house besides his gun and credentials. He did not. Wanting to find a neutral site, they suggested a short ride. Mark and Kathy accompanied the two agents in their car, Mark in the front passenger seat, Kathy in the back. They drove in silence to a location cops tend to feel comfortable in, a McDonald's a few blocks from their house, not far from the Florida turnpike, at a place where the suburbs of Fort Lauderdale and Miami expired beside the Everglades.

Torrence went inside to get two cups of coffee. Mark and Kathy passed.

It had started out proudly in a crisp ceremony at the FBI Academy in Quantico. Now it was ending with three cops and a grieving woman parked outside a fast-food joint, ruefully watching children at play on bright plastic playground equipment, their mothers on guard at tiny white tables.

"I'm sorry it has to be like this. Doing it this way is in the best interest of the bureau," Gavin explained.

"I understand," said Mark.

While they waited for the coffee, Kathy thought of a day that seemed further in the past than it was. On a cool October morning in 1986, the letter they had been expecting for many months finally arrived in the mail at their apartment in Connecticut, in a long envelope bearing the return address, "US Department of Justice, Federal Bureau of Investigation." Their future was inside.

Neither of them had had the nerve to rip it open, so afraid were they that it would say, "No, thanks." They left it unopened on an end table. Mark plunked one-year-old Danielle into the stroller for a hasty walk around the block. Kathy ran into the bedroom.

When Mark got back, Kathy heard him opening it. "Just tell me what it says!" she squealed. He slipped it under the door, face up, and she would never forget the joy and sense of accomplishment that she felt, for both of them, when she looked down and read:

Dear Mr. Putnam:

You are offered a probationary appointment in the Federal Bureau of Investigation, United States Department of Justice, as a Special Agent.

They had laughed and cried; at dinner they drank wine, and at bedtime they made love. And the next day, while Mark was at work, it had all almost come undone. She'd received a phone call from a personnel clerk at the bureau, apologizing that a mistake had been made. The letter was in error; an overlooked review of Mark's medical records had turned up the 1985 shoulder surgery to correct the old soccer injury; the FBI regretted that it could not accept the potential liability this presented. Horrified, Kathy didn't even call Mark to tell him. Instead, she just refused to take no for an answer. For hours, she worked the phone, calling office after office at the Justice Department, until she reached someone in FBI personnel who heard her out. "Please listen to me," she said. "We've been around FBI agents for four years, and frankly, a lot of them are fat guys who couldn't run two blocks if they had to. This man is a perfect physical specimen, I'm telling you. I swear to you, I absolutely guarantee you that my husband will have no problem with agent training; we'll sign whatever waiver you want for your liability. You have to do this."

And, unbelievably, they did. She'd talked him back in. The next week, Mark, as happy as she had ever seen him, was on his way to Quantico, marveling at the tenacity of the woman he loved.

Now that they had their coffee, the agents were ready to get back to the office. Numbly, Kathy watched her husband pass his credentials, his gun and holster, his pager, and office keys to Gavin. He then handed over his letter of resignation.

Gavin cast a look back to Kathy. "I want you to know, if there is anything we can do for you, we'll be there for you." It was a nice thing to say. She knew it had no meaning.

And that was the end of the bureau business. Susan had been found. Mark had confessed. His resignation was official. The rest was up to the State of Kentucky. Mark and Kathy didn't want a ride back. They got out of the car and walked home silently along the sandy shoulder of the road.

17

In Freeburn, Shelby Jean Ward knew that Susan had been found when she got a call from John Paul Runyon late Monday, asking if she could come to his office the next morning at nine o'clock. He wouldn't say why, but she could tell from the tone of his voice.

Runyon and Captain Rose from the state police were already there when she arrived, shaken and subdued. They told her that Susan's remains had been found and tentatively identified.

"Mark Putnam?" she asked.

"Mark Putnam," Runyon replied. "He confessed last night." Knowing how sensitive the matter was, Runyon tried to explain the necessity of a plea arrangement.

"Why, it's cold-blooded murder, John Paul," she protested.

Rose read her Putnam's confession. Runyon then went over the main points of the prosecution's case, which came down, he said, to the fact that there was no evidence without that confession. He said that a sixteen-year sentence was substantial, far in excess of the average for manslaughter.

Shelby, who had never actually met Mark Putnam but who had pushed so hard to find out what had happened between Mark and her missing sister, was not buying that. She left his office in a tearful fury, and Runyon knew he had a problem on his hands even before he got the grand jury into session to prepare the indictment. But he didn't know what else he could do. On Tuesday, June 12, Mark Putnam would be brought to Pikeville to plead guilty. He would be in prison that night. Until then, Runyon hoped that the situation could be kept quiet.

The Wednesday-morning edition of the *Williamson* (W. Va.) *Daily News*, the paper that circulated in the Tug Valley carried a small story with the headline "Unidentified Body Found Near Pikeville." The story didn't identify the body and said only that the state police and the FBI were involved in the investigation.

Shelby and her brother Billy Joe filled in the details for anyone who wanted to know. By Wednesday, the news that an FBI agent had been implicated in the death of a young woman was moving on the Associated Press wire out of Pikeville.

"It's cold-blooded murder to me. My family's all upset about this," Shelby told a reporter from the *Miami Herald*, which had been alerted to the story because it involved an agent assigned to the Miami FBI Bureau. "What was so bad is when he took the body and dumped it over the hill like it was nothing," Shelby said.

"Like some dog," said Billy Joe

Other reporters soon gathered details of the sordid relationship between Susan Smith and Mark Putnam. "She was possessed by him, madly in love with him," Shelby said. "We tried to get her to date other people, but she didn't even want to talk about it. She swore that it was his baby. She wouldn't even have had that baby if it belonged to somebody else. She was even going to name it after him if it was a boy." Shelby described how she had warned Susan to "quit threatening" Mark about the baby. "She wanted him to leave his wife. She was threatening to tell his wife about the baby and he was scared to death."

On Monday, June 11, when she came to the courthouse to testify to the grand jury, Shelby was surrounded by reporters and cameras. "Because he was a big FBI, famous and everything, they don't want him to get justice," she said, denouncing the plea agreement, which had not yet been publicly disclosed. "I don't care what the clique in there says. To me it was brutal murder. Brutal, brutal murder."

Grand juries are pliant tools of the prosecutor, but there is no law that says a grand jury can't get something into its head and refuse to go along, especially with the media going full tilt on Shelby's impassioned denunciation of the deal as a miscarriage of justice, a cover-up orchestrated by the feds, in collusion with the prosecutor. It was hard to argue reasonably in so overheated an atmosphere, especially given the public sympathy flowing toward the victim's tearful sister and other family members. It was highly unlikely, but Runyon knew that if grand jury members decided they were being bamboozled, they did have the legal authority to defy the commonwealth attorney, ignore the practical realities, dig in their heels, and return a murder indictment. That would present Runyon with the worst of all possible scenarios—not only would the plea agreement be null and void, but he would have to prosecute a case on which he had no evidence, on a charge he could not support. Politically, it would be a debacle.

Runyon and his staff had worked diligently all week to prepare a presentation designed to foreclose that possibility. When the grand jury opened its session Monday morning, Runyon called Richard Ray as the first witness. He had the state police detective describe his long and frustrating investigation, beginning with his bewilderment over the FBI's role in delivering Susan Smith to the Landmark motel in the first place, and his uncertainty about the activities of Ron Poole after she was reported missing. Ray said he was surprised to learn that Poole "was doing this more or less on his own—he didn't have an official investigation going."

"At the time that you determined that she was at the Landmark motel, did you find anyone that actually saw him [Mark] with her?" Runyon asked.

"No we didn't. We couldn't find anybody that saw them together, nobody at all."

Turning to the plea agreement, Runyon asked, "Up until the time that he openly was Mirandized and waived his rights on June 4, 1990 . . . did you have any admissible evidence or evidence that you could obtain a criminal charge against Mark Putnam?"

"No, we didn't."

"You didn't have a body then?"

"Didn't have the body. I suspected that she was probably over in the Freeburn area somewhere, and I was pretty sure that she was dead, but didn't have any information that we could have charged him with."

In his testimony, Jim Huggins reiterated that point. The plea bargain, he stressed, was the only viable option. "We had no choice whatsoever—or Mr. Runyon didn't. If he hadn't entered into this agreement, we wouldn't be here today. We would have an unsolved homicide, or would have worse than that—an unsolved homicide where we know who did it, but we would not have a body."

Much to the annoyance of the state police and especially Richard Ray, Huggins took the opportunity to give the FBI credit for solving the case, saying he wished the bureau had gotten involved sooner "but unfortunately we didn't enter it as a joint investigation until the first of May, and we had the case solved in two weeks."

A juror asked Huggins pointedly what had taken the FBI so long to get involved.

"I think the girl's history as being a runaway, and a lot of questions about her past, would indicate to the agents or the detective at the time that maybe she ran away with some other group, she's going to show up in a few months. I don't believe that initially it was taken as serious. No one really wanted to believe that an FBI agent committed a murder, in my opinion."

Captain Rose testified that, without the agreement, "that fellow would have walked. He would never have pulled one day in the penitentiary." On the question of premeditation, Rose added, "I personally do not believe that he intended to kill her. He didn't know she was going to be at the motel. He came back here for court, and there she was. The evidence that we obtained during the investigation was that he actually tried to avoid her during the week I believe as somebody said, had he actually planned to do it, he would have done a lot better job than the job he done."

Since she had been the main source of pressure on the police throughout the year that her sister was missing, Shelby Jean Ward was an important witness. But it was clear that she had no evidence that gave legal weight to her insistence on a murder indictment. The grand jury quickly saw that her knowledge of the relationship between Susan and Mark was strictly hearsay. Shelby conceded that all she knew about Mark was what Susan was telling her.

"Did she tell you that she would come to Pikeville and see Mark Putnam?"

"Yes."

"You don't have personal knowledge, I take it, that she did, but that she told you she did—you weren't over there when she met with him?"

"No, she told me she did. And also Ron Poole, an FBI agent working along with Mark, he said that Susan was coming there and seeing Mark and going out with him on dates, and he said that he knew—she would set and tell him about, you know, that she was pregnant by him. They talked about it. But I never did see them together. I've never seen the guy. I've talked to him on the phone. He called my house several times wanting to know if she was there, and sometimes I would tell him she wasn't when she was because I didn't want her fooling with him."

"But you didn't have any personal knowledge of whether they met or didn't, or what their relationship was, other than what she advised you of?"

"No. She would get ready and come over here [to Pikeville] and see him, and she told me they would go out on dates."

Before dismissing Shelby, Runyon wanted her firmly on the record about whether she understood and agreed with the plea arrangement. "Incidentally," he said, "I doubt you are aware that all the officers that have testified, even Richard Ray, have testified that we had no choice, that if we had not done this, he would be walking free today without any punishment—without any. Do you understand it and accept it as being the thing that had to be done, but not the desirable thing from the standpoint of our wishes or our likes?"

"Yes," Shelby replied.

"That until he confessed and revealed where the body was, that we had no evidence on which to even base the charge—have you been advised about that?"

"Well, he took a polygraph test and he failed that, you know, but they say you can't use that in court . . ."

"That's right . . . Well, if you felt that without this plea agreement, we have no charge at all, would you agree that this is the best we could do?"

"Yes."

After working well into the night and early the next morning, the day Mark was coming to court, the grand jury handed up the indictment in the form Runyon had wanted. It read:

Detective Ray's initial investigation into Susan Smith's disappearance produced no hard evidence regarding her whereabouts. . . . Because a body had not been located, the case remained an investigation into a missing person. . . . As possible motives and suspects were eliminated by the officers, the scope of the investigation focused primarily on one person, Mark Steven Putnam. . . . The Kentucky State Police, the Federal Bureau of Investigation, the United States Attorney and the Commonwealth's Attorney . . . discussed that although Mark Steven Putnam had a motive and the opportunity to kill Susan Smith, and although circumstantial evidence indicated he had, no eyewitnesses were available, and no physical evidence existed sufficient to support a criminal charge against him. Most importantly, no homicide charge could be supported because no body had been found and no other evidence of the killing existed. It was decided and agreed upon by all concerned that further investigation would be unlikely to reveal the location of the body or other evidence conclusively linking Putnam to the killing. A decision was made to enter into negotiations with Putnam through his attorney.

. . . In return for the complete disclosure of the location of the body of Susan Smith and the manner in which she died, the Commonwealth agreed to recommend a 16-year term of imprisonment if Putnam would agree to plead guilty to first-degree manslaughter.

. . . The Grand Jury during this investigation had made available to it various legal principles and the constraints that they placed upon this investigation, and under which the law enforcement officers and the prosecutors were compelled to operate. . . . On the case at hand, all of the information necessary to establish the legal requirement [for the charge] was furnished by the defendant only after he had been assured as

to the recommendations of the Commonwealth. The Grand Jury was further informed that these plea negotiations were entered into under the limitations and constraints imposed by Rule 11 of the Criminal Rules of Procedure, which provide that any statements, admissions or incriminating facts that are disclosed during the negotiations cannot be used against the accused unless a plea agreement is ultimately reached and finally consummated.

It is our opinion that the plea agreement should be ratified and accepted by the court.

The Grand Jury is not unmindful that a death has occurred. However, we are also not unmindful of the fact that without the cooperation of Putnam and his attorney, most probably the body of Susan Smith would never have been found and the case would never have been solved.

The Grand Jury invited the sister of the victim, to wit, Shelby Ward . . . [who] concluded by acknowledging that although the punishment to be received by the accused does not satisfy her, she now fully understands that without the accused's voluntary confession and disclosure of where the body was left, no charge whatsoever could be brought against the accused. She is satisfied that this is the most that can be achieved by this Grand Jury.

The Grand Jury is also aware of the Commonwealth Attorney's concern for the family of Susan Smith and the desire at all times to be able to bring this matter to a conclusion for their peace of mind. The decision of how best to proceed when faced with the facts and the circumstances which John Paul Runyon and the investigators were given was most difficult. The decision made, without question, was correct, appropriate, and in the best interest of the family and the citizens of this Commonwealth.

It is the Grand Jury's opinion that the charge of man-slaughter and the recommendation of 16 years in prison reflect the realities of this case. Obviously Putnam would not cooperate with the investigators and reveal the location of the body without assurances that the Commonwealth would recommend less than the maximum possible sentence. The information given by Putnam and his plea of guilty have two positive results. First, the family of Susan Smith can now know her fate and can begin to adjust and reconstruct their lives with this painful knowledge. Second, a guilty man will be punished for his crime.

The Grand Jury sincerely hopes that this inquiry by a duly assembled and randomly selected Grand Jury of 12 impartial Pike County citizens will help to clear up some of the erroneous, irresponsible and seemingly deliberate false statements disseminated by the media.

On her way into the courtroom to hear Mark's plea, Shelby got caught with a loaded .38 in her purse, wrapped in a thick cotton sock. It set off the metal detector when she passed through. "I just plumb forgot I had that gun," she explained. She was promptly disarmed and two state troopers accompanied her to her seat.

Up front, waiting for the judge, Runyon rolled his eyes when he was told what had caused the commotion in the back of the courtroom. Mark, waiting with his lawyer in the witness room, didn't know anything about it. A few cops milled around in the jury room, and Mark caught the eye of Bert Hatfield and tried a feeble joke that he regretted immediately: "You remember when you told me that girl was trouble?" Bert winked and made a small clicking noise with his tongue.

"There's a lot of media out there," a court marshal said apologetically, explaining to Mark that he would have to handcuff him after the plea for the benefit of the cameras from the Lexington television stations. Mark appreciated the consideration of being told what to expect.

He considered his court appearance a technicality, since in his own mind the verdict had already been given and the sentence was in place. This allowed him to brace himself for the ordeal with a measure of concealed contempt. Had things worked out for him in Pikeville, Mark had expected to be a key investigator in the federal probe of political and judicial corruption in eastern Kentucky. He had to accept the cruel irony of standing there, accused and guilty under the scornful gaze of several people whom he had once anticipated he would help indict.

It was the first time he had ever appeared in court dressed in anything other than a neat business suit. Instead, he wore blue jeans, sneakers, a white shirt unbuttoned at the collar. Only the fact that his shirt was wet with sweat and clinging to his back betrayed the deeply conflicting emotions he felt as he stood at the defense table. The room smelled of fresh paint. Every seat in the little courtroom was taken, and spectators were crowded at the entrance, straining to see inside. He could hear whispers and titters. Whenever he turned his head, he saw faces hidden by cameras. The still cameras made nervous fluttering sounds; the television cameras were silent and watchful.

Court was called into session. Pike circuit judge Bayard Collier opened the proceedings with a soliloquy on the majesty of the law. Drifting out of time and place, Mark thought about bracelets. At the academy, they called handcuffs "silver bracelets." They had explained that the bracelets had both practical and psychological functions: one to disable a prisoner, the other, sometimes equally important, to humiliate him. Mark rubbed his wrists together, wondering how they would feel.

"It was sixteen years or nothing at all," Judge Collier was intoning from the bench, calling Mark back to attention. "If I had not accepted, or expected to deny, the motion to accept the plea, then according to the law I would have had to tell Putnam and his attorney that in advance. At that point, he simply would have withdrawn his confession and we would have been back to square one." The judge peered down portentously at the cameras. "No evidence, no case." Shutters chattered in response.

The judge looked at Mark and asked if he was in agreement with the terms of the plea arrangement.

Mark forced himself not to clear his throat and said, firmly and loudly, "Yes, sir, I am." The judge didn't meet his stare. He appeared to Mark as if he were at the end of a long tunnel.

A voice whispered in Mark's ear to put his hands behind his back. A drop of sweat collected on his eyebrow just at the top of his vision. The cuffs snapped on with the resonance of a car door slamming. The cameras clucked with satisfaction. The judge imposed the sentence. The whole thing was over in less than a half hour. Having no idea where he was going, Mark said good-bye to his lawyer and was led out of the courtroom by two marshals.

A few days before the court session, Runyon, unable to convince Shelby that he had negotiated the best deal he could get, had advised her, "Hell, Shelby, if you don't understand what I'm telling you, go get you a lawyer, somebody you trust, to explain it for you."

The next day, Runyon had received a phone call from Larry Webster, a tough-talking young Pikeville lawyer whose business cards depict a bungalow set in a mountain holler. Webster often defended hill people in criminal cases. Runyon distrusted him with grave wariness, believing that he harbored political ambitions. But Runyon at least credited him for having a modicum of intelligence, and he thought Webster would have set Shelby straight.

"Look, Larry, explain it to her," Runyon said.

But Webster was staking out a new claim. "Well, the FBI could have done more."

"Larry, I'm in a position now where that's immaterial. They *didn't*. We're beyond that point."

The morning of Mark's court appearance, Webster, representing Shelby and other members of her family, filed a civil action charging that Mark Putnam "wrongfully caused the death of Susan Smith." Webster said he would be asking "millions of dollars" in punitive damages. From that point on, the suit would be a silent factor in much of the controversy that was about to occur over the plea arrangement and confession.

Runyon had anticipated a certain amount of backlash. "Mountain people think that certain people can get *anything* done," he would later say. "They're real quick to say, 'Well, hell, he was bought off'—and I have to admit with a certain degree of justification." But he was surprised and somewhat overwhelmed by the resonance of Shelby's protests, reflected in a strong and negative reaction in the out-of-town papers. Runyon had expected controversy, but he hadn't expected anyone to say he'd let the killer off with a light sentence. He was proud of the bargain he had driven.

Yet it was true that the plea arrangement was drafted and adjudicated in a way that precluded any public examination of the complexities of the case—including the questionable performance of the FBI both in tolerating the exploitation of informants like Susan Smith and in neglecting to investigate aggressively when circumstances indicated that one of its agents was involved in a scandal and perhaps a crime. The killer was in and out of court in a flash, and the record reflected only his formal seven-page written confession. There was no opportunity for dispassionate examination of the events that had led to the crime.

With the victim's aggrieved family denouncing the result, this was a recipe for a kind of media reaction that fed not on information but on well-placed and quite reasonable sounding innuendo. Runyon was about to learn that he couldn't control it with a few phone calls and an avuncular chat.

After the sentencing, Runyon held his first press conference in eighteen years as Pike County commonwealth attorney.

"Someone here this afternoon asked if justice has been rendered," Runyon said. "Justice is a result of doing the best you can with what you have. Justice, like beauty, is in the eye of the beholder." Without the confession, authorities had "absolutely no evidence," he said. "Not one scintilla or shred of evidence to bring a charge or convict this man."

"Well, what if the body was found?" he was asked.

"Believe me, they couldn't have ever found it." He didn't mention that by the time Mark told them where the body was, the ravine was about to be filled in by the mining company. He tried to explain that he saw only two options when Mark's lawyer phoned to discuss a deal: "To hang up the phone and do nothing, or to start negotiations of some kind."

Why did the suspect confess, then?

"I happen to believe that his conscience played a major role, conscience and a hope to save his soul." The prosecutor happened to believe that it was as simple as that.

The prosecutor had been annoyed by the FBI's official dismissal of the matter as a state case, and Runyon insisted that Terry O'Connor from the Lexington office attend the press conference to answer questions. Runyon had no intention of letting the FBI off the hook, but the questions were perfunctory and reflected no interest in the systemic problem underlying the case. Media apathy enabled the FBI man to say merely, "This incident has damaged the FBI's reputation and its most valuable asset, that being the public trust. We are following up on this, and I would expect some administrative changes to result from it."

It would be the last official statement the FBI would make on the case.

Meanwhile, Shelby had her own reckoning with the law. The state police officers stayed with her through the sentencing proceedings and then took her to headquarters in Pikeville, where she was cited for carrying a concealed weapon and released on her own recognizance in time to get back to the courthouse a few blocks away and talk to reporters out front.

What about the gun charge? "I told them, 'Lord, I wasn't going to do nothing. I wouldn't shoot nobody at all. I always keep my pistol in my purse, but when I get out of the car, I take it out and put it on the seat. This morning I forgot.'"

Runyon didn't think she intended to shoot Mark Putnam either, no matter how it looked. In eastern Kentucky, carrying a gun in your purse was something even the best of people might do. Runyon could recall a tearful phone call he had received a few years ago from a prominent Pikeville woman who had gone to Washington, DC, on a trip and ended up in federal custody. It seems she had forgotten about the pistol in her purse when she went on a White House tour. Runyon had to make a number of phone calls to get her out of jail and have the charges dropped.

Shelby's explanation about the gun was at least plausible, although one state police official maintained that she had really brought in the weapon for "publicity purposes." The fact was, for a woman with a gun charge over her head, Shelby was getting a lot of publicity denouncing as a slap on the wrist the sentence for the man who killed her sister. "This is the dirtiest county I've ever seen in my life," she said. "I think they're covering everything up."

In the hubbub over the plea agreement and Mark Putnam himself, it was easy to lose sight of the victim. And Shelby was determined that that not happen. Even though they fought, the sisters had been close—it was to Shelby whom Susan turned when she was most in trouble. Whatever else might be said about Susan, she had been exploited and abandoned by an institution that employed her and by a man she trusted. Shelby was determined that attention be paid to Susan even if she did tend to trumpet her own role in her sister's life.

"She was more like a daughter to me than a sister," Shelby told the *Williamson Daily News*, published in a small coal city up the Tug Fork on the West Virginia side. She said she had warned Susan to stop seeing Mark "because he was married and had a family. And also, I didn't want her to because I felt she was in danger, that he was using her as an informant, informing on people around where she lived and I lived and she was staying with me. I felt like we were all in danger because of her fooling with him. . . . He had a violent temper, she told me that."

Later in the summer, scheduled to appear in court on the misdemeanor gun charge, Shelby retracted her denunciation of the prosecutor's office: "I do apologize; he, Runyon, was right and I was wrong. I just didn't understand what they were telling me before." She insisted that her about-face had nothing to do with the gun charge: "I was not told to make an apology. I hold my hand to God, I have never been coerced. I talked to my mom and dad and we all think John Paul Runyon and the state police done real good on this."

Why the change of heart? "Once I got my rest and got to thinking about it, they just did the best they could with what they had. The FBI is the one to blame. I got no cooperation from the FBI and, in fact, was insulted by one of their agents. An FBI agent killed my sister and the FBI tried to cover it up. I believe the role that the FBI played should be thoroughly investigated and a full public disclosure made."

Still, she expressed sympathy for Mark. "I do feel sorry for the boy," she said, having had her first look at him in the courtroom. "He did look pitiful." She explained that her Sister was "so in love with him" that she wouldn't heed her warnings about the dangers of working as an informant. Susan "just went crazy" when Mark told her that he and his wife would adopt the child if it was his. "Right to this day, I don't think she would want us to say anything about Mark." But Shelby added, "There is no excuse for what he done and he will pay for the rest of his life. I don't think he really meant to kill her. He just panicked." Still, she said, "I will never forgive him for what he did to my sister; I just hope that one of these days he can forgive himself."

The peace Shelby decreed with the prosecutor's office did not hold for long. After the gun charge was dropped, she changed her position and again withdrew her apology, "I didn't mean a word of it," she said.

Shelby's instincts for publicity were unfailing. The prosecutor's office, which had been quietly pleased with the sentence extracted from the negotiations with Putnam was pummeled in the press for letting the killer off lightly. While the state's most respected newspaper, the *Courier Journal* in Louisville, applauded the plea arrangement, the only daily newspaper circulated throughout eastern Kentucky, the *Lexington Herald Leader,* set a tone that would influence other newspapers and television stations in Lexington. In the absence of detailed information about the investigation, assertions were treated as fact. One editorial stated, "Putnam once threatened Smith when she talked to him about the pregnancy"—an allegation made solely by Shelby.

An editorial in the *Ashland* (Ky.) *Daily Independent*, denounced the "light sentence" given to Mark Putnam and proclaimed that a "murder charge would have been more appropriate." Among the grounds it cited, inaccurately, were that there was "evidence of Putnam's involvement in Smith's death before his confession"; that "an argument between Smith and Putnam could apparently be heard in the motel"; and that "a cracked windshield in the rental car indicated that a scuffle could have taken place," which ignored the fact that the windshield was repaired long before anyone had reason to believe Susan Smith was dead.

Runyon thought such editorials were idiotic and encouraged wild conspiracy theories, but he also believed that they validated one of his favorite axioms: "A lie can go around the world twice before the truth gets its socks on."

In Pikeville, of course, the controversy reached feud proportions immediately. Shelby's lawyer, Larry Webster, had a regular column in the twice-weekly Pikeville paper, the *Appalachian News-Express*, which ran under the pen name Red Dog. He wrote, "It used to be that the crooks had to do their own killing of informants. The government is so efficient now that they do it for the crooks. The agent who strangled that girl sure was lucky he didn't accidentally kill her in a car wreck. He could get life for that."

Meanwhile, the newspaper's publisher, LeJeune Waggoner, offered these tips in a column under the headline "How to Get Away with Murder":

1. Be sure and commit the crime in eastern Kentucky, preferably Pike County.
2. Make sure your victim is poor and white. Do not kill a minority or a man.

3. Make sure the prosecution, grand jury and judge dance to your jig.

4. Be specific where you want to spend your time. Do not accept any ole Kentucky state pen.

5. Be sure and make enough money to be a yuppie so you can hire a fancy out-of-state lawyer.

6. It helps if the taxpayers furnish the money to buy drinks and other party favors. Most any man can impress girls if Uncle Sam is paying the tab.

7. Remember hillbillies from eastern Kentucky are kind of second-class citizens and sometimes you can kill two for the price of one—it helps if you're the father of one.

The prosecutor's defenders rushed to respond. Ten members of the grand jury released a statement denouncing Waggoner's column as "irrational and without any basis in fact."

"From a prosecutor's perspective, sixteen years was pretty darn good," William B. Johnson, the president of the Kentucky Association of Defense Attorneys told reporters. Frank Haddad, a past president of the same association, said that as a defense lawyer he would never have considered trying to make a deal with a prosecutor who had no evidence. "I would have said, 'Bring your indictment and let's go to trial.' They would never have been able to make the case."

Unaccustomed to public criticism, agitated at having not only his ability but his integrity challenged, Runyon went on a Lexington television program called "Your Government" to defend his actions. "It'll stand out, in my opinion, as one of the few cases, if not the only case, in Kentucky where a man's conscience has driven him to plead guilty to murder and take sixteen years in the penitentiary," he insisted. "I don't have many people coming into my office and saying, 'Look, I'm a criminal, I violated the law, and I want you to send me to the penitentiary.'

"When we started out on this plea agreement, obviously, when he was willing to confess, he wasn't willing to take the maximum penalty when we had no case. I probably would have been a little easier on John Q. Public—this boy was in a position of trust. He was an FBI agent."

David Wolf, the forensic anthropologist conducting the autopsy on Susan's remains at his laboratory in Frankfort, made no secret of his contempt for the FBI, which he had long regarded as haughty and not suitably respectful toward state officials such as himself. Though seriously ill with cancer, Wolf also had another reason to insert himself as publicly as possible in the controversy in Pikeville. A Hollywood production company had made inquiries about obtaining the rights to the stories of various principals in the case. Hearing about this, Wolf thought of an old television program, "Quincy, M.E." which had starred Jack Klugman as a crusty medical examiner. Already, Wolf was wondering out loud who would play himself.

This prospect evidently had an impact on the conduct of an autopsy that would normally have taken only a few days. At the end of the week, after Mark had already pled guilty, Wolf was still at work cataloging the remains.

Susan's family wanted to have a funeral on Wednesday, June 20. The Friday before, Wolf was asked to return the remains, but he declined, saying that his work was only one-quarter finished. Shelby, charging that Wolf was engaged in a "science project," not an autopsy, went to Runyon's office for help. Runyon notified Charles Morris, the county coroner, and said that he would comply with the request to have the remains returned for burial. But he warned them both, "If you want anything additional on an autopsy, you better get it before you bury this girl."

"The poor little thing's been laying out long enough," Shelby said. "We just think it would be best to have her buried because Mommy and Daddy have been worried enough."

Runyon had his assistant prosecutor, Rick Bartley, call Wolf. Bartley had to threaten an indignant Wolf with a court order to have the remains released.

But even before they arrived from Frankfort, Shelby again changed her position. She now insisted that the autopsy be resumed immediately, placing the state in the position of having to refuse publicly. The criminal case was closed, said David Jones, the administrator of the state medical examiner's office. "We are a state agency. We can't do an investigation to assist someone in civil litigation."

The family lacked the money to pay a private pathologist to do an autopsy for its lawsuit, Shelby responded. Furthermore, she said, the funeral could go ahead only if someone could be found to pay for that.

Runyon phoned Alice Eldridge, who owned the Phelps Funeral Home, where Susan's remains were being sent, and asked, "Alice, what's your absolute bottom-line price on a nonprofit funeral?"

Alice did some quick calculations on the old Burroughs adding machine on her desk. "Five hundred dollars, John Paul."

Runyon made more calls, and a purchase order was drafted for the Pike County Fiscal Court. Under *Description of Goods* on the form it read, *Burial of body found on Harmon's Branch*. A maximum payment of five hundred dollars was specified under *Aid to Needy*.

Alice Mullins Eldridge had founded her funeral home in the late 1950s with her first husband, Haskell, who died in 1983. The pride she took in her position was reflected in her "business cards," actually cardboard hand-fans with balsam handles, imprinted with the name of the funeral home, a stanza of inspirational poetry, and under that the words *Alice Eldridge, Lady Embalmer & Director*.

Alice's second husband, Luther Eldridge, was a coal miner who played gospel hymns on the electric organ in the parlor during funerals. As a member of one of Peter Creek's oldest families, he was a fourth cousin to Susan's mother.

Alice knew that burying Susan Smith would be a thankless task, but she resolved to bring as much dignity and forbearance as she could to the job. Aware of the notoriety of the case, she made careful note of what was inside the box before preparing the remains for burial.

The family told her they wanted to have a public viewing of the closed casket at her funeral parlor. "Shelby wanted to put on a big show," Alice would later say. She was the kind of woman who took in strays of all sorts, and she felt great sadness over the short life and tragic death of Susie Smith. She worked hard to make the funeral as decorous as she could. She placed the pitiful remains in a child-size Excello fiberglass casket, "a good child's casket." The grave marker was small, about the size of a cereal box, but not cheap—it was bronze and engraved: "Susan Daniels Smith—1961–1989."

Susie Smith went to her grave surrounded by the people she had known all of her life. Family and neighbors, about forty in all gathered in the viewing room of the Phelps funeral home with the Reverend DeWitt Furrow, pastor of the Peter Creek Presbyterian Church.

As Luther loomed over the organ, the mourners sang hymns, and the service concluded with "The Rose," the sad ballad by Amanda McBroom that was made famous by Bette Midler. It was Susan's favorite, and it the lyrics use to make her cry.

The next day, a sheriff's car led a small procession of vehicles through Phelps, around the mountain to Freeburn, and up the steep path beside the creek in Barrenshee Hollow, to the Eldridge family plot on the side of the hill next to the frame house where Susan had grown up.

The gravediggers were three muscular local boys, Billie Joe Wolford, Gregory Prater, and Kenneth Wolford. Alice paid them $300 of the $500 allotted for the funeral.

Addressing the mourners, the preacher asked, "How could this ever happen in America, in Pike County? With as many Christian people as there are among us, how could this have ever happened? Yet it did happen and it was very real. We see and read about it every day. We never think it will happen to us, but it is. And every one of us is part of the guilt." He took as his text the Lamentations of Jeremiah:

> She weeps bitterly in the night,
>   tears on her cheeks;
> among all her lovers
>   she has none to comfort her;
> all her friends have dealt treacherously with
>   her,
> they have become her enemies.

Mark Putnam left the Pikeville courthouse with two state police officers and no idea where he was going. He felt himself being carried along like a stick on a current, head down through a sea of yapping faces, cameras scattering like gulls. Propelled headlong, balance awry with manacled wrists, he fell into the backseat of the police cruiser, his feet pushed in like cargo; the vehicle lurched forward as if besieged in a motorcade. He righted himself, pressed his cheek against the cool glass, not caring about the pictures.

At a brief stop at the state police post he stared mutely at fingertips stained with fingerprint ink. Firm hands on his shoulder, averted eyes. Men stumped by uncertain protocol. "Hang in there," said one, and a second one affirmed the sentiment gruffly. "Hey, Mark," another said, with nothing to add to the greeting. Said still another, with clumsy kindness, "Hey, you want a sandwich or something?" Cops. Not knowing words to say, they were glad to see him leave.

To where they did not say, except that it was on an airplane. Two detectives with whom he once worked cases were assigned to drive him up to Lexington in a new Crown Victoria. En route, making talk from the backseat, Mark said, "You guys are coming up in the world." Up front, Det. Joel Newsome, the big man at the wheel, replied silently with stricken eyes in the rearview mirror. But the cuffs were off for the ride. And in the hills they relaxed a little. Riding shotgun, Det. Claude Tackett, tall and wiry, sat back, draped his arm across the seat, shifting a bit to display more of his face, and told the prisoner as if sharing a secret, "We're going to Otisville, New York. Wherever the hell that is."

Where it was, mostly, was out of sight. The bureau had been worried about major media attention—in fact, there was far less than anybody had anticipated, undoubtedly because places like Pikeville seldom show up on the media radar screens and the publicity of the Putnam case had been a contained explosion, quick and local. Otisville was a medium-security federal prison in the foothills of the Catskill Mountains, coincidentally near the last big stretch of the Appalachian Trail.

Mark said, "Claude, you remember when I first arrived in Pikeville, you were the only detective who traded business cards with me?"

Claude remembered and said that he was sorry about the way it worked out. He coughed and fell silent

Mark asked about a robbery case he knew they had going. Neither replied. Joel's eyes found his in the mirror. That was the moment Mark realized he was no longer a cop.

The weather was nice, a warm and fragrant afternoon with big clouds in the sky like sails on top of the hills. They fell silent to the hum of the road winding down from the mountains into the open bluegrass flatland of Kentucky radiant in late-spring-time sunlight.

On the New Circle Road skirting busy Lexington the driver stiffened, gaped at signs and exit ramps flying by with billboards, slowed to forty.

"Do you know where the airport is?" Joel asked.

"Joel, I am not rightly sure."

From the backseat Mark said softly, "You can take Versailles Road, two exits ahead." He pronounced the word the local way: *Ver-SALES.* Joel frowned, watching for the turn.

On the plane, neutral turf, they were more accommodating and less troubled with him in the middle seat. The state cops stared out the window on takeoff and landing, like people who don't fly much and are still thrilled with the sight.

There was a two-hour layover at O'Hare before the connection to New York. They made him feel comfortable, not obviously watching while he ducked into the men's room, clearing their throats and standing back away while he went to call Kathy collect. Clinging to the phone, he glanced up at a television just inside a bar and saw his own image flicker across the screen, his eyes wide with fear that might have looked furtive in the instant sweep of the frame, words he could not make out imposed beneath. His face disappeared and the picture rearranged itself into the generic visage of a Chicago anchorman changing the subject. Kathy, numbly composed, told him that the television pictures from Pikeville had been on the Miami news—they hadn't managed to track her down in Sunrise for the requisite reaction—and on CNN, but not on the network news programs, which she and Chris had monitored from the bedroom so the children wouldn't see.

★   ★   ★

On the second leg of the flight Mark dug out of his pocket a photograph of himself and the children. He and Danielle and little Mark all had their arms outstretched, as if beckoning to the photographer. Kathy, as usual, had taken the picture; she seldom appeared in family photos.

The twin-engine plane touched down in darkness at a quiet airport in a small city called Middletown. Near the terminal, three uniformed New York state policemen waited, arms folded with impatience, flinty eyes shifting from one to the other as the three men got off the plane and approached across the asphalt.

"Which one of you men is the prisoner?"

Feeling foolish, Mark raised his hand. Ignoring the Kentucky officers, two of the New York State cops grabbed him, locked his arms in theirs, and duckwalked him over to one of their cars, then pushed him onto the hood and roughly patted him down. Jerking his arms back violently for cuffing, one of the cops used the opportunity to yank Mark's elbows upward, sending a searing jolt through his shoulders that almost knocked him out. As he reeled, his eyes hot with rage, Mark thought of the occasions he had done the same thing to a particularly distasteful prisoner, a cheap cop stunt to release a little aggression and send a painful message about who was in charge.

They drove for a long time on country roads over dark rolling farmland, the Kentucky troopers in the car behind. One of the New York cops told his partner that this prisoner wasn't the only "hotshot fed" who belonged in jail, but he would do for now.

Mark worried about how he would handle himself. Contempt and rude treatment from state cops were one thing; in prison, with the cops on the other side of the bars, it was going to be a different story. As he rode, he devised a new challenge for himself, handling that inevitable first confrontation with another prisoner eager to confront a cop in jail—not backing down, not whining, complaining, or asking for help. Above all, handling it like a man and not behaving in any way that would embarrass the FBI.

Ahead, against a black sky, on the crest of a hill, he saw the prison in white light. Razor wire glinted like ice atop a twenty-foot fence that curled around drab buildings with blazing windows. The gate swung open; he was taken from the car and hustled inside without a chance to say good-bye to the Kentucky boys, who stood back from the glare. The transformation was as abrupt as it was total: The papers and photograph in his pocket were taken away, a bundle of clothing was thrust into his arms. He was stripped naked and stood there appraised and poked by men who, he thought with his own initial flash of contempt, did this every day for a living.

Steeling himself, propelled along a gleaming hallway through gates that doubled like decompression chambers, he kept his chin up. Mentally, he groped to find a new role for himself. He toyed with the fantasy that he was not in prison as a killer, but as a cop on the ultimate undercover mission—lengthy, arduous, and extremely dangerous. He imagined himself still a special agent of the FBI, no matter what they said. He had a job to do and responsibilities to uphold. And he would prevail, he vowed, even if they kept him there until the very last day of his sixteen years.

In October of 1990, four months after Susan's body was found, Shelby Jean Ward went to court to file harassment and criminal-trespass charges against her brother Billy Joe, a day after he helped their father, Sid, to petition to replace her as administrator of Susan's estate.

Shelby's lawyer later filed an administrative complaint with the Justice Department charging that FBI negligence "was a proximate cause of the death of Susan Smith." The claim alleged that agents Ron Poole and Terry Hulse "were negligent in failing to see that the relationship between Smith and Putnam was terminated, failing to take steps to protect Smith from the consequences of that relationship, and failing to see that Smith received personal protection from Putnam," who, the claim alleged, had been placed "under an extreme amount of pressure . . . to carry out some untoward act on learning of the pregnancy." The claim charged that Mark "furthered not only his own purposes but also the purposes of the FBI" in killing Susan, since various criminal cases that Mark helped to prosecute with Susan's assistance could have been jeopardized by disclosure of the relationship between the two.

In May of 1991, eleven months after Susan was buried, Shelby and other family members who had filed the wrongful death lawsuit against Mark obtained a court order to have the body exhumed for a second autopsy to be conducted by Wolf. The forensic anthropologist spent nearly a year on the task but died before it was completed. The state's chief medical examiner, Dr. George R. Nichols, then stepped in and concluded: "The identity of the decedent as Susan Daniels Smith is confirmed by odontologic comparison. Further, it is my opinion that the findings are consistent with suffocation."

As for Susan herself, she left no letters. She barely left behind photographs. Like Kathy, Susan was usually the one who took the pictures.

In May 1992, a year after her remains had been exhumed, Susan was reburied in another spot farther up Barrenshee Hollow, next to her brother Raymond Daniels, who had been killed earlier in the year in a car wreck. Only a handful of people, including her father, Sid, and her sister, Shelby, stood by in a cold drizzle to see her laid once more to rest.

Four months afterward, while researching this book, I walked across the plank bridge over Peter Creek to Johnson Bottom, where Kenneth Smith was living in a trailer with the two children, Miranda and Brady.

A relaxed and amiable if wary host, still barefoot on an early fall day, Kenneth, who denied ever physically abusing Susan, spoke about his relationship with Susan with apparent affection mixed with consternation, especially when I asked him what he thought she saw in Mark Putnam. He stroked his chin before replying, "Well, I don't want to be bragging on myself, but Mark Putnam was no better looking than I am." Pondering the question further, he said, "I guess it was just that he made her feel like she was important. Susie always wanted to feel good about herself. And for a while, I guess, she did."

Saying good-bye outside, Kenneth introduced me to young Brady, a fresh-faced, blond-haired boy of seven who had just skidded up to the trailer in a cloud of dust with three young friends on bicycles.

Looking me over in a place where outsiders are nothing but trouble, one of the young boys asked, "Brady, is that the man that killed your mama?"

Kathy Putnam sold the condo and most of their furniture in Fort Lauderdale and moved with her children to Minnesota to be near Mark, who was transferred from Otisville to a federal prison in Rochester, Minnesota. A year later, she and the children returned to Connecticut, living with the help of welfare payments.

She remained bitter about what she felt was the FBI's disinclination to thoroughly reevaluate its policies about the use of informants in general, as well as the training and supervision of agents in an office like Pikeville. "Left unchecked, the FBI remains a law unto itself," she said.

Three years after he went to prison, she continued to proclaim her love and support for her husband. On sleepless nights, she blamed herself for not being able to prevent the tragedy.

"In hindsight, it's always easy to see the mistakes, and I feel that I messed up the worst of all three of us. I knew Mark's position and I knew what Susan was thinking. What I didn't see was that there was too much going on for all of us, Mark, Susan, and me, to be able to evaluate it on our own.

"We each had our own agenda. For Susan, Mark was the only man she ever knew who treated her with respect. She never woke up in the morning, opened her eyes, and felt that she meant something to someone. Was it so wrong for her to want him for herself?

"I was fighting a different battle. I knew how much Mark's job meant to him, but I could see that it was beginning to destroy us. I was determined to get out of Pikeville, desperately trying to hold on to the part of us that existed before. Doing that, I lost Mark. Poole was interfering, and Susan saw her opportunity.

"I know that Mark didn't understand all of what was going on. He only saw me at home, coming apart at the seams. He had never seen me like that before. We were on a collision course, and there are no rules in that kind of game."

Kathy said she is haunted by the thought of Susan. "I never sleep more than three hours at a time. Some nights, I actually wake up with the phone in my hand, thinking I'm talking to her."

Meanwhile, Kathy struggled to provide as normal a life as she could for the two children and to shore up her husband in prison. In the summer of 1993, she was making plans to move back to Minnesota to be near him.

"He tells me from prison, 'I think about the kids, how I screwed up their lives'—and I say, 'You can't think about that anymore, Mark. It's done. You have a responsibility here, and that's not to give up, and not to become a product of that place. Your responsibility is to come back to us as the man we knew. Think about what we still have. We love each other—we have something many people never find. We have beautiful, healthy children who are getting through this. Time is all that's between us. Time will pass and we'll be okay.'"

In prison, Mark endlessly analyzed the circumstances that led to his downfall, looking for wisdom in hindsight. "I often think about whether Susan was really pregnant. I don't think she was. If she was, I don't think now that it could have been mine. That's one of the places I get totally aggravated with myself—in the hysteria of the moment, I never looked, in a cool way, at the situation. The baby was most likely someone else's, if there even was one. She certainly believed there was, but then Susan believed a lot of things.

"I broke my standards. That was the compelling reason that I had to do what I did in confessing. Was I stupid? I don't know. Here I am for the next twelve or fourteen years, whatever. Maybe I am just stupid. If I could take back those two minutes in that car . . .

"But I had a responsibility to live up to, and I failed it. For what I did, I sentenced myself. I didn't have to give myself up, I know that better than anybody. And even then, I didn't have to take sixteen years. Confessing was the only way I could see of even being able to start over with a clean slate.

"I know I could be on the beach right now with my family in Florida. I lost all of that. I lost my children's childhood, and they lost their father. But I also know that now I can sleep at night; I can look myself in the mirror. I couldn't do that for a whole year. Slowly, I am becoming at peace with myself.

"Why am I going to lie to anybody at this point about a trivial issue such as where and when I slept with her? I admitted to killing somebody. Anything else pales. It's the most unconscionable thing you can do to somebody. By admitting it and doing the time that I have to do, I did the thing that I thought would square it away as much as I humanly could, by taking my punishment like a man, by accepting full responsibility for my own actions. This will be the worst thing that will ever happen to me, and I can only go one place from here: straight up."

Just as his wife did, Mark worried that he would sound cold about Susan. "I cared for her. She accepted me when I first got there, when a lot of other people didn't. For that reason, I was very grateful to her. She helped me to get on the map. I felt a certain amount of gratitude. She hung in there with me. She was as patient with me as I was with her.

"I felt a great amount of pity for her, for her upbringing and for the environment she had to live in. In that respect, I cared for her. I wanted to help her.

"The most important thing is that Susan lost her life because of me. I didn't mean to kill her, but that changes nothing, because I did kill her.

"I had to explain all of this to Kathy. Can you imagine just coming home and telling your wife, 'I'm going to jail. I killed somebody, Kathy'? At that point, my life was so miserable internally that I thought, 'Just put me in jail and throw away the key. I deserve it.' I had let the situation exacerbate, and it never should have happened.

"But I did the crime. I gave myself up when anyone else might say I didn't really have to. What was gained from that? Well, Susan's parents know where their daughter is, which they didn't know for a year, and Susan's children know. What else? I can't think of anything else.

"I walk around here, I can't *believe* I'm in prison. I ask, 'How did this happen to you?' It's just unfathomable to me that I'm here. But dammit, I did it, I have to live with the consequences.

"And now I can live with myself. There are no secrets between Kathy and me anymore. When I come home, if she is still there for me, I know there're going to be problems, but we're going to beat it. There's just no question in my mind.

"One of the things that hurts me most is the effect on my relationship with my son—we never got to know each other. Danielle and I had five years together, five good years. My son knows me as a voice on the phone."

In prison, he read and reread the letters he got from his daughter, especially the first one, folded and creased until it was nearly in tatters:

Dear Old Pop:

I got this special paper for writing to you. I hope you like it. I have been a very good girl. I have been helping Mommy around the house sometimes without even being asked. I have been eating all my suppers. I stay up later now because I am older than my brother. And I should be able to. He is still being a pain. But I love him anyway. I can't wait until we'll be able to visit you and give you hugs and kisses. I want you to know that we are ok. We miss you but we are taking care of business. You take care of yourself for us. Eat good, sleep good, and brush your teeth. I got your letters and my heart puffed with love. Please write when you can and I will. I love you as big as the universe. Be good, and be careful.

Love,

Danielle Your #1 Girl

EPILOGUE

This sad story became sadder on February 5, 1998, when Kathy Putnam died at the age of thirty-eight. "Mrs. Putnam was found dead in her Manchester, Conn., home by her 13-year-old daughter, Danielle" and had died of "an apparent heart attack," the Associated Press reported.

After Kathy's death, her parents, Carol and Ray Ponticelli, took Danielle and Mark Jr. into their home in Manchester until Mark was released from prison in the fall of 2000. Kathy's parents always remained close to Mark. "He's a wonderful man. It was a crime of passion," Carol told the *Hartford Courant* when Mark was released, his sentence reduced from sixteen years to ten for good behavior. A prison department spokesman said that Mark had been a "model inmate," who volunteered in the chapel and commissary and took classes in maintaining heating and cooling systems.

Mark remarried and is living in the South, as are Danielle and Mark Jr.

After I interviewed him over several days in 1992 in a federal prison in Rochester, Minnesota, I had stayed in touch by mail with Mark until early 1999. I remained in close touch with Kathy for many years after *Above Suspicion* was published in 1993, while she struggled to keep her marriage and family together. She remained deeply wary of Ron Poole, whom she saw as a half-baked but nevertheless sinister Iago—scheming, jealous, and sexually obsessed with Susan. Poole's incessant interferences were "contributing factors in causing the death of Susan Smith," Kathy asserted in an eight-page statement to the FBI in March 1992. "I wish to make it known to the FBI that I am terrified of Ron Poole," she said.

I had interviewed Kathy at length at her home in Connecticut in 1992, and for years afterward I spoke frequently with her on long phone calls. She was invariably honest and forthright; she always insisted that nothing be held back, that nothing was out of bounds in her deeply personal recollections, even things that were profoundly painful and sometimes embarrassing to her. Kathy was brave. I admired her enormously.

A local newspaper in Connecticut said that heavy drinking had contributed to Kathy's sudden death. From prison in 1998, Mark answered my condolence letter with a long reply, in which he discussed his anguish about his wife's emotional distress. "Joe, she couldn't shake the deep depression which engulfed her, nor would she accept the fact that she had a problem. Over the years her condition deteriorated to the point where suicide was a common theme to our nightly calls. No matter what the family and I attempted to do, she shut us out. Her condition was exacerbated by the fact that she was drinking heavily. Unfortunately, the kids bore the brunt of her capriciousness. It got to the point where she wouldn't let me talk to the kids alone, and wouldn't let Ray and Carol see them," he wrote, referring to Kathy's parents. His letter, several months after her death, added, "The kids and I have indeed grown closer as a result of our loss and have a steely determination to succeed."

I should note that in hours of one-on-one interviews in prison in 1992 and in letters to me, Mark never stopped expressing shock and remorse. "I can't accept what I have done to my wife and kids," he wrote to me from prison. "As I look around my environment, my insides scream that I don't belong here, yet I know deep down I need to fulfill my societal obligations. I try to put myself in the place of Susan's family and yes, I would want me away for a long time."

In 2000, two years after Kathy's death and the same year that Mark was released from prison, Ron Poole died at the age of fifty, after a twenty-year career as an FBI special agent. An FBI investigation into Poole's actions in Pikeville veered into other cases in eastern Kentucky after 1990. Among them was the rogue agent's role in advocating the release from jail of a convicted killer who then went on to commit multiple murders during the time he was also an informant for Poole. In another case in 1990, Poole's undercover work was cited in a successful sting operation that led to federal bribery convictions of four eastern Kentucky county sheriffs and a police chief—but even that case raised questions about the agent's behavior: A county sheriff testified that he had declined to work with Poole because he "appeared to be more interested in having sex with a woman he was sent to investigate."

In 1991, the *Lexington Herald-Leader* excoriated the FBI in an editorial. "If the FBI has a woodshed, it should take Ron Poole there for some serious career counseling. Clearly, the FBI needs to take a long, close look at its policies and practices involving informants."

The internal FBI investigation concluded with a censure, demotion, and suspension of forty days without pay for Poole, and a censure and suspension of fourteen days without pay for Terry Hulse, the supervisor in Covington who was responsible for the Pikeville regional office 215 miles away. However, despite his scheming and manipulations, the FBI investigation found that Poole was unaware that Mark had killed Susan until Mark made his confession.

In 2016, Jim Huggins, the FBI supervisor who conducted the investigation that led to Mark's confession, told me that the bureau's existing procedures for handling informants were "tightened" after the Putnam case. In general, said Huggins, who is now retired, a supervising agent's job is to closely evaluate the use of and payments to informants. "If you've been around a while, you should be able to tell when something isn't right. With a female informant especially, like when Mark told Hulse, 'Listen, she visited the office and brought me a gift.' Bingo, that's when the first light goes off. So you call up Mark and say, 'What the hell is going on here, buddy?' Which opens a dialogue. There's your opportunity to have a talk with a young agent, and it's where an older mentor who has been around for a while makes the difference."

In 1990, Susan's family filed a wrongful death suit against Mark Putnam. A federal bankruptcy judge awarded $463,837 in compensatory damages and $500,000 in punitive damages against Putnam, who had filed for personal bankruptcy in prison in 1993. "We got the judgment against him and never could identify any assets in his name. It was not collectable," said Larry Webster, the Pikeville attorney who filed the lawsuit.

In Pikeville in 1991, Det. Richard Ray was named Trooper of the Year by the Kentucky State Police. Ray took his plaque and resigned, saying he was disgusted by the department's general penny-pinching on investigations, including the Putnam case. He is now retired.

John Paul Runyon, the Pike County commonwealth attorney, was reelected unopposed to a sixth term in 1992. Runyon remained convinced that Mark Putnam never meant to kill Susan Smith. "I believe it was accidental," he said in 1992. He remained distressed by what he regarded as the FBI's casual attitude toward using informants, and by what he saw as its failure to heed warnings sent up by the Putnam fiasco. "I was very emphatic. They sent agents to my home to talk to me about it, and I told them flat-out, if there's one thing you need to learn from this case, if nothing else, you need to take a real close look at how you deal with informants—what kind of protection you give them and what concern you have for them. I told them, if you don't have a policy already, you need to develop one, and if you have a policy, by God, you need to start enforcing it."

Runyon, who had discussed his role in the Putnam prosecution at length with me in Pikeville in 1992, died in 2015 at the age of ninety.

As for Susan's children, her son, Brady, died several years ago after overdosing on a combination of methadone and Xanax. Miranda is married with a child, and living near Phelps, Kentucky. Kenneth is living quietly in the same area.

In the summer of 2016, I went to see Shelby Ward, who, at sixty-one, still lived beside the Tug Fork River in Freeburn. Unfortunately, Shelby said she was unable to discuss the quarter-century-old case and its aftermath, including a surprising long-distance friendship that had developed many years earlier between her and Kathy Putnam. After Mark went to prison, Kathy reached out to Shelby. Though the two women had never met, and Shelby was the first person to suspect that Mark had killed her sister, they became friends through long phone calls of the sort that Kathy often had with Susan. In an interview in 1992, Shelby said that Kathy "would talk of waking up in the middle of the night with the telephone receiver in her hand, swearing she had been talking with Susan."

The material in this book all comes from my own conversations with the people involved, as well as from police and FBI files, court records, and historical research. There are numerous passages in this book of reconstructed dialogue. These were always derived from the recollections of at least one person who was directly involved in the conversation. In dialogue involving Susan Smith, I satisfied myself that what someone recalled her saying in a specific instance was also consistent with what other people who knew her recalled about her attitudes and state of mind at the time. I depended on Mark Putnam's recollections to reconstruct the final conversation between him and Susan.

As a journalist I have written thousands of stories, including more than nine hundred columns for the *New York Times*. Most of them quickly fade in memory, but the details of this one have haunted me for twenty-five years, partly because *Above Suspicion* is fact-based journalism that is also a narrative tragedy involving complex personalities and events in a compelling setting. Meanwhile, I have always been curious about and sympathetic toward Susan Smith, the only one of the principal characters that I was, of course, unable to speak with.

Susan, as everyone who knew her agreed, could drive you nuts with her prattling and her fables and exaggerations, and her pitiful desperation to get herself out of the circumstances and geography that held her. As Kathy Putnam always told Susan: Choices have consequences; goals can be set and achieved; there is usually a way out, especially if you're young and smart and so personable (as Susan definitely was) that the world is actually inclined to cut you some slack and meet you more than halfway.

"That girl was just likeable," Bert Hatfield, the deputy sheriff who first befriended Mark as a rookie agent new to the territory in 1987, told me in the summer of 2016. "She was so convincing, no matter what bullshit she was talking. Her personality was just that good. People liked her, me included. But Susie always wanted more out of life than she was able to get. She didn't know how to go about it, even when the answers were so clear."

Much of what I learned about Susan's real personality, as opposed to the one assigned to her by gossips, came from detailed and deeply emotional recollections by Kathy Putnam, who should have been Susan's adversary, given the circumstances, but who, even in the depths of her despair, always considered her a friend whom she had lost.

Larry Webster, the Pikeville attorney who represented Shelby Ward and the rest of Susan's family after she was killed, still had a vivid impression of her a quarter century later. He said, "I hate to be stereotypical, but she was kind of typical of a lot of young mountain women. They just have a certain charm to them, and their sexuality is kind of overt and unashamed, but sort of innocent in a way. I'm sure Mark Putnam was charmed by Susan, who was different from any girl he knew before—unlike his wife, who was probably kind of prudish and had money, the kind of wife he needed to marry." Of course, Kathy (whom Webster never met) didn't have "money," but she did project outward poise and, to Susan's hungry eye, a cosmopolitan style that may have seemed exotic in Pikeville at the time.

People in Freeburn who remember Susan, including her family, all seem to have accepted the idea that she and Mark had a long, intense affair that lasted for two years and included torrid assignations in motels and even, as Susan bragged to friends, at the Putnams' home in Pikeville during the time when Kathy traveled back to Connecticut for the birth of their second child.

It certainly makes the story more cinematic to envision the sweaty young lovers, dashing lawman and perky mountain girl, tangled in the bedsheets. But I myself don't buy it. I believe the truth is sadder than that. In his confession, and in subsequent conversations with me in prison in which I took him over key details again and again, looking for discrepancies that I never found, Mark consistently maintained that sex with Susan was quick and opportunistic, certainly not planned (he didn't even have condoms), and that it had occurred over a period of months starting in December 1988, not years, as some accounts based entirely on local speculation insisted. These things supported his accounts: The unequal power relationship between the two, underpinned by his sense of status and propriety, if not morality; the Putnam home in Pikeville had nosy neighbors who were vigilant about neighborhood comings and goings; and Mark had no good reason that I could ascertain to lie about the sex after he admitted to killing her.

"The times I had sex with her always took place in the car, and I never had sex with her at my house or at a motel," he said in his confession statement on June 4, 1990—which he repeated to me on several occasions.

In the winter of 2016 I learned that Phillip Noyce, the Australian director of films such as *Salt*, *The Quiet American*, and *Clear and Present Danger*, had agreed to adapt *Above Suspicion* as a movie. Phillip spent weeks driving around eastern Kentucky scouting locations, but he ruled out Pikeville and instead chose Harlan, a gloomy little town of 1,800 in the Kentucky coal-belt about eighty-five miles southwest of Pikeville.

"Pikeville doesn't look like Pikeville anymore," he told me when I visited the Harlan location in July 2016 as filming was underway. Emilia Clarke (famous for playing Daenerys Targaryen, the "Mother of Dragons" in the hit HBO fantasy series *Game of Thrones*) was playing Susan Smith and Jack Huston (who played the title role in the 2016 remake of the biblical epic *Ben-Hur*) was cast as Mark Putnam. Sophie Lowe played Kathy Putnam.

Revisiting the region for the first time since 1992, I was surprised by how right Phillip was. Pikeville today does not look much like the sleepy county seat I encountered in 1992. A new twenty-five-acre University of Pikeville campus and medical center sprawls down a hill overlooking downtown, across the street from two new hotels. Main Street and Courthouse Square have been spruced up with new facades and even outdoor stages. There's a flashy new seven-thousand-seat concert and sports events arena called the Eastern Kentucky Expo Center, which opened in 2005. These expensive improvements were all part of an ambitious publicly financed plan to beautify Pikeville as a center for regional tourism in eastern Kentucky.

Larry Webster, who has practiced law from his office near the courthouse for over a quarter century, chuckled and explained: "They put all these big buildings up and created an illusion of more prosperity than you will actually find here," Webster said. "After that TV series on the Hatfield–McCoy feud created all this interest, people started roaring in here to see everything—but really there ain't much to see. All we can do really is put up signs saying 'This is where something happened.'"

The producers and the director of the movie version of this book, to their great credit, were adamant about filming in eastern Kentucky, even though the remoteness of the region—it's more than two hours from any significant urban center—added extra expense to the budget, not to mention major logistical burdens. The producers firmly believed that geography itself was a character in the book, and they affirmed the concept of "authenticity of place"—enough so to spend months with a movie crew encamped in a little town with so few amenities.

Above Suspicion links three people, a young man who wanted affirmation in his long-sought job as an FBI agent and two women who emotionally orbited him, each impelled by her own conflicted desires, each tragically unaware that a terrible collision lay ahead. In a work necessarily restricted to fact-based journalism and what can be reasonably interpreted from those facts, Mark Putnam was a far easier character to draw than the two women. The challenge, for both book and movie, was to reflect what is increasingly known in literature, including the literature of cinema, as the "female gaze."

One afternoon during the filming of *Above Suspicion*, Emilia spoke passionately about her desire to bring Susan to life and capture the sad utility of her dreams. She told me she had read everything she could get her hands on about Susan. In fact, she had already worn out two copies of *Above Suspicion*—"They're all dog-eared and I've scrawled all over them," she said. On location, she devoured my background notes and lengthy transcripts from tapes of Kathy and Mark's reflections on Susan compiled twenty-five years before.

As we spoke, Emilia switched effortlessly between her native British accent and the eastern Kentucky "hillbilly" twang that she had been perfecting for months. When she did the final take, bathed in ethereal blue light as Phillip Noyce softly called "Action!" and repeated those last sad lines about the death of dreams, I realized that, in a way that written words alone did not adequately achieve, this young actress had worked magic and brought forth a vision that I recognized as Susan Smith.

After the movie wrapped in mid-July I drove across the mountains to Pikeville, and then onto Route 23 north of town, toward the mountain where Susan's body had lain in weeds and strip-mine debris for nearly a year until Mark's confession. The Goldenrod Motel and Marlow's are gone, and there are no coal trucks spewing black nuggets as they hurtle north. That's because the boom and bust cycles of coal are over. In 2015, as cheap and less polluting fuels like natural gas won out, coal production in eastern Kentucky was at its lowest in eighty years. One after the other, the giant coal-producing companies have gone bankrupt, leaving behind devastated landscapes, poisoned streams, and billions of dollars in cleanup costs to be borne by taxpayers.

The place where Susan lay is at the summit of a former strip mine. Two weathered park benches sag in the mud. The dirt bikes that Mark heard whizzing nearby when he laid Susan's nude body in the ravine have given way to all-terrain vehicles and an equestrian center that attracts riders on trails lacing through reclaimed slopes. From the crest of the hill, the mountains of Appalachia are stacked like bread loaves on the horizon.

The roads corkscrewing through the hills from here to Freeburn have not changed much since the days when Bert Hatfield taught Mark Putnam how to grit his teeth, take his foot off the brake, and drive like a hell-bound hillbilly. Treacherous turns leading to tiny hamlets with rusting cars parked outside trailers and an astonishing profusion of steepled saltbox churches with electric signs warning of a apocalyptic visions of a Rapture soon to come.

At the end of such death-defying highways lie the isolated old coal-camp towns like Freeburn, population 399, sustained by government checks and social inertia, largely unchanged in the quarter century since I first came here.

Bert Hatfield still presides over his small used-car lot beside the stubby bridge across the Tug to West Virginia. I talked to him in his office inside a cramped trailer, at a desk piled high with papers and files, with a police scanner to the side, though he said that he believes his days in law enforcement are numbered.

"The drugs are worse than I ever saw before, and I thought I seen it all," he said. In conjunction with law enforcement crackdowns on pain pills, as well as marijuana and cocaine, the chemical formula that concocts this social dysfunction and criminality has been altered, most graphically seen in a deadly new epidemic of cheap heroin tricked out with an opioid called fentanyl that boosts its potency by more than 50 percent.

"I don't even know these kids," Bert said. "I used to be able to say, listen, I know your father or your sister, but there's a new element coming around now that doesn't even think the same way. In law enforcement, you better be able to change with the times or get out, and I'm ready to get out."

As the local cop who first introduced Mark to Susan, a girl he grew up with in Freeburn, Bert still had strong feelings about her. "Susie had been my informant for years before I introduced Mark to her," he said. "She gave me valuable information, and she did the same for Mark."

Was he aware of the sexual relationship that developed between the two?

"Like everybody else, I heard talk, especially from what she was telling folks. But Mark and I spent a lot of hours together and I never saw that side of him, and he never mentioned anything like that to me. Toward the end, I did warn him about getting too involved with this girl, that she was running her mouth pretty bad. I did try to send some red flags up for him, but I think he took it personally, as me butting in. We drifted apart over that."

As so many others did, Bert blamed the FBI for lax supervision of a hard-charging, eager-to-succeed young agent who eventually got into a situation he could not control. "I think they threw him to the wolves," he said.

Across the river, seven miles up the road on the West Virginia side, lies Matewan, the coal town where Susan Daniels was born in 1961, the fifth of nine children of Sid and Tracy Daniels of Barrenshee Hollow in Freeburn, Kentucky.

When Susan was a child, the two-block-long downtown in Matewan had shops, including Nenni's Department Store, a tailor, and a cobbler. At Christmas and Easter, miners' families from all over the Tug Valley would dress in their Sunday best, Susan's among them, and flock to the festively decorated Nenni's.

But by the mid-1970s, Matewan was a faded town. It had been

ripped apart by the Tug river floods, boom-and-bust cycles of coal, and the violent class struggles as the miners attempted to unionize. Young Susan knew she needed to get out, any way possible.

On a breezy July afternoon in 2016, I wandered into Matewan's somnambulant downtown. The streets were almost empty. I peered into the souvenir shop's window to look at the display of Hatfield–McCoy tchotchkes. A wood-burned plaque was displayed prominently:

HATFIELD–McCOY

FUED

1865–1890

And yes, "feud" was misspelled.

I walked down to the river, across from Main Street. After a 1977 flood wiped out most of the town, the Army Corps of Engineers had built a great concrete floodwall, decorated with scenes from the Battle of Matewan, that runs a quarter mile along the Tug. At the base of the steps to the river, mayflies swarmed around me. I parted my way through nettles and ferns and cattails to the riverbank to watch a boy, maybe thirteen years old, paddle by in a broken-down canoe with exposed and splintered slats. The boy waved and swirled downriver on the Tug's fast northbound tumble down to the Ohio, the river access to the big cities of the Midwest.

Where did that boy think he was going in a busted old canoe? Did he have a plan to return against that swift current? Or was he, like Susan, simply adrift on a stream?

Finally, I realized, it was time for a journalist to put his notes away. History pointedly cleared its throat in forlorn little Matewan, where Susan Smith first had her notions, where ghosts now drifted in smoky tendrils on the lonesome holler of the wind.

IMAGE GALLERY

Mark Putnam as a child, with his father, Walter.

Mark Putnam in college, playing soccer.

Mark Putnam at his graduation from the FBI academy.

Kathy Putnam.

Mark, Kathy, and Danielle Putnam, 1986.

Pikeville, Kentucky.

Main Street, Pikeville.

Federal Courthouse; location of the FBI office in Pikeville.

Susan Smith in her seventh grade yearbook.

Susan Smith in grade school.

Kenneth and Susan Smith.

Barrenshee Hollow in Freeburn, where Susan grew up.

Danielle, Mark, and Mark Jr. in Florida.

A nightly ritual: Mark reading a bedtime story to Danielle and
Mark Jr. in Florida.

Mark, Mark Jr., and Danielle reading the newspaper in Florida.

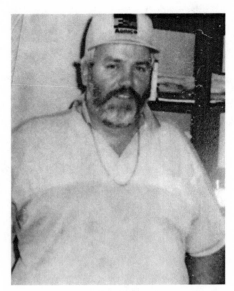

Ron Poole, 1991.

Detective Richard Ray at the site where Susan's body was found.

Commonwealth Attorney John Paul Runyon.

Retired FBI supervisor Jim Huggins, 2016.

Sherriff's Deputy Bert Hatfield at his car lot in Freeburn, 2016.

The author on the set of the film adaptation with actor Emilia
Clarke, who is playing Susan Smith, in 2016.

ABOUT THE AUTHOR

Joe Sharkey was a weekly columnist for the *New York Times* for nineteen years. Previously, he was an assistant national editor at the *Wall Street Journal* and a reporter and columnist with the *Philadelphia Inquirer*. The author of four books of nonfiction and one novel, Sharkey is currently an adjunct professor of journalism at the University of Arizona. He and his wife live in Tucson.

JOE SHARKEY

FROM OPEN ROAD MEDIA

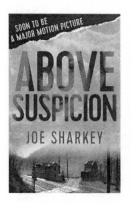

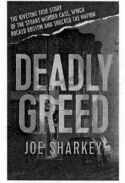

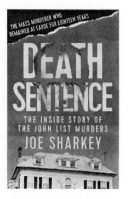

OPEN ROAD

INTEGRATED MEDIA

INTEGRATED MEDIA